ORGANIZATIONAL WRONGDOING AS THE "FOUNDATIONAL" GRAND CHALLENGE

RESEARCH IN THE SOCIOLOGY OF ORGANIZATIONS

Series Editor: Michael Lounsbury

Recent Volumes:

Volume 55:	Social Movements, Stakeholders and Non-Market Strategy
Volume 56:	Social Movements, Stakeholders and Non-Market Strategy
Volume 57:	Toward Permeable Boundaries of Organizations?
Volume 58:	Agents, Actors, Actorhood: Institutional Perspectives on the Nature of Agency, Action, and Authority
Volume 59:	The Production of Managerial Knowledge and Organizational Theory: New Approaches to Writing, Producing and Consuming Theory
Volume 60:	Race, Organizations, and the Organizing Process
Volume 61:	Routine Dynamics in Action
Volume 62:	Thinking Infrastructures
Volume 63:	The Contested Moralities of Markets
Volume 64:	Managing Inter-organizational Collaborations: Process Views
Volume 65A:	Microfoundations of Institutions
Volume 65B:	Microfoundations of Institutions
Volume 66:	Theorizing the Sharing Economy: Variety and Trajectories of New Forms of Organizing
Volume 67:	Tensions and Paradoxes in Temporary Organizing
Volume 68:	Macrofoundations: Exploring the Institutionally Situated Nature of Activity
Volume 69:	Organizational Hybridity: Perspectives, Processes, Promises
Volume 70:	On Practice and Institution: Theorizing the Interface
Volume 71:	On Practice and Institution: New Empirical Directions
Volume 72:	Organizational Imaginaries: Tempering Capitalism and Tending to Communities Through Cooperatives and Collectivist Democracy
Volume 73A:	Interdisciplinary Dialogues on Organizational Paradox: Learning from Belief and Science
Volume 73B:	Interdisciplinary Dialogues on Organizational Paradox: Investigating Social Structures and Human Expression
Volume 74:	Worlds of Rankings
Volume 75:	Organizing Creativity in the Innovation Journey
Volume 76:	Carnegie goes to California: Advancing and Celebrating the Work of James G. March
Volume 77:	The Generation, Recognition and Legitimation of Novelty
Volume 78:	The Corporation: Rethinking the Iconic Form of Business Organization
Volume 79:	Organizing for Societal Grand Challenges
Volume 80:	Advances in Cultural Entrepreneurship
Volume 81:	Entrepreneurialism and Society: New Theoretical Perspectives
Volume 82:	Entrepreneurialism and Society: Consequences and Meanings
Volume 83:	Digital Transformation and Institutional Theory
Volume 84:	Organizational Wrongdoing as the "Foundational" Grand Challenge: Definitions and Antecedents

RESEARCH IN THE SOCIOLOGY OF ORGANIZATIONS ADVISORY BOARD

RESEARCH IN THE SOCIOLOGY OF
ORGANIZATIONS   VOLUME 85

ORGANIZATIONAL WRONGDOING AS THE "FOUNDATIONAL" GRAND CHALLENGE: CONSEQUENCES AND IMPACT

EDITED BY

CLAUDIA GABBIONETA
University of York, UK

MARCO CLEMENTE
ZHAW School of Management and Law, Switzerland

and

ROYSTON GREENWOOD
University of Alberta, Canada & University of Edinburgh, UK

United Kingdom – North America – Japan
India – Malaysia – China

Emerald Publishing Limited
Howard House, Wagon Lane, Bingley BD16 1WA, UK

First edition 2023

British Library Cataloguing in Publication Data
A catalogue record for this book is available from the British Library

ISBN: 978-1-83753-283-4 (Print)
ISBN: 978-1-83753-282-7 (Online)
ISBN: 978-1-83753-284-1 (Epub)

ISSN: 0733-558X (Series)

Printed and bound by CPI Group (UK) Ltd, Croydon, CR0 4YY

ISOQAR certified
Management System,
awarded to Emerald
for adherence to
Environmental
standard
ISO 14001:2004.

Certificate Number 1985
ISO 14001

INVESTOR IN PEOPLE

CONTENTS

List of Figures and Tables   *ix*

About the Editors   *xi*

About the Contributors   *xiii*

List of Contributors   *xvii*

Foreword   *xix*

**Introduction: Organizational Wrongdoing as the "Foundational"
Grand Challenge: Consequences and Impact**
Claudia Gabbioneta, Marco Clemente and Royston Greenwood   *1*

**Chapter 1   The Certification Effect of New Legislation:
CEO Accountability for Misconduct After Sarbanes-Oxley**
Jo-Ellen Pozner, Aharon Mohliver and Celia Moore   *11*

**Chapter 2   Goofus or Gallant? An Attribution-Based Theory
of Misconduct Spillover Valence**
Jung-Hoon Han, Timothy G. Pollock and Srikanth Paruchuri   *35*

**Chapter 3   "Crowd Contamination"? Spillover Effects in the
Context of Misconduct Allegations**
Brigitte Wecker and Matthias Brauer   *53*

**Chapter 4   Peers: Powerful or Negligible? A Systematic Review
on Peer Factors and Internal Whistleblowing**
Behnud Mir Djawadi, Sabrina Plaß and Sabrina Schäfers   *73*

**Chapter 5   I Report If They Report: The Role of Media in
Whistleblowing Intentions on Fraud and Corruption**
Sebastian Oelrich   *101*

Chapter 6   Networked Whistleblowing, Counter-Hegemony and the Challenge to Systemic Corruption
Iain Munro and Kate Kenny   *121*

Chapter 7   Historical Approaches to Researching Organizational Wrongdoing
Adam Nix and Stephanie Decker   *141*

LIST OF FIGURES AND TABLES

Chapter 1

Fig. 1a. Distribution of Firms in the Full Sample, by Free Float
(up to $60 Billion) and Market Capitalization
(up to $1 Trillion).   19

Fig. 1b. Distribution of Firms Included in the Final Sample by
Free Float (up to $500 Million) and Market Capitalization
(up to $6 Billion).   20

Fig. 1c. Firms Excluded (Unshaded) and Those Included (Shaded)
in the Final Sample.   20

Table 1. T-tests for Equality of Means Between Firms that are
Exempt from Section 404 (Free Float < $75 million) and
Those That are Not Exempt (Free Float Between $75 and
150 Million), $N = 84$.   21

Table 2. Descriptive Statistics and Correlations.   23

Table 3. Linear Probability Models Predicting CEO Change and
CFO Change After Restatement.   24

Fig. 2.   Statistical Significance (z-scores) of the Coefficient on the
Interaction Term for Sarbanes-Oxley X Exempt Using
Different Thresholds of Public Float.   25

Table 4. T-Tests for Equality of Means Before and After
Sarbanes-Oxley.   26

Table 5. Replication of the Full Model (Table 3, Model 2) Using
Non-Restating Firms.   26

Table 6. Replication of the Full Model (Table 3, Model 2) Using
Firms with Public Floats of $50–$125 Million.   27

Chapter 2

Fig. 1.   Conceptual Framework.   45

Chapter 3

Fig. 1.   Illustration of Anticipation, Evaluation, and Reaction to
Allegations in the Automotive Industry.   56

Fig. 2.   Investor Reaction Explained by Investor Anticipation and
Evaluation.   57

Table 1. Descriptive Statistics and Correlations.   62

Table 2. Regression Results Predicting Investor Reaction to a Focal
Allegation.   63

Fig. 3.   Influence of Allegation Prevalence Among Other Firms
on Investor Reaction to a Focal Allegation.   64

Chapter 4

Fig. 1.   Framework with Seven Subcategories of Peer Factors and
             Internal Whistleblowing (Influences & Consequences).   78
Table 1.   Identified Articles About Peer Influences on Internal
             Whistleblowing.   79
Table 2.   Identified Articles About Peer Consequences After Internal
             Whistleblowing.   89
Table 3.   List of Proposed Research Gaps, Research Paths & Exemplary
             Research Questions.   93

Chapter 5

Fig. 1.   Hypothesized Moderation-Mediation Model.   106
Table 1.   Correlation Matrix.   108
Fig. 2.   Perceived Media Coverage of Fraud and Corruption Overview.   109
Table 2.   PLS SEM Results of Moderation-Mediation Analysis.   111
Fig. 3.   Moderation MEDIA × CORR_CO.   112
Fig. 4.   Moderation MEDIA × RETAL.   113
Table 3.   OLS Regressions with Sociodemographic and Country
             Dummy Controls.   114

Chapter 6

Table 1.   Counter-Hegemonic Whistleblowing Practices and Alliances.   134

Chapter 7

Table 1.   Historically Informed Approaches to Researching
             Organizational Wrongdoing.   148

ABOUT THE EDITORS

Claudia Gabbioneta holds a Chair in Accounting and Management at the School for Business and Society at University of York. Her research interests include professions, organizational wrongdoing, and professional misconduct. Her work has been published in prestigious international journals, such as *Accounting, Organizations and Society, Human Relations, Work, Employment and Society*, and *Research in the Sociology of Organizations*. She is a Senior Editor of *Organization Studies* and sits in the Editorial Board of the *Journal of Management Studies* and the *Journal of Strategic Contracting and Negotiation*. She has organized several PDW at the Academy of Management and EGOS on organizational wrongdoing and corporate scandals and was an invited panelist at the sub-panel on organizational wrongdoing at the 2019 EGOS colloquium.

Marco Clemente is a Professor of Management and Sustainability, Head of Research Center at the ZHAW, School of Management and Law. His research interests include business ethics, sustainability, organizational misconduct, and corporate scandals. He has analyzed a variety of contexts, including automotive, advertising, and sports. He has published in leading academic journals, including the *Academy of Management Review*, *Journal of Management Inquiry*, and *Research in the Sociology of Organizations*. He has organized several PDWs at the Academy of Management and EGOS on organizational wrongdoing and corporate scandals.

Royston Greenwood graduated from the University of Birmingham in the UK. He is Professor Emeritus at the University of Alberta, and Professorial Fellow at the University of Edinburgh. He is a Fellow of the Academy of Management, Honorary Member of the European Group for Organization Studies, and Fellow of the Royal Society of Canada. His research interests include organizational and institutional change from an institutional perspective. His research has been published in various journals including the *Administrative Science Quarterly, Academy of Management Journal, Academy of Management Review,* and the *Academy of Management Annals*. He is a former chair of the OMT Division of the Academy of Management, and former editor of the *Academy of Management Annals*.

ABOUT THE CONTRIBUTORS

Matthias Brauer is a Professor of Strategic and International Management at the University of Mannheim, Germany. He received his DBA and his habilitation from the University of St. Gallen, Switzerland. His primary research domain is corporate strategy and governance, with particular interest in how financial investors and analysts influence and respond to firms' major strategic decisions and actions.

Stephanie Decker is a Professor of Strategy at Birmingham Business School and a Visiting Professor in African Business History at the University of Gothenburg, Sweden. Her work focuses on historical approaches in Organization Studies and Strategy, and she has published in journals such as *Academy of Management Review, Human Relations, Journal of Management Studies, Organization, Business History Review,* and *Business History.* She is joint editor-in-chief of *Business History,* on the editorial board of *Organization Studies, Journal of International Business Studies* and *Accounting History,* and Co-Vice Chair for Research & Publications at the British Academy of Management.

Behnud Mir Djawadi is a Research Fellow at the Management Department at Paderborn University (Germany). His research interests include behavioral and experimental economics, as well as organizational behavior, health economics, public economics, and business ethics. Mainly, he uses microeconomic or organizational theory along with concepts of behavioral economics, and the method of economic experiments in both the lab and the field to investigate behaviors and outcomes, and to design institutions and individual incentives for behavioral change. Currently, he is the Secretary of the Society for the Advancement of Behavioral Economics (SABE).

Jung-Hoon Han is an Assistant Professor of Management at the Trulaske College of Business, University of Missouri. He received his PhD from the Pennsylvania State University. His research focuses on the sociocognitive processes shaping firms' behaviors and outcomes with an emphasis on the role of social evaluations such as status, reputation, and celebrity.

Kate Kenny is a full Professor of Business and Society at University of Galway. She has held research fellowships at the Edmond J. Safra Lab at Harvard University and Cambridge's Judge Business School. Her work has been published in *Organization Studies, Organization, Gender Work and Organization, ephemera* and *Human Relations* among other journals. Her books include *Whistleblowing: Toward a New Theory* (Harvard University Press, 2019), *The Whistleblowing Guide*

(Wiley Business, 2019, with W. Vandekerckhove and M. Fotaki), *Understanding Identity and Organizations* (Sage 2011, with A. Whittle and H. Willmott), and *Affect at Work: The Psychosocial and Organization Studies* (Palgrave 2014, with M. Fotaki). She serves on the editorial boards of *Human Relations, Organization,* and *Organization Studies*.

Aharon Mohliver is an Assistant Professor of Strategy and Entrepreneurship at London Business School and was a Visiting Scholar at Yale School of Management. He has taught Strategy for the London and Dubai EMBA programmes at London Business School, as well as Strategic Management courses for MBA, MiM and MiF, and the Ph.D Sociological Foundations of Strategy courses. His research centers on liminal practices – actions that are in a normative "gray area" – and how these impact audience perceptions, scandals, strategic choices, profitability, and competitive advantage. He studies liminal practices in a wide variety of settings, for example, his most recent work has been on liminal practices and the physician networks fuelling the American prescription drug epidemic, the religious affiliation of nursing homes and elderly neglect and abuse and the strategic use of audiences political polarization to increase profits. Understanding liminality helps organizations navigate – gray areas by designing practices and processes that will avoid costly ethical failings while retaining, or even increasing its competitive advantage. For policymakers, this work can inform policies to reduce misconduct by mitigating liminality, instead of later policing it as a crime. He earned his B.A. in Politics, Philosophy and Economics from The Hebrew University and holds a Master's in Finance and Strategy from the Hebrew University and a Ph.D. from Columbia Business School.

Celia Moore is a Professor of Organisational Behaviour in the Department of Management and Entrepreneurship at Imperial College Business School, where she also directs the Centre for Responsible Leadership. Prior to Imperial, she was on the faulty at London Business School and Bocconi University in Milan, Italy, as well as a Visiting Scholar at Harvard Business School. Her research and teaching sits at the intersection of leadership and ethics. She is particularly interested in supporting individuals to enact their moral agency responsibly. Most recently, she has focused on how individuals navigate morally consequential decisions in their professional lives and challenge legitimate authority figures when they feel morally compelled to do so. She earned her B.A. in Philosophy from McGill University and holds Master's in Public Administration from Columbia University's School of International and Public Affairs. She completed her doctoral work at the Rotman School of Management at the University of Toronto.

Iain Munro is a Professor of Leadership and Organization at the University of Newcastle. His work has been published in *Organization Studies, Organization, Human Relations, Business Ethics Quarterly,* and the *Journal of Business Ethics*. He has authored a book on *Information Warfare in Business: Strategies of Control and Resistance* (London: Routledge, 2005). He serves on the editorial boards of *Human Relations, Organization,* and *Organization Studies*.

Adam Nix is a Lecturer in Responsible Business at the University of Birmingham and an Associate of the Lloyd's Centre for Responsible Business. His research interests include historical research into digital-era business and understanding how wrongdoing and irresponsibility exist in organizational and market contexts.

Sebastian Oelrich is a Post-Doc Researcher of Financial and Management Accounting at Technische Universitaet Dresden, Germany. His research focuses on prevention and detection mechanisms against fraud, including whistleblowing, social-control agents, corporate culture, as well as their interplay. He also gives lectures on fraud and business ethics.

Srikanth Paruchuri is B. Marie Oth Professor of Business Administration in Mays School of Business at Texas A&M University. He holds a PhD from Columbia University. His research focuses on the consequences of significant events to associated actors and on the role of social networks in firm innovation. He has published in several journals including *Academy of Management Journal, Strategic Management Journal*, and *Organization Science*. He has served as an Associate Editor at *Academy of Management Journal* and is currently serving on several editorial boards.

Sabrina Plaß is a PhD candidate at the Management Department at Paderborn University (Germany). Her research interests include CSR, corporate sustainability, business ethics, and behavioral economics. Her current research focuses on experimental studies on whistleblowing and conceptual investigations on corporate digital responsibility.

Timothy G. Pollock is the Haslam Chair in Business and Distinguished Professor of Entrepreneurship in the Haslam College of Business, University of Tennessee – Knoxville. His research focuses on how social evaluations – such as status, reputation, celebrity, and stigma – social capital, impression management activities, and media accounts influence market dynamics, firm outcomes such as market valuations and media coverage, and a variety of corporate governance structures and strategic decision-making outcomes. He is also interested in how entrepreneurs' experiences and organizational resource endowments influence their strategic decision-making. His research has won numerous awards and been published in all the top management journals. He is also an International Research Fellow with the Centre for Corporate Reputation at Oxford University, a Research Fellow with Haslam's Neel Corporate Governance Center, has served as an Associate Editor for the *Academy of Management Journal*, and served on the executive committees of the Organization and Management Theory Division of the *Academy of Management* and the Organization Science Division of *INFORMS*.

Jo-Ellen Pozner is an Associate Professor of Management and Entrepreneurship at the Leavey School of Business at Santa Clara University. Before Santa Clara, she was on the Faculty of the Haas School of Business, University of California, Berkeley. Her research focuses on questions of corporate governance and social evaluation, especially the reputational and labor market effects of misconduct at the organizational level on boards of directors. Her current work focuses on the social processes through which publics make sense of and evaluate others in light of wrongdoing. She graduated with a PhD in Management and Organizations from the Kellogg School of Management, Northwestern University, and holds an MBA from the Stern School of Business, New York University, a Masters in Economics from the School of Advanced International Studies, Johns Hopkins University, and a BSFS in International Economics from the School of Foreign Service, Georgetown University.

Sabrina Schäfers is a PhD candidate at the Management Department at Paderborn University (Germany). Her research interests include business ethics, behavioral economics, social norms, and whistleblowing. Her current research focuses on the experimental investigation of effective measures to improve whistleblowing behavior in organizations.

Brigitte Wecker is a Doctoral candidate in Strategic Management at the University of Mannheim, Germany. Prior to joining academia, she worked as a Consultant for McKinsey & Company. Her current primary research interest is corporate misconduct.

LIST OF CONTRIBUTORS

Matthias Brauer	University of Mannheim, Germany
Stephanie Decker	University of Birmingham, UK
Behnud Mir Djawadi	Paderborn University, Germany
Jung-Hoon Han	University of Missouri, USA
Kate Kenny	University of Galway, Ireland
Aharon Mohliver	London Business School, UK
Celia Moore	Imperial College Business School, UK
Iain Munro	University of Newcastle, UK
Adam Nix	University of Birmingham, UK
Sebastian Oelrich	Technische Universität Dresden, Germany
Srikanth Paruchuri	Texas A&M University, USA
Sabrina Plaß	Paderborn University, Germany
Timothy G. Pollock	University of Tennessee – Knoxville, USA
Jo-Ellen Pozner	Santa Clara University, USA
Sabrina Schäfers	Paderborn University, Germany
Brigitte Wecker	University of Mannheim, Germany

FOREWORD

Research in the Sociology of Organizations (RSO) publishes cutting edge empirical research and theoretical papers that seek to enhance our understanding of organizations and organizing as pervasive and fundamental aspects of society and economy. We seek provocative papers that push the frontiers of current conversations, that help to revive old ones, or that incubate and develop new perspectives. Given its successes in this regard, RSO has become an impactful and indispensable fount of knowledge for scholars interested in organizational phenomena and theories. RSO is indexed and ranks highly in Scopus/SCImago as well as in the Academic Journal Guide published by the Chartered Association of Business schools.

As one of the most vibrant areas in the social sciences, the sociology of organizations engages a plurality of empirical and theoretical approaches to enhance our understanding of the varied imperatives and challenges that these organizations and their organizers face. Of course, there is a diversity of formal and informal organizations – from for-profit entities to non-profits, state and public agencies, social enterprises, communal forms of organizing, non-governmental associations, trade associations, publicly traded, family owned and managed, private firms – the list goes on! Organizations, moreover, can vary dramatically in size from small entrepreneurial ventures to large multi-national conglomerates to international governing bodies such as the United Nations.

Empirical topics addressed by *Research in the Sociology of Organizations* include: the formation, survival, and growth or organizations; collaboration and competition between organizations; the accumulation and management of resources and legitimacy; and how organizations or organizing efforts cope with a multitude of internal and external challenges and pressures. Particular interest is growing in the complexities of contemporary organizations as they cope with changing social expectations and as they seek to address societal problems related to corporate social responsibility, inequality, corruption and wrongdoing, and the challenge of new technologies. As a result, levels of analysis reach from the individual, to the organization, industry, community and field, and even the nation-state or world society. Much research is multi-level and embraces both qualitative and quantitative forms of data.

Diverse theory is employed or constructed to enhance our understanding of these topics. While anchored in the discipline of sociology and the field of management, *Research in the Sociology of Organizations* also welcomes theoretical engagement that draws on other disciplinary conversations – such as those in political science or economics, as well as work from diverse philosophical traditions. RSO scholarship has helped push forward a plethora theoretical conversations on institutions and institutional change, networks, practice, culture, power, inequality, social movements, categories, routines, organization design and change, configurational dynamics, and many other topics.

Each volume of *Research in the Sociology of Organizations* tends to be thematically focused on a particular empirical phenomenon (e.g., creative industries, multinational corporations, entrepreneurship) or theoretical conversation (e.g., institutional logics, actors and agency, microfoundations). The series publishes papers by junior as well as leading international scholars, and embraces diversity on all dimensions. If you are scholar interested in organizations or organizing, I hope you find *Research in the Sociology of Organizations* to be an invaluable resource as you develop your work.

Professor Michael Lounsbury
Series Editor, *Research in the Sociology of Organizations*
Canada Research Chair in Entrepreneurship & Innovation
University of Alberta

INTRODUCTION: ORGANIZATIONAL WRONGDOING AS THE "FOUNDATIONAL" GRAND CHALLENGE: CONSEQUENCES AND IMPACT

Claudia Gabbioneta, Marco Clemente and Royston Greenwood

ABSTRACT

Organizational wrongdoing is still very much prevalent in today's society. Traditional and social media are full of examples of organizations engaging in unethical or illegal behavior. While it is difficult – if not impossible – to establish whether the ever-increasing number of reported cases of wrongdoing is due to an actual increase in the phenomenon (objectivist view of wrongdoing) or to more attention being paid to it (social-constructivist view of wrongdoing), the fact remains that organizational wrongdoing seems to have become the norm rather than an exception in our everyday life. This is concerning, as organizational wrongdoing tends to undermine trust in fundamental institutions, such as the Market, the State, Religion, and Law, and may lead to them being replaced by other – sometimes less desirable – institutions or create an "institutional void." Because of its potential impact on established institutions, organizational wrongdoing deserves to be closely monitored and further examined. This volume of Research in the Sociology of Organizations *is an attempt to draw attention to the theoretical and empirical relevance of the topic, consolidate and extend the knowledge accumulated in this area of research, and highlight potential direction for future research. The volume focuses in particular on the variegated consequences and impact of organizational wrongdoing.*

Organizational Wrongdoing as the "Foundational" Grand Challenge: Consequences and Impact
Research in the Sociology of Organizations, Volume 85, 1–10
Copyright © 2023 by Claudia Gabbioneta, Marco Clemente and Royston Greenwood
Published under exclusive licence by Emerald Publishing Limited
ISSN: 0733-558X/doi:10.1108/S0733-558X20230000085001

Keywords: Organizational wrongdoing; misconduct; scandals; corruption; unethical behavior; grand challenge; social evaluation

INTRODUCTION

In 2021, in opening the pages of a newspaper, one could not keep up with the number and frequency of reports on wrongdoing by organizations. In March, the U.K. Financial Reporting Council (FRC) commenced an investigation into Deloitte over its audit work of car dealership chain Lookers for the years 2017 and 2018.[1] The audit became part of an investigation by the Financial Conduct Authority (FCA), with allegations of fraud and black holes in Lookers' accounts. Although the FCA subsequently dropped its investigation, the FRC decided to carry out a full investigation of Deloitte's work. In effect, the FCA was implicitly probing Deloitte's role as a protector of the market system.

In July of the same year, both the former chief executive officer and the chief financial officer of telecommunications company FTE Networks, were arrested and charged with accounting fraud among a series of crimes, including the embezzling of millions of dollars from the company to pay for private jet use, luxury automobiles, personal credit cards, unauthorized wire transfer, stock issuances, and unauthorized salary increases.[2]

In September 2021, the Securities and Exchange Commission fined New York City-based telecom Pareteum Corp. $500,000 for overstating its revenue by approximately $42 million over six quarters and for providing false information to its auditors.[3] In the same month, Kraft Heinz agreed to pay $62 million as part of a settlement with the Securities and Exchange Commission for improper accounting that led to the restatement of several years of financial reporting, and, in December, Peter Armbruster – the former chief financial officer of trucking and logistics company Roadrunner Transportation Systems – was convicted for his role in a complex securities and accounting fraud scheme.[4]

The above cases are just a few examples of companies that have been investigated or found guilty of financial misbehaviors within a few months. Such wrongdoings are not novel (Cooper et al., 2013): Enron (e.g., Arnold & de Lange, 2004; Coffee, 2001; Fox, 2003; Healy & Palepu, 2003; McLean & Elkind, 2013; Unerman et al., 2004) and Parmalat (e.g., Ferrarini & Giudici, 2006; Gabbioneta et al., 2013; Melis, 2005) are infamous earlier examples. But they do seem to keep attracting considerable and growing attention. Other venues and forms of organizational wrongdoing are also in the spotlight and are receiving significant media coverage internationally, such as the Weinstein and the Epstein scandals or the Roman Catholic Church's abusive treatment of indigenous children in residential schools, to cite a few.

Implications for Institutional Trust

It is difficult to establish conclusively whether instances of organizational wrongdoing are on the increase or whether the seemingly growing list is an outcome of media interest and its sharper ability to uncover and expose such behaviors. As unreported instances of organizational wrongdoing are difficult, if not impossible, to observe, the media are the main source of information on organizational wrongdoing that one can draw upon (Roulet & Clemente, 2018, Clemente et al., 2016, Roulet & Pichler, 2020). The media, however, do not offer an objective, impartial representation of events (Clemente & Gabbioneta, 2017). Rather, by framing an event as an instance of wrongdoing, the media act as social control agents (Greve et al., 2010, Palmer, 2012), separating rightful from wrongful behavior and contributing to the categorization of that event as wrongdoing.

However, the increase in the number and frequencies of reported instances of organizational wrongdoing, whether due to an actual increase in the phenomenon (objectivist view of wrongdoing) or a social construction by the media (social-constructivist view of wrongdoing), can and may irreparably undermine trust in fundamental institutions, such as the Market, the State, Religion, and Law (on this point, see also Lounsbury, forthcoming). These institutions are the foundation of our society, and they enable it to function and survive. If faith in these institutions erodes, they can become replaced by other, sometimes less desirable alternatives, (Zucker, 1986). For example, in Italy in the second half of the nineteenth century, the lack of trust in the newly formed State – due to the absence of central government institutions at the local level and repeated episodes of corruption and wrongdoing – was associated with the emergence and development of various criminal organizations (e.g., Cosa Nostra in Sicily, 'Ndrangheta in Calabria, and Camorra in Campania) that seemed to offer an answer to the problems and uncertainties experienced by the population at the time (Dickie, 2004). Similarly, the series of sex scandals that hit the Catholic Church in the United States and elsewhere resulted in a loss of trust in this institution and a sharp decrease in the number of its members, some of which moved away from religion as a whole or joined more extreme congregations (Piazza & Jourdan, 2018). Or, again, the lack of trust in the functioning of the financial market in the aftermath of the wave of financial scandals taking place at the turn of the century, of which Enron and Parmalat are only the most egregious examples, was followed by a resurgence of barter and, more generally, of several non-market-based forms of exchange (e.g., Goff, 2009; Marin & Schnitzer, 2002). Moreover, if the lack of trust in institutions becomes widespread, it might be used to justify populist and even violent challenges to taken-for-granted norms and behaviors, which constitute the pillars of our society.

The consequences of organizational wrongdoing, in other words, could be profoundly disruptive. Furthermore, with more and more scholarly attention directed toward other grand challenges, such as climate change, social inequality, and sustainability, and multiple calls for scholars to study the Sustainable Development Goals (George et al., 2016), we should not forget that solving corruption (Castro et al., 2020) and other forms of organizational wrongdoing is a "foundational" grand challenge that underlies many others. As the UN puts it, "acting against corruption is imperative to achieving the recently adopted Sustainable Development Goals, which aim to end poverty, protect the planet, and ensure prosperity for all, amongst others" (UNDOC, 2020).

Hence, the motivation for this volume of *Research in the Sociology of Organizations* is to draw attention to the theoretical and empirical relevance of the topic, to consolidate and extend the knowledge being accumulated in this area of research, and to highlight potential directions for future research. This volume focuses in particular on the variegated consequences and impact of organizational wrongdoing, which we discuss below.

ORGANIZATIONAL WRONGDOING AS THE "FOUNDATIONAL" GRAND CHALLENGE: CONSEQUENCES AND IMPACT

This volume, *Organizational Wrongdoing as the "Foundational" Grand Challenge: Consequences and Impact*, includes seven papers and focuses on the consequences of organizational wrongdoing, and the role of whistleblowing. It also includes a methodology paper.

Remedial Actions After Organizational Wrongdoing

The first study in this volume examines the remedial actions that firms can take to recover from wrongdoing. Pozner, Mohliver, and Moore argue that organizational theory offers conflicting perspectives on whether new legislation will increase or decrease pressure on firms to take remedial action following misconduct. The dominant perspective posits that new legislation increases expectations, amplifying pressures to take remedial action. A more recent perspective, however, suggests that the mere expectation that a firm is required to meet more stringent regulatory requirements will influence relevant audiences to certify firms as legitimate. This certification effect, in other words, buffers firms, reducing the pressure to take remedial action after misconduct. Using a temporary, largely arbitrary exemption from a key provision of the Sarbanes-Oxley Act, the Authors find that firms that were *not* required to meet all the regulatory standards of good governance were 45% *more* likely to replace their CEOs following the announcement of an earnings restatement after Sarbanes-Oxley. On the other hand, firms that were required to meet all of the Sarbanes-Oxley's provisions were 26% *less* likely to replace their CEOs. The Authors conclude that these results show some unexpected negative consequences of introducing new legislation as a means of curbing organizational wrongdoing.

Spillover Effects of Organizational Wrongdoing

The second and third papers in this volume focus more particularly on the so-called spillover effects of organizational wrongdoing, whereby "innocent" firms (bystanders) are affected by wrongdoings committed by other firms. This area of research has grown significantly in the last few years but produced mixed results. Whereas some studies provide evidence of negative spillover effects accruing to bystander firms (Barnett & King, 2008; Jonsson et al., 2009; Paruchuri &

Misangyi, 2015), other studies document positive spillover effects (Naumovska & Lavie, 2021; Paruchuri et al., 2019; Piazza & Jourdan, 2018). Moreover, while some studies have found spillover to be driven by *similarities* in product offerings, industry membership, or category membership (Jonsson et al., 2009; Naumovska & Lavie, 2021; Paruchuri et al., 2019), other studies have also considered the role that organizational *differences* can play (Paruchuri et al., 2019; Piazza & Jourdan, 2018). More research is needed to uncover when a positive or negative spillover is more likely to occur and to uncover the underlying mechanisms driving them.

Han, Pollock, and Paruchuri address both of these questions by drawing on attribution and expectancy violations theories. These Authors argue that a spillover's valence (i.e., being positive or negative) depends on the locus of attributions made by stakeholders: isolated attribution – i.e., when the causes of the wrongdoing are attributed to the perpetrator alone – results in positive spillovers; in contrast, systemic attribution – i.e., when the wrongdoing's causes are perceived as indicative of a systemic problem shared among a broader set of organizations – leads to negative spillovers. The Authors further maintain that the nature of the wrongdoing – whether it is a capability or integrity failure – and its prevalence within a perpetrator and other firms, influences the attributions of stakeholders, and ultimately the spillover's valence. By theorizing when a positive vs. a negative spillover is more likely, and by moving the explanations of the mechanisms behind each of them beyond mere category membership, the Authors enhance our current understanding of spillover effects.

Wecker and Brauer also focus on spillover effects but examine more specifically whether the number of prior allegations against *other* firms has implications for a firm currently facing an allegation. Building on behavioral decision theory, the Authors argue that the relationship between allegation prevalence among other firms, and investor reaction to a focal allegation, is an inverted U-shaped arising from the combination of two effects. In the absence of prior allegations against other firms, investors fail to anticipate the focal allegation, and hence react particularly negatively (the "anticipation effect"). In the case of many prior allegations against other firms, investors also react particularly negatively because investors perceive the focal allegation as more warranted (the "evaluation effect"). Examination of 8,802 misconduct allegations against US firms between 2007 and 2017, provides support for the predicted, inverted U-shaped effect, and thus complements recent misconduct spillover research by highlighting that, not only can a current allegation against an individual firm "contaminate" other, unalleged firms, but, that prior allegations against other firms can "contaminate" an individual firm currently facing allegations.

Whistleblowing and Organizational Wrongdoing

The next three papers in this volume turn to the examination of whistleblowing. Whistleblowing – "the disclosure by organization members (former or current) of illegal, immoral, or illegitimate practices under the control of their employers, to persons or organizations that may be able to effect action" (Near & Miceli, 1985, p. 4) – has proved to be an effective way to unveil – and to some extent, deter – organizational wrongdoing (e.g., Keenan, 2000). It is therefore important to examine the factors that may promote, or, on the contrary, hinder it.

Djawadi, Plaß, and Schäfers conduct a systematic review of the literature on internal whistleblowing and identify seven thematic clusters of "peer" factors that have been studied: peer involvement in wrongdoing and whistleblowing situations, allegiance to peers and to the organization, behavioral prescription by peers, relationship and experiences with peers, fear of consequences from peers, adverse perceptions that peers have concerning whistleblowers, and adverse actions that peers undertake against whistleblowers. Taken together, these factors offer researchers an informative overview of the peer factors that have been examined to influence the whistleblowing decision, and of the extent to which whistleblowers experience adverse consequences from peers in the aftermath of whistleblowing. This paper provides a useful rationalization and categorization of prior studies on internal whistleblowing.

Oelrich examines the factors that influence the whistleblowing decision by looking at the influence of the media. This paper builds on research on norm activation to develop a moderation-mediation model of whistleblowing that highlights how the media can convey social norms and influence whistleblowing intentions. Using a cross-national survey of employees from China, Germany, and Russia ($n = 1,159$), Oelrich hypothesizes and finds that media criticism of corruption and fraud directly influences employee attitudes toward corruption as well as the likelihood that they will blow the whistle. He also finds that media criticism reduces the negative influence of "corrupted" colleagues on the whistleblower's attitude toward corruption, and the negative influence of their fear of retaliation on whistleblowing intentions. These results highlight the media's impact on whistleblowing decisions and illuminate the factors that promote whistleblowing.

Munro and Kenny investigate the whistleblowing decision by looking at the relationship that whistleblowers build with activist social movements. The Authors argue that there is a clear relationship of mutual support between whistleblowing and activist social movements, both in the process of whistleblowing and in furthering the campaigns of the social movements themselves. Alliances with activist social movements can not only mitigate the effects of retaliation against whistleblowers, but can also provide more general support. In addition, whistleblower disclosures can be a vital resource for the work of activists by drawing public attention to widespread corruption and wrongdoing. Whistleblowers can even become activists and be drawn into the social movements. Several whistleblowers have positioned their reasons for blowing the whistle not simply as a matter of public interest, but more broadly as a social protest and civil disobedience. By theorizing the complex and mutual relationship between whistleblowers and activist social movements, the Authors identify another factor that can promote whistleblowing and increase the unveiling and/or deterring of wrongdoing.

Methodological Issues in Research on Organizational Wrongdoing

The last paper in this volume is a methodology paper, in which Nix and Decker demonstrate the valuable insights provided by historical approaches. The Authors draw on a range of practices from history and the social sciences to introduce four historically informed approaches: narrative history, analytically structured history, historical process study, short-term process study. They differentiate these approaches based on their particular affordances and treatment of two key methodological considerations: historical evidence, and temporality. Narrative history makes critical use of social documents and narrative sources that originate from, or refer to, historical events, and it generally covers a long time period, following certain themes or actors through multiple historically relevant contexts. Analytically structured history relies on evidence based on historical norms and procedures, though source selection is guided by an interest in theoretical conceptualization rather than historical events, and focuses on events within a clearly specified period that is dictated by theoretical relevance. Historical process study uses historical sources as data but places this material in its historical context and is guided by an interest in long-term processes, often involving multiple stakeholders. Short-term process study uses contemporary secondary data from an event to reconstruct specific events and employs temporal distance to understand complex and fast-moving dynamics within specific event(s) and processes. By identifying these four historically informed approaches, the Authors point at the importance of history for the study of organizational wrongdoing and offer a valuable methodological roadmap for future research in this area.

FUTURE DIRECTIONS FOR RESEARCH ON ORGANIZATIONAL WRONGDOING

While significantly enhancing our understanding of organizational wrongdoing, the contributions in this volume highlight work that still needs to be done. Future research may further investigate the impact of legislative changes aimed at curbing organizational wrongdoing. Whereas the introduction of new regulation may have positive consequences in some areas, it may also produce unintended negative effects. The paper by Pozner, Mohliver, and Moore, for example, shows that firms subject to most stringent regulatory provisions become less likely to fire their CEO after announcing an earnings restatement than they were before the legislation was enacted, while firms exempt from the same provisions become more likely to replace their CEOs. Future research may look at other pieces of regulation aiming at preventing wrongdoing and examine the extent to which they may have similar unexpected negative consequences.

Another important yet insufficiently addressed question is if, and how, spillover effects are affected by social evaluations, such as status, reputation, celebrity, and stigma. Organizational and management scholars have long recognized social evaluations as an important factor shaping audiences' interpretation of, and reaction to, organizational misconduct, particularly because of their ability to provide audiences with cognitive heuristics that alleviate perceived uncertainty at the onset of misconduct (Bundy & Pfarrer, 2015; Chandler et al., 2020; Dewan & Jensen, 2020; Park & Rogan, 2019). However, they have not investigated how these evaluations may affect the attribution process theorized by Han, Pollock, and Paruchuri. Nor have we learned how social evaluations may influence the expectancy violations by stakeholders. Future studies are needed to analyze how social evaluations combine with social attributions and misconduct valance in causing – or preventing – spillover effects.

Finally, future studies could take a closer look at the relationship between whistleblowing and activist social movements. Munro and Kenny highlight the benefits of a closer relationship between these two actors, but further research is needed to uncover the potential problems associated with this relationship. Is it possible that activist social movements could make instrumental use of whistleblowers, such that the latter see their role more as supporting social movements, than as reporting wrongdoing? Are whistleblowers, in other words, at risk of being "captured" by social movements? The relationship between whistleblowers and activist social movements deserves further examination.

CONCLUSIONS

This volume draws attention to organizational wrongdoing, which has acquired significant momentum in recent years as a consequence of the increase in the number of cases reported in the media. For us, understanding the processes of organizational wrongdoing is of great theoretical and empirical relevance – not least because wrongdoing might contribute to the decline and loss of institutional trust. We consider organizational wrongdoing as a "foundational" grand challenge that affects the ability of our society to solve other grand challenges and attain the Sustainable Development Goals. Our hope is that the breadth and depth of the contributions included in this volume will provide impetus to this area of research by inspiring more scholars to probe this fascinating and fundamentally important topic.

NOTES

1. https://www.frc.org.uk/news/march-2021/investigation-into-deloitte-for-the-audits-of-look; https://www.insider.co.uk/news/deloitte-under-investigation-over-audits-23699445.

2. https://www.justice.gov/usao-sdny/pr/former-ceo-and-cfo-public-telecommunications-company-charged-manhattan-federal-court; https://www.cnbc.com/2021/07/15/fte-networks-executives-charged-with-securities-fraud-conspiracy.html

3. https://www.sec.gov/enforce/33-10975-s; https://www.clearyenforcementwatch.com/2021/09/two-recent-settlements-highlight-heightened-sec-focus-on-accounting-fraud-and-potential-benefits-of-cooperation/

4. https://www.sec.gov/news/press-release/2021-174; https://www.justice.gov/opa/pr/former-chief-financial-officer-publicly-traded-company-sentenced-two-years-significant.

REFERENCES

Arnold, B., & de Lange, P. (2004). Enron: An examination of agency problems. *Critical Perspectives on Accounting, 15*(6–7), 751–765.

Barnett, M. L., & King, A. A. (2008). Good fences make good neighbors: A longitudinal analysis of an industry self-regulatory institution. *Academy of Management Journal, 51*, 1150–1170.

Bundy, J., & Pfarrer, M. D. (2015). A burden of responsibility: The role of social approval at the onset of a crisis. *Academy of Management Review, 40*, 345–369.

Castro, A., Phillips, N., & Ansari, S. (2020). Corporate corruption: A review and an agenda for future research. *Academy of Management Annals, 14*, 935–968.

Chandler, D., Polidoro Jr., F., & Yang, W. (2020). When is it good to be bad? Contrasting effects of multiple reputations for bad behavior on media coverage of serious organizational errors. *Academy of Management Journal, 63*, 1236–1265.

Clemente, M., Durand, R., & Porac, J. (2016). Organizational wrongdoing and media bias. In *Organizational wrongdoing: Key perspectives and new directions* (pp. 435–466). Cambridge University Press.

Clemente, M., & Gabbioneta, C. (2017). How does the media frame corporate scandals? The case of German newspapers and the Volkswagen diesel scandal. *Journal of Management Inquiry, 26*(3), 287–302.

Coffee, J. C. Jr. (2001). Understanding Enron: It's about the gatekeepers, stupid. *Business Lawyer, 57*, 1403–1421.

Cooper, D. J., Tina, D., & Palmer, D. (2013). Fraud in accounting, organizations and society: Extending the boundaries of research. *Accounting, Organizations & Society, 38*(6–7), 440–457.

Dewan, Y., & Jensen, M. (2020). Catching the big fish: The role of scandals in making status a liability. *Academy of Management Journal, 63*, 1652–1678.

Dickie, J. (2004). *Cosa nostra. A history of the Sicilian mafia*. Palgrave Macmillan.

Ferrarini, G., & Giudici, P. (2006). Financial scandals and the role of private enforcement: The Parmalat case. In J. Armour & J. A. McCahery (Eds.), *After Enron: Improving corporate law and modernising securities regulation in Europe and the US*. Hart Publishing.

Fox, L. (2003). *Enron: The rise and fall*. John Wiley & Sons.

Gabbioneta, C., Greenwood, R., Mazzola, P., & Minoja, M. (2013). The influence of the institutional context on corporate illegality. *Accounting, Organizations and Society, 38*(6–7), 484–504.

George, G., Howard-Grenville, J., Joshi, A., & Tihanyi, L. (2016). Understanding and tackling societal grand challenges through management research. *Academy of Management Journal, 59*, 1880–1895.

Goff, K. G. (2009). The return of barter. *Network Journal, 16*(9), 37.

Greve, H. R., Palmer, D., & Pozner, J.-E. (2010). Organizations gone wild: The causes, processes, and consequences of organizational misconduct. *Annals of the Academy of Management, 4*, 53–107.

Healy, P. M., & Palepu, K. G. (2003). The fall of Enron. *Journal of Economic Perspectives, 17*(2), 3–26.

Jonsson, S., Greve, H. R., & Fujiwara-Greve, T. (2009). Undeserved loss: The spread of legitimacy loss to innocent organizations in response to reported corporate deviance. *Administrative Science Quarterly, 54*, 195–228.

Keenan, J. P. (2000). Blowing the whistle on less serious forms of fraud: A study of executives and managers. *Employee Responsibilities and Rights Journal, 12*, 199–217.

Lounsbury, M. (Forthcoming). The problem of institutional trust. *Organization Studies*.

Marin, D., & Schnitzer. M. (2002). *Contracts in trade and transition: The resurgence of barter*. MIT Press.

McLean, B., & Elkind, P. (2013). *The smartest guys in the room: The amazing rise and scandalous fall of Enron*. Penguin Group.

Melis, A. (2005). Corporate governance failures: To what extent is Parmalat a particularly Italian Case? *Corporate Governance: An International Review, 13*, 478–488.

Naumovska, I., & Lavie, D. (2021). When an industry peer is accused of financial misconduct: Stigma versus competition effects on non-accused firms. *Administrative Science Quarterly, 66*(4), 1130–1172.

Near, J. P., & Miceli, M. P. (1985). Organizational dissidence: The case of whistle-blowing. *Journal of Business Ethics, 4*(1), 1–16.

Palmer, D. (2012). *Normal organizational wrongdoing: A critical analysis of theories of misconduct in and by organizations*. Oxford University Press.

Park, B., & Rogan, M. (2019). Capability reputation, character reputation, and exchange partners' reactions to adverse events. *Academy of Management Journal, 62*, 553–578.

Paruchuri, S., & Misangyi, V. F. (2015). Investor perceptions of financial misconduct: The heterogeneous contamination of bystander firms. *Academy of Management Journal, 58*, 169–194.

Paruchuri, S., Pollock, T. G., & Kumar, N. (2019). On the tip of the brain: Understanding when negative reputational events can have positive reputation spillovers, and for how long. *Strategic Management Journal, 40*, 1965–1983.

Piazza, A., & Jourdan, J. (2018). When the dust settles: The consequences of scandals for organizational competition. *Academy of Management Journal, 61*, 165–190.

Roulet, T. J., & Clemente, M. (2018). Let's open the media's black box: The media as a set of heterogeneous actors and not only as a homogenous ensemble. *Academy of Management Review, 43*,
327–329.

Roulet, T. J., & Pichler, R. (2020). Blame game theory: Scapegoating, whistleblowing and discursive
struggles following accusations of organizational misconduct. *Organization Theory, 1*, 1–30.

UNDOC. (2015). United Nations Office on Drugs and Crime. Retrieved September 14, 2022, from
https://www.unodc.org/unodc/en/frontpage/2015/December/breakthechain-this-international-
anti-corruption-day.html

Unerman, J., & O'Dwyer, B. (2004). Enron, WorldCom, Andersen et al.: A challenge to modernity.
Critical Perspectives on Accounting, 15(6–7), 971–993.

Zucker, L. G. (1986). Production of trust: Institutional sources of economic structure, 1840–1920.
Research in Organizational Behavior, 8, 53–111.

CHAPTER 1

THE CERTIFICATION EFFECT OF NEW LEGISLATION: CEO ACCOUNTABILITY FOR MISCONDUCT AFTER SARBANES-OXLEY

Jo-Ellen Pozner, Aharon Mohliver and Celia Moore

ABSTRACT

We investigate how firms' responses to misconduct change when the institutional environment becomes more stringent. Organizational theory offers conflicting perspectives on whether new legislation will increase or decrease pressure on firms to take remedial action following misconduct. The dominant perspective posits that new legislation increases expectations of firm behavior, amplifying pressure on them to take remedial action after misconduct. A more recent perspective, however, suggests that the mere necessity to meet more stringent regulatory requirements certifies firms as legitimate to relevant audiences. This certification effect buffers firms, reducing the pressure for them to take remedial action after misconduct. Using a temporary, largely arbitrary exemption from a key provision of the Sarbanes-Oxley Act, we show that firms that were not required to meet all the regulatory standards of good governance it required became 45% more likely to replace their CEOs following the announcement of an earnings restatement after Sarbanes-Oxley. On the other hand, those that were required to meet all of Sarbanes-Oxley's provisions became 26% less likely to replace their CEOs following a restatement

Organizational Wrongdoing as the "Foundational" Grand Challenge: Consequences and Impact
Research in the Sociology of Organizations, Volume 85, 11–33
Copyright © 2023 by Jo-Ellen Pozner, Aharon Mohliver and Celia Moore
Published under exclusive licence by Emerald Publishing Limited
ISSN: 0733-558X/doi:10.1108/S0733-558X20230000085002

announcement. Ironically, CEOs at firms with a legislative mandate intended to increase accountability for corporate misconduct shoulder less blame than do CEOs at firms without such legislative demands.

Keywords: Organizational misconduct; Sarbanes-Oxley; legislative certification; CEO turnover; symbolic management; regulation

Governments enact laws to govern firm behavior, often to prevent or minimize their wrongdoing. These laws specify appropriate rules of conduct, establish monitoring mechanisms, and outline punishments for deviations. A dominant theoretical perspective on the effect of legislation on firm behavior focuses on the various ways new laws increase pressure on firms to behave appropriately. These include imposing direct pressure on firms to comply with legal demands (DiMaggio & Powell, 1983), generating indirect pressure on them to signal their compliance through symbolic gestures (DiMaggio & Powell, 1983; Meyer & Rowan, 1977; Scott, 1995), and prompting them to take remedial action following suspicions that they have violated the new regulatory standards (Pfarrer et al., 2008; Pozner, 2008).

An alternative theoretical perspective, however, suggests that new legislation could have the opposite effect. Research has found that meeting stricter regulatory demands certifies firms as legitimate (Anderson et al., 1999; Rao, 1994; Sine et al., 2007), making it easier for them to manage stakeholder impressions and guide reactions to negative events (Elsbach & Sutton, 1992; Pfeffer, 1981). Ultimately, this may lead to less scrutiny of firm behavior and easier deflection of negative attention (Rao, 1994). In other words, firms can use the legal mandate to meet new regulatory requirements to signal that they are appropriate, valid, and desirable within a social system (Scott, 1987; Zucker, 1986). Thus, firms required to comply with new legislation are "certified" by it, increasing the likelihood that they will be endorsed by prominent institutional actors (Aldrich & Fiol, 1994; Hannan & Carroll, 1992), a key building block in both cognitive and sociopolitical legitimacy (Meyer & Rowan, 1977; Shane & Foo, 1999). This perspective suggests that firms subject to new legislative requirements may, ironically, be at least partially shielded from the consequences of violating them.

In this paper, we focus on the certification effect that the Sarbanes-Oxley Act of 2002 provided to firms that were required to fully comply with its new regulatory requirements. Sarbanes-Oxley defined corporate governance standards and mandated that Chief Executive Officers (CEOs) and Chief Financial Officers (CFOs) be personally liable for fraudulent financial statements. We theorize that the more stringent standards of corporate governance that Sarbanes-Oxley imposed on certain firms partially insulated them from the consequences of a restatement, lessening the pressure to take their senior executives to task. On the other hand, the subset of firms that were exempted from its most stringent provisions would not enjoy the same endorsement, forcing them to demonstrate fitness in other ways. Our fundamental argument is that facing revelations of misconduct after announcing an earnings restatement, firms that are not required to comply with legislative provisions pertinent to that misconduct substitute for the absence of legislative certification by engaging in visible remedial action (CEO replacement).

We test whether exemption from Section 404, a key provision of the Sarbanes-Oxley Act requiring that firms strictly enumerate and defend the robustness of their internal controls, affected the likelihood that a firm replaces its CEO in the aftermath of misconduct. Replacing the CEO is a costly and highly visible decision (Gomulya & Boeker, 2014; Zavyalova et al., 2012) that heralds the seriousness of a firm's efforts to remedy the root causes of its misdeeds (Devers et al., 2009; Pozner, 2008). We find that firms that are exempt from Section 404 of Sarbanes-Oxley replace their CEOs following a restatement announcement at a significantly higher rate after Sarbanes-Oxley than they did before the enactment of the legislation, whereas firms that are similar on all relevant observable dimensions but are required to comply with Section 404 are less likely to replace their CEOs after the legislative change. We provide detailed evidence that exempt firms are remarkably similar on observable financial characteristics and governance variables to non-exempt firms. Within the bounds of archival studies, therefore, we can reasonably treat the firms just above and just below the threshold that triggers exemption as otherwise similar, and essentially randomly treated by the "certification effect" of the legislation.

The difference in remedial action between exempt firms and non-exempt firms holds for CEOs – whose replacement is highly visible (Gangloff et al., 2014), but whose connection to earnings restatements is arguably indirect – but not for CFOs, whose connection to earnings restatements is direct (Geiger & North, 2006), but whose replacement is less notable. That we find no effect for the likelihood of CFO replacement suggests that the increased rate of CEO replacement for firms exempt from Section 404 is driven by the importance of a symbolic act than it is by holding those most directly responsible for the financial statements to task.

THE CERTIFICATION EFFECT OF LEGISLATION

Much of the work on the effect of legislation on the institutional environment and firm behavior addresses how firms adapt to meet more demanding legislative standards (DiMaggio & Powell, 1983; Meyer & Rowan, 1977). A newer perspective suggests that firms may benefit from regulatory change: because many firm attributes are not directly observable, stakeholders rely on signals that they are behaving appropriately (Aldrich & Fiol, 1994; Rao, 1994), and the higher expectations that follow regulatory change provide a signal of organizational fitness to external audiences. One type of signal that external audiences interpret positively involves standards; meeting management standards such as ISO 9000 or ISO 1400, for example, certifies firms as competent in specific domains (Gray et al., 2015; Montiel et al., 2012). Relatedly, Rao (1994) finds that victories in product competitions held by respected and independent intermediaries certified winners, leading to presumptions of victors' competence and increasing their chances of survival.

Certification signals conformity with expectations but can be easily decoupled from underlying realities. Once certified, firms may comply only partially, if at all, with the criteria required for certification (Fiss & Zajac, 2004; Sine et al., 2007), yet still benefit from the certification effect. After receiving ISO 9000 certification, for example, process compliance in medical device firms steadily deteriorated (Gray et al., 2015). The presence of the requirements signals firms' legitimacy, even if compliance with those requirements is only symbolic or even non-existent. We highlight how the mere enactment of new legislation certifies firms required to comply with its stricter regulatory requirements and term this benefit a *certification effect*. Certification buffers firms from the external scrutiny that non-certified firms face, reducing the need to expend resources to demonstrate organizational fitness (Aldrich, 1999; Rao, 1994).

Absent a certification effect, firms must find other ways to demonstrate fitness. Okhmatovskiy and David (2012) argue that organizations may substitute for compliance with a similar act, which they acknowledge can be either symbolic or substantive. This substitution response shifts stakeholder attention away from non-compliance and toward adherence to an alternate standard. Though firms ideally address misconduct in a substantive way, symbolic management – sending clear, visible signals that the firm is taking costly steps to meet stakeholders' expectations and ensure legitimacy – is also a common response (Fiss & Zajac, 2006; Gangloff et al., 2014; Westphal & Zajac, 1998). After misconduct, addressing its root causes quietly may not send a clear enough signal to external audiences that the firm is serious about change, slowing its path to restored legitimacy (Pfarrer et al., 2008). Building on this insight, we argue that firms exempt from legislative requirements designed to ensure integrity in financial reporting may need stronger signals of reparative action than firms certified by the legislation. In contrast, firms required to comply with new standards will be buffered from negative evaluation, lessening their need to send such signals.

CEO Change After a Financial Restatement

A particularly visible form of organizational misconduct is the restatement of corporate earnings. Restatements are the correction of material errors in disclosures previously filed with the Securities and Exchange Commission (SEC) that can result from legitimate errors or "accounting irregularities," fraudulent misapplication of accounting rules, or manipulation of facts, although it is often difficult to distinguish between intentional and unintentional misstatements. Regardless of whether they reflect fraud, most material earnings restatements are understood as admissions of negligence or misconduct. Restatements have meaningful consequences, including the loss of shareholder value (Akhigbe et al., 2005; Palmrose et al., 2004), impaired credibility of future financial disclosures (Farber, 2005), diminished future earnings expectations, and an increase in the cost of capital (Hribar & Jenkins, 2004).

Given the potential of restatements to elicit negative organizational consequences, most restating firms take some form of remedial action to elicit positive interpretations from external audiences (Busenbark et al., 2019; Hersel et al., 2019). CEO replacement is a common remedial measure after restatements (Arthaud-Day et al., 2006; Gangloff et al., 2014). Stakeholders typically attribute responsibility for perceived wrongdoing to the chief executive (Hersel et al., 2019), making CEO replacement a salient signal of a firm's commitment to redressing the wrongdoing. A CEO's connection to earnings restatements is more symbolic than direct, however, and replacement may be more about signaling that the firm is taking reparative actions rather than it is about enacting effective means of repairing the firm's corporate governance and financial reporting weaknesses (Boeker, 1992; Gangloff et al., 2014).

The Role of Legislative Certification in CEO Change After Misconduct

The period surrounding the passage of the Sarbanes-Oxley Act provides a rich context in which to study legislative certification effects. Also known as the "Public Company Accounting Reform and Investor Protection Act," Sarbanes-Oxley was passed in 2002 following the corporate accounting and earnings manipulation scandals that dominated news cycles and policy debates during the preceding two years. Its goal was to increase the reliability of corporate financial statements by elaborating the responsibilities of corporate boards of directors, increasing internal accountability for the accuracy of financial disclosures, and enacting penalties for non-compliance. Among other provisions, the 64-page Act required the CEO and CFO to verify the accuracy of firm financial statements personally.

Not all firms were equally beholden to all of Sarbanes-Oxley's requirements, however. One of the most important aspects of this legislation is Section 404, which mandates that firms have external experts review their internal controls and disclose weaknesses that are discovered, generating external pressure to improve internal processes (Coates & Srinivasan, 2014). By creating an incentive to penalize senior leadership in the wake of misconduct and heightening expectations of appropriate corporate governance, Sarbanes-Oxley also increased the salience of CEO replacement as a signal of a firm's commitment to sound management and oversight (Gomulya & Boeker, 2016; Hillman et al., 2011). Thus, Sarbanes-Oxley increased the expectations of senior leadership accountability of all firms but provided only those certified by it with means to explain away mismanagement and restore legitimacy without taking meaningful action. We argue the certification effect of Sarbanes-Oxley will mean that firms required to comply fully with the law will be less likely to replace their CEO after misconduct. In contrast, firms that are exempt from key Sarbanes-Oxley provisions will substitute for their comparative lack of legislative certification with the visible and costly signal of CEO replacement.

H1. After Sarbanes-Oxley, the rates of CEO replacement following a restatement announcement will (a) decrease for firms subject to its provisions, and (b) increase for firms exempt from them.

The Role of Legislative Certification in CFO Change After Misconduct

Research shows that, like CEOs, CFOs are likely to be replaced after an earnings restatement (Agrawal & Cooper, 2016; Feldmann et al., 2009). Though both are key members of the C-suite, the CFO controls the integrity of a firm's financial reporting in a more direct way than the CEO. If the firm's aim is truly to ensure the veracity and integrity of their financial reporting after misconduct, the replacement of a CFO is more relevant as a remedial act. But replacing a CFO is less visible than replacing a CEO, and thus is a weaker signal to external audiences, and carries less symbolic value. To explore whether the certification effect of the legislation is primarily symbolic, we contrast the likelihood of replacing the CEO with the likelihood of replacing the CFO as a function of legislative change.

If replacing executives following revelations of wrongdoing were designed to address issues leading to the misreporting most directly, we would expect CFO turnover trends to mirror those of CEO replacement. We would further expect this effect to be amplified following legislation specifically mandating C-suite accountability for the veracity of financial reports. Studies confirm that CFO turnover increased in the post-Sarbanes-Oxley period in response to non-fraudulent earnings restatements (Burks, 2010). Thus, the legislation did increase CFO accountability in at least some intended ways, though the remedial actions required after fraudulent restatements likely differ from those required for more benign reasons. If CFO replacement rates were not to change appreciably after the legislation in parallel with CEO replacement, it would provide evidence that CEO replacement was necessary as a symbolic management strategy in response to misconduct.

We test whether the hypothesized changes with respect to CEO replacement after the enactment of Sarbanes-Oxley are also observable for CFOs. Support for this hypothesis would indicate that firms exempt from the legislation have a desire to improve their corporate governance substantively and address the root causes behind the need to restate. On the other hand, if we found support for increased rates of CEO replacement for exempt firms but no support for increased rates of CFO replacement for those firms, this would suggest that exempt firms are managing stakeholder impressions more symbolically than directly.

H2. After Sarbanes-Oxley, the rates of CFO replacement following a restatement announcement will (a) decrease for firms subject to its provisions, and (b) increase for firms exempt from them.

METHODS

Empirical Setting

We situate our study in the context of earnings restatements and the Sarbanes-Oxley Act. Section 404 requires external experts to review firms' internal controls and disclose any weaknesses, generating pressure to improve controls (Coates &

Srinivasan, 2014), which is costly and places a considerable burden on small firms (Advisory Committee on Smaller Public Companies, 2006). To avoid imposing this disproportional cost on small firms, legislators created a temporary exemption for firms with a public float[1] of $75 million, which became permanent in September 2010 (SEC, 2010).

This "temporary" exemption allows us to establish an unusually clear causal argument. While arguments about the cost of compliance are related to firm size, the exemption is based on public float, which is only loosely coupled with size. The public float cutoff of $75 million for Section 404 exemption was arbitrary, corresponding only to the SEC's regulation around the accelerated filing of annual statements,[2] suggesting that exempt firms are similar to non-exempt firms just above the compliance threshold. As the threshold was set in a largely arbitrary political process, we consider it to be exogenous and unknowable *a priori*, allowing us to contrast the behavior of Section 404-exempt firms to those of non-exempt firms. The unpredictable sequence of extensions provides a quasi-natural experiment, providing an appropriate setting to assess the legislation's impact on firm behavior (Arping & Sautner, 2013; Iliev, 2010).

Data

Our sample of restating firms was drawn from two databases issued by the U.S. Government Accountability Office (GAO): restatements announced between January 1, 1997, and June 30, 2002 (U.S. Government Accountability Office, January 17, 2003), and restatements announced between July 1, 2002 and June 30, 2006 (U.S. Government Accountability Office, August 31, 2006). The GAO database only includes cases due to "so-called 'aggressive' accounting practices, intentional and unintentional misuse of facts applied to financial statements, oversight or misinterpretation of accounting rules, and fraud" (U.S. Government Accountability Office, 2002, p. 72). Of the population of 2,309 restatement announcements, complete data were available for 752 restatements from 410 firms. We include the first restatement for each firm to avoid inflating the number of observations.

Dependent Variables. We test firm responses to restatements using *CEO change* and *CFO change*, which take on a value of 1 if the CEO or CFO was replaced within the 365-days following the restatement announcement, and a value of 0 otherwise. These data were collected from media reports and corporate 8-K filings with the SEC.

Independent Variables. Our primary independent variable is an interaction of *Post-Sarbanes-Oxley* and *Exempt from Section 404*. *Post-Sarbanes-Oxley* takes a value of 1 if the restatement was announced after the Sarbanes-Oxley Act was signed on July 30, 2002, and 0 if the restatement preceded the legislation. *Exempt from Section 404* was assigned a value of 1 if the restating firm was below the $75 million public float threshold for exemption from Section 404; a value of 0 indicates a requirement to comply with Section 404 during the quarter in which the restatement was announced. The interaction *Post-Sarbanes-Oxley* X *Exempt* *from Section 404* takes a value of 1 if the firm was exempt from Section 404 after Sarbanes-Oxley's passage.

Control Variables. Media attention is an important driver of CEO turnover (Pozner et al., 2019; Wiersema & Zhang, 2013) and may vary between exempt and non-exempt firms. We account for baseline levels of media attention with *Number of Articles about the Company*, a count of articles mentioning the focal firm in the year before restatement, gathered from the *Lexis-Nexis* news service. We also measure the number of articles that included the word "restatement" for the 365 days beginning with restatement announcement to proxy for external pressure, but exclude articles published after the CEO turnover announcement; we label this variable *Number of Articles about the Restatement.*

We also include controls for firm size and performance. *Market Capitalization* measures the value of stock outstanding, calculated 21 trading days before the restatement announcement. We also include *Return on Assets*, capturing average firm profitability for three years, collected using the *CRSP/Compustat* merged database.

To ensure that our independent variables capture only the variance attributable to the act of restating rather than characteristics of the restatement itself, we include four measures of restatement severity. The dummy variable *Increased net income* is included because restatements that raise net income generally elicit fewer penalties than those that do not (Akhigbe et al., 2005). This measure was drawn from public filings in the SEC's *EDGAR* database. We include a dummy variable for restatements driven by *error involving fraud,* which engender particularly adverse outcomes (Hennes et al., 2008). *Number of quarters restated*, a count of the number of reporting periods corrected in the restatement, captures the duration of the problem underlying restatement. Finally, we include *Restatement was prompted by the firm;* if a restatement was prompted by the SEC or external auditor, the focal firm failed either to find or to disclose its improper accounting, potentially increasing the importance of the firm to take remedial action.

Identification Strategy

Our empirical test relies on comparing two groups of firms that are similar along all dimensions except for Section 404. We thus compare firms below the $75 million exemption threshold to the rest of the firms in the "micro-cap" category, which includes firms with up to $150 million public float and market capitalization no larger than $1.5 billion, resulting in a final sample of 84 firms. We report the results of several robustness checks as well as models testing our hypotheses on broader samples, which increase our sample size to 210 firms. Generally, we err on the side of precision over sample size, which reduces statistical power but increases the chances that the effects we identify can be attributed to the exemption rather than omitted variables. A firm with a public float of $70 million is likely to differ on multiple dimensions from a firm with a public float of $500 million, but not necessarily from a firm with a public float of $100 million.

Our statistical identification relies on the similarity of two groups of firms ("Exempt from Section 404" and "Not Exempt from Section 404") with respect to the characteristics associated with CEO replacement in the wake of restatements.

Two attributes of the firms in our sample lend confidence to this assumption. First, although firm size correlates with CEO dismissal, public float is only weakly related to firm size (correlation of 0.4). Similarly, there is no difference in the mean rate of pre-Sarbanes Oxley CEO replacement between exempt and non-exempt firms; a two-sample t-test finds a similar rate across the two groups ($t = 1.58$).

Second, our sample occupies a small part of the distribution of firm size within the population of publicly traded corporations. Public firms vary in value from a few million dollars to hundreds of billions of dollars. When the threshold of $75 million free float was created, it represented the smallest 0.00018% of public firms; adding firms with free floats larger than $75 million but smaller than $150 million (our comparison group) increases the threshold by only 0.0003%. Fig. 1a represents the entire distribution of firms as a function of market capitalization (y-axis) and free float (x-axis); the figure-in-figure represents the section of the range from which our sample derives. In the entire distribution, the range of market capitalization extends to $1 trillion, and the range of free float extends to $60 billion. Fig. 1b zooms in from Fig. 1a, while Fig. 1c documents the parts of the distribution where our sample lies; within this bracket, exempt and non-exempt firms should not differ systematically.

We further restrict our sample by excluding firms with market caps higher than that of the largest exempt firm (the horizontal dashed line), as well as firms that have public float larger than $150 million. Unreported analysis demonstrates that firms excluded from the comparison set are dissimilar, while firms included in the comparison set are similar in terms of profitability, number of quarters restated, number of analysts following, and network centrality in the network of directors, justifying this empirical choice.

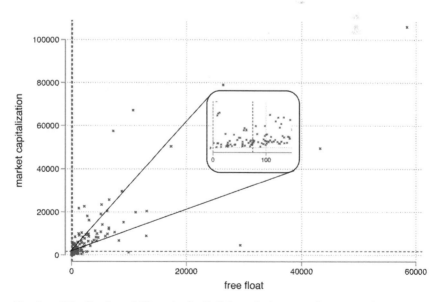

Fig. 1a. Distribution of Firms in the Full Sample, by Free Float (up to $60 Billion) and Market Capitalization (up to $1 Trillion).

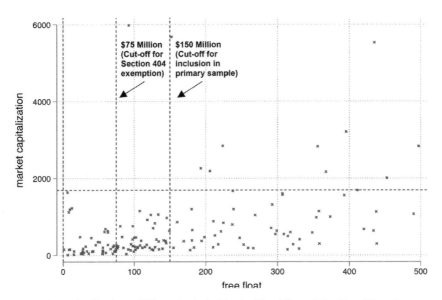

Fig. 1b. Distribution of Firms Included in the Final Sample by Free Float (up to $500 Million) and Market Capitalization (up to $6 Billion).

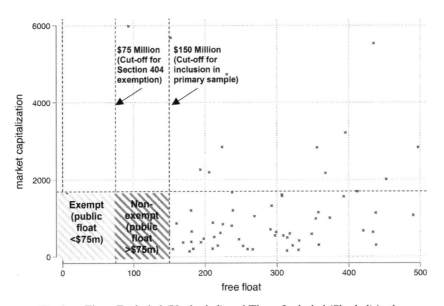

Fig. 1c. Firms Excluded (Unshaded) and Those Included (Shaded) in the Final Sample.

Lastly, we test for differences between exempt and non-exempt firms (with a free float between $75 and $150 million) on observables in Table 1. The two groups are identical on all but two dimensions: non-exempt firms have higher market

Table 1. *T*-tests for Equality of Means Between Firms That are Exempt from Section 404 (Free Float < $75 million) and Those That are Not Exempt (Free Float Between $75 and 150 Million), *N* = 84.

	$1m–$75m Float		$75m–$150m Float		*p* value
	Mean	SD	Mean	SD	
Market capitalization	265	309	389	295	0.06
Number of employees	2.9	4.0	4.4	7.1	0.21
Number of directors	11.7	4.1	13.2	4.3	0.10
Number of articles about the company one year before the restatement	62	175	130	430	0.34
Number of articles about the restatement	1.33	3.30	1.36	2.48	0.96
Number of analysts following the stock	0.92	0.82	1.10	0.56	0.22
Book to market ratio	0.86	0.60	0.70	0.54	0.19
Net profit margin	−0.15	0.52	−0.08	0.30	0.44
Return on equity	−0.08	0.75	−0.06	0.41	0.86
Return on assets	0.04	0.21	0.07	0.18	0.58
Return on assets (prior year)	0.09	0.21	0.11	0.08	0.60
Return on assets (two years ago)	0.14	0.19	0.11	0.09	0.34
Capital ratio	0.28	0.25	0.29	0.38	0.94
Cash ratio	1.02	1.57	0.65	0.79	0.17
Quick ratio	1.96	1.83	1.49	0.98	0.15
Current ratio	2.56	2.12	2.14	1.15	0.27
R&D to sales ratio	0.04	0.12	0.05	0.10	0.76
Amended quarterly reports	0.56	0.50	0.49	0.51	0.52
Replaced CEO	0.28	0.45	0.31	0.47	0.75
Replaced CFO	0.12	0.32	0.22	0.42	0.19
Replaced auditor	0.19	0.39	0.11	0.32	0.33
Days until CEO replacement	232	103	140	92	0.09
Days until CFO replacement	116	57	142	95	0.67

capitalization ($\mu = 389$, $\mu = 265$, $p = 0.06$) and replace their CEOs more quickly ($\mu = 142$ days, $\mu = 232$ days, $p = 0.09$) than exempt firms.[3] The groups do not differ on the likelihood of CEO replacement ($p = 0.75$), CFO replacement ($p = 0.19$), pre-restatement media attention ($p = 0.34$), or post-restatement media attention ($p = 0.96$). We control for systematic differences in size in our empirical analysis.

Model. We use a linear probability model with robust standard errors, represented as:

$$y_i = \alpha + \beta_1 Exempt_i + \beta_2 SOX + \beta_3 (Exempt \times SOX) + \beta X_i + \varepsilon_i.$$

in which *y* is a dummy variable taking the value 1 if the CEO changed after the restatement in models 1 and 2 and value 0 otherwise. In models 3 and 4, the variable takes the value 1 if the CFO changed after the restatement and value 0 otherwise. *Exempt from Section 404* is a dummy variable taking the value 1 if the firm is smaller than the threshold required to comply with Section 404 ($75 million in public float on the last day of the second quarter), *Post-Sarbanes-Oxley* takes the value 1 if the restatement occurred after Sarbanes-Oxley's passage. *X* is a vector of controls. The coefficient of interest is the interaction term, Post-Sarbanes-Oxley X Exempt from Section 404, which captures the change in likelihood that firms exempt from Section 404 after Sarbanes-Oxley passed will replace the CEO or CFO compared to firms required to comply with the legislation. A one-unit increase in the independent variable translates to a βx100 percent change in the dependent variable (CEO replacement and CFO replacement). Replications of all analyses using both logit and probit models show stronger statistical significance for our variable of interest, but with less easily interpreted results.

Results

We report descriptive statistics and correlations in Table 2. Table 3 reports the results of a linear probability model of the likelihood of CEO and CFO turnover for the sub-sample of firms with free float smaller than $150 million.

Model 1 reports the results for the linear probability models regressing CEO change on *Post-Sarbanes-Oxley* and *Exempt from Section 404*. In model 2, we add the interaction of *Post-Sarbanes-Oxley* X *Exempt from Section 404*. The coefficient for *Post-Sarbanes-Oxley,* representing the change in likelihood that non-exempt firms replace their CEO following a restatement after Sarbanes-Oxley, is negative and significant, indicating firms subject to Sarbanes-Oxley's most stringent provisions were 26% *less* likely to replace their CEOs following a restatement announcement than before the legislation was enacted. The interaction term is positive and significant, indicating that exempt firms were 45% *more* likely to replace their CEOs following a restatement announcement than before Sarbanes-Oxley. In raw terms, before Sarbanes-Oxley, 1 of 6 CEOs at restating firms below the $75M threshold was replaced (17%), as were 6 of 27 CEOs at firms above it (22%); after Sarbanes-Oxley, 8 of 17 CEOs at exempt firms (47%) were replaced after restating, while only 8 of 34 CEOs at non-exempt firms (24%) were dismissed. These results provide support for *H1*.

Models 3 and 4 replicate the analysis for CFOs. The results demonstrate that the likelihood of CFO replacement did not change as a function of the legislation for either exempt or non-exempt firms. This analysis fails to provide support for *H2*.

Robustness Checks. Our identification strategy is centered on the assumption that when Sarbanes-Oxley passed, exempt and non-exempt firms were equally likely to replace their CEO in response to announcing restatements. To address the concern that our choice of comparison group influences this result, we conducted a falsification test, re-running our models using additional arbitrarily defined comparison groups, to confirm that the results do not hold when we use thresholds different from $75 million.

We reran all models to test how the significance of the primary independent variable changed as a function of two additional counterfactual threshold levels for exemption from Section 404 ($60 million and $90 million), and eight different threshold levels for inclusion in the comparison group, ranging from $150 million to $500 million in increments of $50 million. We then chart how the *z*-score of the coefficient of *Sarbanes-Oxley* X *Exempt from Section 404* varies for each of these

Table 2. Descriptive Statistics and Correlations.

	N	Mean	SD	1	2	3	4	5	6	7	8	9	10	11
1	CEO change	84	0.29	0.46											
2	CFO change	84	0.18	0.38	0.24**										
3	Exempt from Section 404	84	0.49	0.50	-0.07	-0.15+									
4	Post Sarbanes-Oxley	84	0.59	0.50	-0.04	0.07	0.30*								
5	No. articles 1 year prior to restatement	84	99.5	336.5	0.14	-0.01*	-0.11	0.06							
6	No. articles about the restatement	84	1.38	2.94	0.39**	0.29*	-0.01	0.20	0.11						
7	Market cap 21 days pre-restatement ($M)	84	319	304	-0.04	-0.04	-0.18	0.10+	0.11	0.15					
8	Three-year average ROA	84	0.09	0.15	0.13	-0.14	-0.01	-0.11	-0.08	0.06	0.19				
9	Restatement increased income	84	0.24	0.43	-0.05	-0.11	-0.05	-0.04	0.03	-0.18	-0.24	-0.17			
10	Number of quarters restated	84	4.78	4.44	0.10	0.03	0.02	0.07	-0.01	0.15	-0.07	0.08	-0.15		
11	Restatement due to fraud	84	0.07	0.26	0.12	-0.01	-0.09	-0.33**	-0.07	-0.08	-0.07	0.09*	-0.04	0.14	
12	Restatement prompted by the firm	84	0.76	0.43	-0.13	-0.03	0.05	-0.13	0.05	-0.12	-0.05	-0.04	-0.02	0.15	0.04

Note: ** $p < 0.01$, * $p < 0.05$, + $p < 0.10$.

Table 3.   Linear Probability Models Predicting CEO Change and CFO Change
After Restatement.

	(1)	(2)	(3)	(4)
	CEO Change	CEO Change	CFO Change	CFO Change
Exempt from Section 404	−0.043	−0.321*	−0.163*	−0.237*
	(0.085)	(0.137)	(0.078)	(0.098)
Sarbanes-Oxley	−0.058	−0.260*	0.061	0.007
	(0.099)	(0.129)	(0.088)	(0.135)
Sarbanes-Oxley X Exempt from Section 404		0.453**		0.120
		(0.167)		(0.153)
Number of articles about the company	0.000	0.000	0.000	0.000
	(0.000)	(0.000)	(0.000)	(0.000)
Number of articles about the restatement	0.062***	0.061***	0.038**	0.038**
	(0.0134)	(0.015)	(0.013)	(0.013)
Market capitalization	0.000	0.000	0.000	0.000
	(0.000)	(0.000)	(0.000)	(0.000)
Three-year average return on assets	0.364	0.332	−0.377	−0.385
	(0.289)	(0.255)	(0.298)	(0.313)
Restatement resulted in increased income	−0.000	−0.009	−0.118	−0.121
	(0.116)	(0.111)	(0.103)	(0.103)
Number of quarters restated	0.003	0.008	−0.004	−0.002
	(0.011)	(0.011)	(0.009)	(0.009)
Restatement due to fraud	0.216	0.203	0.030	0.027
	(0.217)	(0.225)	(0.193)	(0.194)
Restatement prompted by the firm	−0.109	−0.080	0.018	0.025
	(0.115)	(0.113)	(0.109)	(0.110)
Constant	0.338*	0.381*	0.297+	0.309+
	(0.169)	(0.169)	(0.153)	(0.158)
Observations	84	84	84	84
R-squared	0.233	0.282	0.163	0.168

Notes: Robust standard errors in parentheses.
*** $p < 0.001$, ** $p < 0.01$, * $p < 0.05$, + $p < 0.10$.

permutations. The results are plotted in Fig. 2. The lines represent how the z-score varies for different comparison groups and the real ($75 million/solid line) and counterfactual ($60 million/dotted line, and $90 million/dashed line) thresholds.

If our effect were spurious, the $75 million public float threshold would not be inherently meaningful and we would expect other thresholds to explain CEO departure. As the figure shows, however, $75 million is the only consistently meaningful threshold, and our key independent variable remains significant for all comparisons, while no other public float thresholds reflect z-scores of 1.64 or higher. This strongly suggests that $75 million is a meaningful threshold, supporting our assertion that exemption from Section 404 drives CEO replacement, rather than other omitted variables that correlate with public float. This provides further evidence that the $75 million public float threshold, though arbitrary, became a meaningful threshold separating firm behavior in response to earnings restatements.

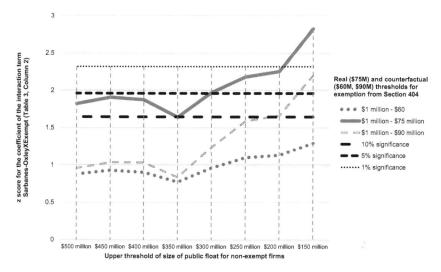

Fig. 2. Statistical Significance (*z*-scores) of the Coefficient on the Interaction Term for Sarbanes-Oxley X Exempt Using Different Thresholds of Public Float.

We also assume parallel trends between firms smaller than $75 million public float and firms $75–$150 million with respect to CEO replacement. If exempt firms become more likely than firms just above the threshold for exemption to replace their CEO between 1996 and 2006, our identification of the effect of Sarbanes-Oxley may be an artifact of violating the parallel trends assumption of a difference-in-difference model. To address this, we test for a difference in the likelihood of CEO replacement before Sarbanes-Oxley between the two groups and find none ($t = 1.56$).

We also compare firm characteristics and the likelihood of CEO replacement before and after Sarbanes-Oxley and find no systematic differences on a variety of metrics. Table 4 reports sample mean and *t*-statistic tests for equality of means between the firms that announced their restatements before and after the passage of Sarbanes-Oxley. The two groups are statistically identical on all but one dimension that might predict both restatement and CEO replacement: more articles are written about the restatement after Sarbanes-Oxley than before ($p = 0.07$). No systematic difference is found for size ($p = 0.42$), number of directors ($p = 0.71$), number of employees ($p = 0.31$), or replacement of the CFO ($p = 0.52$), or auditor ($p = 0.85$). Nevertheless, their treatment of top managers varies systematically before and after the legislation.

Third, we collected data on CEO replacement for non-restating firms. We found no significant differences in the likelihood of CEO replacement between firms exempt from Section 404 and firms just above the exemption threshold. The results are reported in Table 5.

Another concern is whether there is a difference between firms with a public float just above and just below the cutoff of $75 million. Public float can be

Table 4.   *T*-Tests for Equality of Means Before and After Sarbanes-Oxley.

	Before SOX		After SOX		*p* value
	Mean	SD	Mean	SD	
Market capitalization	297	250	350	340	0.42
Number of employees	2.9	3.9	4.2	6.8	0.31
Number of directors	12.3	4.3	12.6	4.2	0.71
Number of articles about the company one year before the restatement	75	324	111	338	0.62
Number of articles about the restatement	0.67	1.60	1.81	3.46	0.07
Number of analysts following the stock	1.00	0.58	1.02	0.78	0.86
Book to market ratio	0.88	0.66	0.70	0.49	0.15
Net profit margin	−0.11	0.31	−0.11	0.49	0.93
Return on equity	−0.01	0.71	−0.11	0.53	0.46
Return on assets	0.09	0.08	0.03	0.24	0.11
Return on assets (prior year)	0.13	0.07	0.09	0.19	0.27
Return on assets (two years ago)	0.12	0.09	0.13	0.18	0.89
Capital ratio	0.31	0.28	0.27	0.34	0.57
Cash ratio	0.86	1.49	0.81	1.05	0.87
Quick ratio	1.88	1.70	1.61	1.28	0.42
Current ratio	2.61	1.85	2.16	1.56	0.24
R&D to sales ratio	0.06	0.09	0.04	0.12	0.38
Amended quarterly reports	0.44	0.50	0.58	0.50	0.23
Replaced CEO	0.31	0.47	0.29	0.46	0.86
Replaced CFO	0.14	0.35	0.19	0.40	0.52
Replaced auditor	0.14	0.35	0.15	0.36	0.85
Days until CEO replacement	148	98	225	105	0.16
Days until CFO replacement	179	81	110	81	0.21

Table 5.   Replication of the Full Model (Table 3, Model 2) Using Non-Restating Firms.

	(1)	(2)	(3)	(4)	(5)	(6)
	Full Sample	Full Sample	Full Sample	$1m–$150m Public Float	$1m–$150m Public Float	$1m–$150m Public Float
	CEO Change	CEO Change	CEO Change	CEO Change	CEO Change	CEO Change
Exempt from Section 404		−0.0121	−0.026+		−0.047	−0.056+
		(0.0125)	(0.013)		(0.029)	(0.033)
Sarbanes-Oxley		0.00432	−0.004		0.006	−0.008
		(0.0104)	(0.013)		(0.015)	(0.022)
Sarbanes-Oxley X Exempt from Section 404			0.029			0.029
			(0.022)			(0.025)
Market capitalization		0.000	0.000	0.000	0.000	0.000
		(0.000)	(0.000)	(0.000)	(0.000)	(0.000)
Public float	0.000	0.000	0.000	0.000	0.000	0.000

(*Continues*)

Table 5.   (*Continued*)

	(1)	(2)	(3)	(4)	(5)	(6)
	Full Sample	Full Sample	Full Sample	$1m–$150m Public Float	$1m–$150m Public Float	$1m–$150m Public Float
	CEO Change	CEO Change	CEO Change	CEO Change	CEO Change	CEO Change
	(0.000)	(0.000)	(0.000)	(0.000)	(0.000)	(0.000)
Three-year average ROA		0.018	0.017		0.039	0.039
		(0.0247)	(0.025)		(0.058)	(0.058)
Constant	0.0273***	0.032*	0.036**	0.029*	0.088+	0.088+
	(0.006)	(0.019)	(0.013)	(0.015)	(0.048)	(0.048)
Observations	1,211	1,093	1,093	551	509	509
R-squared	0.002	0.003	0.004	0.000	0.008	0.010

Notes: Robust standard errors in parentheses.
*** $p < 0.001$, ** $p < 0.01$, * $p < 0.05$, + $p < 0.1$.

manipulated in ways that other measures of size cannot (Gao, 2016; Gao et al., 2009). We therefore constrained our sample to firms with public floats between $50 million and $125 million, yielding a sample of 50 firms, 19 with public floats of $50–$75 million, and 31 with public floats of $75–$125 million. Firms manipulating public float are more likely to be in this restricted sample than in our primary one. Even using this smaller sample, our results support *H1* but not *H2*; results are reported in Table 6.

Table 6.   Replication of the Full Model (Table 3, Model 2) Using Firms with Public Floats of $50–$125 Million.

	(1)	(2)	(3)	(4)
VARIABLES	CEO Change	CEO Change	CFO Change	CFO Change
Exempt from Section 404	0.024	−0.297+	−0.096	−0.169
	(0.134)	(0.152)	(0.106)	(0.113)
Sarbanes-Oxley	−0.035	−0.250	0.034	−0.015
	(0.133)	(0.151)	(0.133)	(0.171)
Sarbanes-Oxley X Exempt from Section 404		0.579*		0.131
		(0.220)		(0.212)
Number of articles about the company	0.000	0.000	0.000	0.000
	(0.000)	(0.000)	(0.000)	(0.000)
Number of articles about the restatement	0.082*	0.080*	0.032	0.032
	(0.035)	(0.035)	(0.0336)	(0.034)
Market capitalization	0.0001***	0.0001***	0.0001**	0.0001**
	(0.000)	(0.000)	(0.000)	(0.000)
Three-year average return on assets	0.151	0.173	−0.255	−0.250
	(0.241)	(0.184)	(0.289)	(0.309)
Restatement resulted in increased income	−0.010	−0.049	0.018	0.009

(*Continues*)

Table 6.   (*Continued*)

VARIABLES	(1) CEO Change	(2) CEO Change	(3) CFO Change	(4) CFO Change
	(0.117)	(0.121)	(0.147)	(0.146)
Number of quarters restated	0.0112	0.018	0.011	0.013
	(0.018)	(0.018)	(0.016)	(0.017)
Restatement due to fraud	0.286	0.245	0.064	0.055
	(0.274)	(0.245)	(0.202)	(0.206)
Restatement prompted by firm	−0.108	−0.099	−0.181	−0.179
	(0.163)	(0.153)	(0.187)	(0.188)
Constant	0.099	0.174	0.245	0.262
	(0.212)	(0.210)	(0.217)	(0.223)
Observations	50	50	50	50
R-squared	0.363	0.453	0.203	0.208

Notes: Robust standard errors in parentheses.
*** $p < 0.001$, ** $p < 0.01$, * $p < 0.05$, + $p < 0.1$.

DISCUSSION

We investigate the effect of legislative certification on executive turnover after organizational misconduct. We find a significant change in how firms respond to revelations of their misconduct after the enactment of Sarbanes-Oxley, such that firms *exempt* from key provisions of the act become 45% *more* likely to dismiss their CEOs after announcing a restatement than they were before the legislation, while firms that become subject to the strictest provisions of Sarbanes-Oxley become 26% *less* likely to dismiss the CEO in the same situation. We find no similar difference across groups with respect to CFO dismissal. Our analysis suggests the certification effect of the legislation confers legitimacy on firms that are required to comply with it but leaves exempt firms without such cover. These results suggest that Sarbanes-Oxley, ironically, released some CEOs from having to take more accountability for wrongdoing.

Our results provide evidence for the certification effects of legislation. The literature on certification has focused on the legitimacy benefits gained by meeting a professional standard or performance threshold (Anderson et al., 1999; Gray et al., 2015; Rao, 1994). We broaden these findings by showing how the mere enactment of new legislation certifies firms required to comply with its stricter regulatory requirements. Indeed, these firms can be declared fit *despite* evidence they had *not* complied with the new legislative standards. In contrast, exemption from new regulatory requirements, while intended to reduce burdens on small firms, eliminates the certification effect and appears to lead them to take more substantial remedial action. Our results suggest that exempt firms felt compelled to substitute (Okhmatovskiy & David, 2012) for the absence of certification by enacting costly symbolic management strategies after misconduct.

Consistent with existing research, our results suggest that replacing the CEO following misconduct is a means to restore firm legitimacy (Arthaud-Day et al., 2006; Gangloff et al., 2014; Pozner & Harris, 2016). Firms exempt from

Sarbanes-Oxley's most stringent requirements appear to select CEO replacement over CFO replacement as a remedial strategy, even though the CFO has a more direct and substantive role in verifying a firm's financial records than the CEO. It also underscores the importance for exempt firms to send strong signals to external audiences that they will address misconduct, even if replacing the CFO might have done this more directly (Geiger & North, 2006).

Though we found that firms beholden to Sarbanes-Oxley's strictest provisions became less likely to replace their CEOs after announcing a restatement, it would be inaccurate to conclude that Sarbanes-Oxley had a universally negative effect on CEO accountability. In other work using a broader set of firms, we find that Sarbanes-Oxley increased the likelihood of CEO replacement after a restatement, amplified by increased media coverage of corporate misconduct in the post-Sarbanes-Oxley world (Pozner et al., 2019). Relatedly, Gomulya and Boeker (2016) found that Sarbanes-Oxley decreased the extent to which a CEO could count on close ties to board members as protection from dismissal in the aftermath of misconduct. Burks (2010), however, found that Sarbanes-Oxley shifted the disciplinary measures imposed on CEOs for misconduct away from dismissal toward bonus penalties, a change attributed to restatements becoming less severe after the legislation. These conflicting findings indicate that Sarbanes-Oxley had differential effects on CEO accountability depending, at minimum, on firm size, restatement severity, and media attention, as well as whether the firm is beholden to all of Sarbanes-Oxley's legislative requirements. True main effects are always rare; the effect of Sarbanes-Oxley on CEO accountability for misconduct is no exception.

A thought-provoking incidental finding was that non-exempt firms that replace their CEOs after misconduct do so more quickly, though at a lower rate, than exempt firms. Questions about how quickly firms engage in remedial action after misconduct are interesting, as are questions about whether that speed matters to stakeholder evaluations (Pfarrer et al., 2008). Our data, however, are not well-suited to addressing such questions. Future research would benefit from exploring the predictors and consequences of different temporal choices for remedial action following firm misconduct, using a sample more appropriate to those questions.

Our findings also have implications for theory on organizational stigmatization (Devers et al., 2009; Pozner, 2008). While much research has explored what contributes to firm-level stigmatization as well as how firms react to potentially stigmatizing events (Gomulya & Boeker, 2016; Semadeni et al., 2008), our study sheds light on why otherwise similar firms may take different actions in light of potentially negative social evaluations. We show that institutional forces – the certification effect of new legislation – lower stigma for firms beholden to new legislation but raise it for firms exempt from its provisions.

Relevant to this discussion is the fact that the size of a firm's free float is, to some degree, open to manipulation by the company (Gao et al., 2009). Some firms may reduce the magnitude of their free float to avoid having to comply with the demands of Section 404, facilitating shady activity with less scrutiny. This is consistent with the findings summarized in Table 6, which demonstrates that our hypotheses hold with even the most restricted sample. The fact that some may have manipulated free float to avoid regulatory oversight could mean that every firm in that category suffers from some level of stigma-by-association. In this case, accountability pressures from CEOs beholden to the legislation are lessened not only because of the certification effect but also by "cleaning" the category of certified firms from those firms with a tendency toward misconduct who self-select into the non-certified category. Determining what portion of the effect is driven by which mechanism is an interesting direction for future research.

More generally, our findings bolster our understanding of the effect of legislative change on firm behavior. Although research has demonstrated the coercive impact of legislation on market structures and firm practices, ours is one of the first studies to explore how legislative change affects how firms that have already violated the law behave (Pozner et al., 2019, is another). Our results also show clearly that legislation affects the behavior of firms that are outside its circumscribed regulatory reach, as well as the behavior of firms beholden to it – though in ways opposite to the legislation's intent.

While our results indicate that new legislation elicits certification effects that release CEOs from experiencing the same burden of accountability as those who are exempt from the legislation's requirements, we do not want to suggest in any way that Sarbanes-Oxley was ineffective, nor are we claiming that legislative efforts to control misconduct are destined to backfire. Indeed, in other work on the effect of legislative change on firm responses to misconduct, we found that Sarbanes-Oxley increased CEO accountability, both directly and by amplifying the role of the media in spotlighting firms' misdeeds and triggering CEO change (Pozner et al., 2019). Our study has practical implications for firms, particularly those that find themselves on the wrong side of the law, as well as policymakers who want to encourage as many firms as possible to stay on the right side of it. Our results here focus on a small subset of firms to tease out how new legislation may have unintended certification effects that release CEOs from the accountability they ought to shoulder for their firms' misconduct. Policymakers should be sensitive to their potential.

ACKNOWLEDGMENTS

We would like to thank Colleen Stuart, Brandy Aven, Michaela DeSoucey, Simona Giorgi, Andreea Gorbatai, Olenka Kacperczyk, Ming Leung, Kelly Patterson, Seemantini Pathak, Sara Soderstrom, Sameer Srivastava, Adina Sterling, and Mathijs de Vaan, for their comments on earlier versions of this paper. An earlier version of this paper was available on SSRN.

NOTES

1. Public float refers to the total market value of shares in the hands of public investors, excluding insiders and controlling interest stakeholders. This differs from market capitalization, which refers to the total value of shares outstanding, regardless of ownership.

2. The temporary and arbitrary nature of the exemption means that it has been subject to regular debate. In a November 2002 final rule release, the following comment was entered into the published record:

"Comments were mixed on the proposed definition of accelerated filer. Several commenters believed all public companies should be subject to the same filing deadlines, regardless of a company's size or experience in preparing filings. Other commenters agreed with the notion of excluding smaller companies that may not have the necessary resources and infrastructure to report on an accelerated basis. Comments also were somewhat mixed on the proposed use of public float as a method to differentiate between companies. Several commenters thought the $75 million public float threshold was too low...I believe that a public float test serves as a reasonable measure of size and market interest..." (McFarland, 2002).

Correspondingly, the Dodd-Frank Act of 2010 required the SEC to study whether $300 million in public float might be a more reasonable cut-off for Section 404 exemption; proposals have suggested extending the exemption to firms of that size (SEC, 2016).

3. In response to a reviewer's comment that non-exempt firms replacing their CEOs more quickly than exempt firms do suggests that CEOs from non-exempt firms are less protected by certification that we argue, we ran our primary models (which we report in Table 3), with a restricted time window for CEO replacement. When we restrict the time window for CEO replacement to 6 months rather than 12, our results are qualitatively identical in direction and significance.

REFERENCES

Advisory Committee on Smaller Public Companies. (2006, April 23). Final Report to the Securities and Exchange Commission. www.sec.gov/info/smallbus/acspc/acspc-finalreport.pdf

Agrawal, A., & Cooper, T. (2016). Corporate governance consequences of accounting scandals: Evidence from top management, cfo and auditor turnover. *Quarterly Journal of Finance, 07*, 1650014.

Akhigbe, A., Kudla, J., & Madura, R. J. (2005). Why are some corporate earnings restatements more damaging? *Applied Financial Economics, 15*, 327–336.

Aldrich, H. E. (1999). *Organizations evolving*. Sage Publications.

Aldrich, H. E., & Fiol, C. M. (1994). Fools rush in? The institutional context of industry creation. *Academy of Management Review, 19*, 645–670.

Anderson, S. W., Daly, J. D., & Johnson, M. F. (1999). Why firms seek ISO 9000 certification: Regulatory compliance or competitive advantage? *Production and Operations Management, 8*, 28–43.

Arping, S., & Sautner, Z. (2013). Did SOX Section 404 make firms less opaque? Evidence from cross-listed firms. *Contemporary Accounting Research, 30*, 1133–1165.

Arthaud-Day, M. L., Certo, S. T., Dalton, C. M., & Dalton, D. R. (2006). A changing of the guard: Executive and director turnover following corporate financial restatements. *Academy of Management Journal, 49*, 1119–1136.

Boeker, W. (1992). Power and managerial dismissal: Scapegoating at the top. *Administrative Science Quarterly, 37*, 400–421.

Burks, J. J. (2010). Disciplinary measures in response to restatements after Sarbanes–Oxley. *Journal of Accounting and Public Policy, 29*, 195–225.

Busenbark, J. R., Marshall, N. T., Miller, B. P., & Pfarrer, M. D. (2019). How the severity gap influences the effect of top actor performance on outcomes following a violation. *Strategic Management Journal, 40*, 2078–2104.

Coates, J. C., & Srinivasan, S. (2014). SOX after ten years: A multidisciplinary review. *Accounting Horizons, 28*, 627–671.

Devers, C. E., Dewett, T., Mishina, Y., & Belsito, C. A. (2009). A general theory of organizational stigma. *Organization Science, 20*, 154–171.

DiMaggio, P. J., & Powell, W. W. (1983). The iron cage revisited: Institutional isomorphism and collective rationality in organizational fields. *American Sociological Review, 48*, 147–160.

Elsbach, K. D., & Sutton, R. I. (1992). Acquiring organizational legitimacy through illegitimate actions: A marriage of institutional and impression management theories. *Academy of Management Journal, 35*, 699–738.

Farber, D. B. (2005). Restoring trust after fraud: Does corporate governance matter? *Accounting Review, 80*, 539–561.

Feldmann, D. A., Read, W. J., & Abdolmohammadi, M. J. (2009). Financial restatements, audit fees, and the moderating effect of CFO turnover. *AUDITING: A Journal of Practice & Theory, 28*, 205–223.

Fiss, P. C., & Zajac, E. J. (2004). The diffusion of ideas over contested terrain: The (non)adoption of a shareholder value orientation among German firms. *Administrative Science Quarterly, 49*, 501–534.

Fiss, P. C., & Zajac, E. J. (2006). The symbolic management of strategic change: Sensegiving via framing and decoupling. *Academy of Management Journal, 49*, 1173–1193.

Gangloff, K. A., Connelly, B. L., & Shook, C. L. (2014). Of scapegoats and signals: Investor reactions to CEO succession in the aftermath of wrongdoing. *Journal of Management, 42*, 1614–1634.

Gao, F. (2016). To comply or not to comply: Understanding the discretion in reporting public float and SEC regulations. *Contemporary Accounting Research, 33*, 1075–1100.

Gao, F., Wu, J. S., & Zimmerman, J. (2009). Unintended consequences of granting small firms exemptions from securities regulation: Evidence from the Sarbanes-Oxley Act. *Journal of Accounting Research, 47*, 459–506.

Geiger, M. A., & North, D. S. (2006). Does hiring a new CFO change things? An investigation of changes in discretionary accruals. *The Accounting Review, 81*, 781–809.

Gomulya, D., & Boeker, W. (2014). How firms respond to financial restatement: CEO successors and external reactions. *Academy of Management Journal, 57*, 1759–1785.

Gomulya, D., & Boeker, W. (2016). Reassessing board member allegiance: CEO replacement following financial misconduct. *Strategic Management Journal, 37*, 1898–1918.

Gray, J. V., Anand, G., & Roth, A. V. (2015). The influence of ISO 9000 certification on process compliance. *Production and Operations Management, 24*, 369–382.

Hannan, M. T., & Carroll, G. R. (1992). *Dynamics of organizational populations: Density, legitimation, and competition.* Oxford University Press.

Hennes, K., Leone, A., & Miller, B. (2008). The importance of distinguishing errors from irregularities in restatement research: The case of restatements and CEO/CFO turnover. *The Accounting Review, 83*, 1487–1519.

Hersel, M. C., Helmuth, C. A., Zorn, M. L., Shropshire, C., & Ridge, J. W. (2019). The corrective actions organizations pursue following misconduct: A review and research agenda. *Academy of Management Annals, 13*, 547–585.

Hillman, A. J., Shropshire, C., Certo, S. T., Dalton, D. R., & Dalton, C. M. (2011). What I like about you: A multilevel study of shareholder discontent with director monitoring. *Organization Science, 22*, 675–687.

Hribar, P., & Jenkins, N. T. (2004). The effect of accounting restatements on earnings revisions and the estimated cost of capital. *Review of Accounting Studies, 9*, 337–356.

Iliev, P. (2010). The effect of SOX Section 404: Costs, earnings quality, and stock prices. *The Journal of Finance, 65*, 1163–1196.

McFarland, M. H. (2002). *Acceleration of periodic report filing dates and disclosure concerning website access to reports.* https://www.sec.gov/rules/final/33-8128.htm#I

Meyer, J. W., & Rowan, B. (1977). Institutionalized organizations: Formal structure as myth and ceremony. *American Journal of Sociology, 83*, 340–363.

Montiel, I., Husted, B. W., & Christmann, P. (2012). Using private management standard certification to reduce information asymmetries in corrupt environments. *Strategic Management Journal, 33*, 1103–1113.

Okhmatovskiy, I., & David, R. J. (2012). Setting your own standards: Internal corporate governance codes as a response to institutional pressure. *Organization Science, 23*, 155–176.

Palmrose, Z.-V., Richardson, V. J., & Scholz, S. (2004). Determinants of market reactions to restatement announcements. *Journal of Accounting and Economics, 37*, 59–89.

Pfarrer, M. D., DeCelles, K. A., Smith, K. G., & Taylor, M. S. (2008). After the fall: Reintegrating the corrupt organization. *Academy of Management Review, 33*, 730–749.

Pfeffer, J. (1981). Management as symbolic action: The creation and maintenance of organizational paradigms. *Research in Organizational Behavior*, *3*, 1–52.

Pozner, J. E. (2008). Stigma and settling up: An integrated approach to the consequences of organizational misconduct for organizational elites. *Journal of Business Ethics*, *80*, 141–150.

Pozner, J.-E., & Harris, J. (2016). Who bears the brunt? A review and research agenda for the consequences of organizational wrongdoing for individuals. In D. Palmer, R. Greenwood, & K. Smith-Crowe (Eds.), *Organizational wrongdoing* (pp. 404–434). Cambridge University Press.

Pozner, J.-E., Mohliver, A., & Moore, C. (2019). Shine a light: How firm responses to announcing earnings restatements changed after Sarbanes–Oxley. *Journal of Business Ethics*, *160*, 427–443.

Rao, H. (1994). The social construction of reputation: Certification contests, legitimation, and the survival of organizations in the American automobile industry: 1895–1912. *Strategic Management Journal*, *15*, 29–44.

Scott, W. R. (1987). The adolescence of institutional theory. *Administrative Science Quarterly*, *32*, 493–511.

Scott, W. R. (1995). *Institutions and organizations*. Sage Publications.

SEC. (2010, September 15). Final Rule on Internal Control Over Financial Reporting in Exchange Act Periodic Reports Of Non-Accelerated Filers.

Semadeni, M., Cannella, A. A., Fraser, D., & Lee, D. S. (2008). Fight or flight: Managing stigma in executive careers. *Strategic Management Journal*, *29*, 557–567.

Shane, S., & Foo, M.-D. (1999). New firm survival: Institutional explanations for new franchisor mortality. *Management Science*, *45*, 142–159.

Sine, W. D., David, R. J., & Mitsuhashi, H. (2007). From plan to plant: Effects of certification on operational start-up in the emergent independent power sector. *Organization Science*, *18*, 578–594.

U.S. Government Accountability Office. (2002, October 4). *Financial statement restatements: Trends, market impacts, regulatory responses, and remaining challenges.* http://www.gao.gov/new.items/d03138.pdf

U.S. Government Accountability Office. (2003, January 17). *Financial restatement database.* http://www.gao.gov/new.items/d03395r.pdf

U.S. Government Accountability Office. (2006, August 31). *Financial restatement database.* http://www.gao.gov/new.items/d061053r.pdf

Westphal, J. D., & Zajac, E. J. (1998). The symbolic management of stockholders: Corporate governance reforms and shareholder reactions. *Administrative Science Quarterly*, *43*, 127–153.

Wiersema, M. F., & Zhang, Y. (2013). Executive turnover in the stock option backdating wave: The impact of social context. *Strategic Management Journal*, *34*, 590–609.

Zavyalova, A., Pfarrer, M. D., Reger, R. K., & Shapiro, D. L. (2012). Managing the message: The effects of firm actions and industry spillovers on media coverage following wrongdoing. *Academy of Management Journal*, *55*, 1079–1101.

Zucker, L. G. (1986). Production of trust: Institutional sources of economic structure, 1840–1920. *Research in Organizational Behavior*, *8*, 53–111.

CHAPTER 2

GOOFUS OR GALLANT? AN ATTRIBUTION-BASED THEORY OF MISCONDUCT SPILLOVER VALENCE

Jung-Hoon Han, Timothy G. Pollock and Srikanth Paruchuri

ABSTRACT

Despite growing interest in misconduct spillovers – where unimplicated bystand-ers' stock prices, reputations, resources, and opportunities are positively or neg-atively affected by others' misconduct – theory about spillovers' antecedents has largely focused on industry or product similarity, and has used the same characteristics to argue for both positive and negative spillovers. Furthermore, limited research has considered both positive and negative spillovers together, instead focusing on one kind of spillover or the other in isolation, thereby cre-ating a lack of theoretical integration within the literature. In this chapter, we draw on attribution theory and expectancy violations theory to explain when and how misconduct incurs positive and negative spillovers. We argue that a spillover's valence depends on the locus of attributions made by stakeholders, where the misconduct's causes are attributed to the perpetrator alone (i.e., an isolated attribution) – resulting in positive spillovers – or the misconduct's causes are perceived as indicative of a systemic problem shared among a broader set of organizations (i.e., a systemic attribution), leading to nega-tive spillovers. We further suggest that the misconduct's nature and misconduct

Organizational Wrongdoing as the "Foundational" Grand Challenge: Consequences and Impact
Research in the Sociology of Organizations, Volume 85, 35–51
Copyright © 2023 by Jung-Hoon Han, Timothy G. Pollock and Srikanth Paruchuri
Published under exclusive licence by Emerald Publishing Limited
ISSN: 0733-558X/doi:10.1108/S0733-558X20230000085003

*prevalence within a perpetrator and among other firms influences stakehold-
ers' attributions, and ultimately the spillover's valence. Our theory contributes
to the organizational misconduct literature by providing a unifying theoretical
framework to understand both positive and negative spillovers.*

Keywords: Organizational misconduct; spillover; attribution theory;
expectancy violations; stakeholder reactions; cognition and perceptions

When you were a kid, and another kid (it could have been a sibling, or a friend)
did something wrong, did you end up sharing the blame whether you did anything
wrong or not? Or, did you come out looking better? That is, like the children's
cartoon about brothers Goofus and Gallant, were you seen as a "screw-up" or
"the good kid," and what affected whether you received the undeserved praise or
vilification?

In the last 15 years, management scholars have given significant attention to
a similar issue: how a firm's misconduct affects innocent bystanders (Barnett &
King, 2008; Jonsson et al., 2009; Naumovska & Lavie, 2021; Paruchuri et al.,
2019; Pontikes et al., 2010; Zavyalova et al., 2012). The dominant view of this
phenomenon has been that audiences often extend their punitive reactions to
others within the same category, thereby incurring negative spillovers (Barnett &
King, 2008; Jonsson et al., 2009; Paruchuri & Misangyi, 2015). However, coun-
tervailing findings have recently emerged that misconduct can also incur positive
spillovers to uninvolved bystanders (Naumovska & Lavie, 2021; Paruchuri et al.,
2019; Piazza & Jourdan, 2018), creating a confusing overall image where some
bystanders suffer, while some benefit from other organizations' misconduct.

Further complicating the matter, prior research has focused on perpetrator
and bystander similarities in product offerings, industry membership, or category
membership as the basis for both positive and negative spillovers (Jonsson et al.,
2009; Naumovska & Lavie, 2021; Paruchuri et al., 2019), although the positive
spillover camp has also considered the role organizational differences play in
affecting a spillover's valence (Paruchuri et al., 2019; Piazza & Jourdan, 2018).
We are aware of only one study that has simultaneously considered both positive and negative spillovers. Naumovska and Lavie (2021) argued and found that
negative spillovers prevail the greater the market overlap between perpetrators
and bystanders, up to a point, after which the positive spillover effects of competition begin to dominate. They also argued that positive spillovers occur as
market overlap increases, and when evaluators use fine-grained market classifica-
tions. However, advancing research on misconduct spillovers requires more comprehensive theorizing about the antecedents of positive and negative spillovers
and their underlying mechanisms that goes beyond just category co-membership
(Naumovska & Zajac, 2022). Developing a more comprehensive understanding
of when a positive or negative spillover is more likely to occur requires understanding why stakeholders make the particular attributions (Roehm & Tybout,
2006) that lead to positive and negative spillovers.

In this chapter, we build theory predicting misconduct spillover valence using attribution theory (Heider, 1958; Kelley & Michela, 1980; Martinko et al., 2011) and expectancy violations theory (Burgoon, 1978; Burgoon & Hale, 1988; Burgoon & Le Poire, 1993; Kim, 2014). Attribution theory has generated valuable insights into how audiences form causal inferences and evaluative judgments (Kelley & Michela, 1980; Martinko et al., 2011). Management and organizational scholars have used attribution theory to study stakeholders' responses to organizational crises (Bundy & Pfarrer, 2015; Lange & Washburn, 2012) and ascribe responsibility for negative outcomes (e.g., Gomulya et al., 2019), primarily focusing on how internal or external misconduct attributions shape stakeholders' reactions to perpetrators (Bednar et al., 2015; Love & Kraatz, 2017). Scholars have employed expectancy violations theory to understand how stakeholders react to positive and negative surprises (Pfarrer et al., 2010), and how firms use different impression management techniques to manage negative expectancy violations (Elsbach, 2006; Graffin et al., 2016).

We argue that stakeholders' attributions have implications for bystanders as well as perpetrators, because attributional processes are highly relational in nature (Eberly et al., 2011; Lange & Washburn, 2012). That is, whether stakeholders attribute a misconduct incident to the perpetrator only (i.e., make an "isolated attribution") or view it as indicative of a common problem among a larger group of firms (i.e., make a "systemic attribution") is a key determinant of the misconduct spillover's valence, because this attribution shapes stakeholders' perceived generalizability of the perpetrator's culpability (Paruchuri & Misangyi, 2015). Thus, our theory differs from prior work focused on category characteristics alone (Barnett & King, 2008; Naumovska & Lavie, 2021). Focusing just on category characteristics by definition means that spillovers can only occur within that industry or category. In contrast, because we view the locus of audiences' attribution as the central theoretical mechanism, our theory allows for the possibility that misconduct spillovers can occur across dissimilar industry categories, depending on how the attribution process unfolds.

In developing our theory, we first establish the relationship between the locus of attribution and the valence of the spillover, proposing that more isolated attributions have a greater influence on the likelihood of positive spillovers, and more systemic attributions have a greater influence on the likelihood of negative spillovers. Next, we theorize about how the nature of the misconduct – whether it is a capability or integrity failure (Connelly et al., 2016; Mishina et al., 2012) – affects the locus of attribution. We also consider how the extent to which the misconduct's prevalence within the perpetrator organization (Greve et al., 2010) and among organizations in the broader environment (Zavyalova et al., 2012) influences the locus of attribution. We further theorize that these different prevalence dimensions also moderate the relationship between the locus of attribution and the spillovers' valences in different ways.

Our theoretical framework contributes to the organizational misconduct literature by moving the focus from common category membership and competitive overlaps to the attributional processes underlying stakeholders' assessments that drive positive and negative spillovers. In doing so, we clarify the boundary conditions for the long-observed phenomenon of negative spillovers, and the newly emerging research stream on positive spillovers. By extending insights from attribution theory, we provide a theoretical basis for distinguishing between the antecedents of positive and negative spillovers, thereby offering guidelines on when positive or negative spillovers are more likely to occur that can extend beyond typical industry-based categorical boundaries.

AN ATTRIBUTION-BASED THEORY OF MISCONDUCT SPILLOVERS

The Locus of Attribution and Spillover Valence

Attribution theory's central premise is that when confronted with incidents that deviate from expectations or widely accepted norms (as is the case with organizational misconduct [Greve et al., 2010; Paruchuri et al., 2019]), observers actively seek explanations for the incident and make causal inferences – in other words, they make attributions (Heider, 1958; Weick, 1995). These attributions, however, tend to be "far from logical and thorough" (Fiske & Taylor, 1991, p. 553), because people frequently form instantaneous judgments about the perpetrators and their misconduct despite generally lacking detailed information about the actual causes and consequences (Bundy & Pfarrer, 2015; Lange & Washburn, 2012). Rather, what matters the most in attributing blame to the perpetrator is whether the perceived locus of causality is internal or external to the actor (Eberly et al., 2011; Kelley & Michela, 1980). All else equal, stakeholders disapprove more strongly of internally attributed misconduct, because internal attributions imbue greater responsibility to the actor (Bednar et al., 2015; Bundy & Pfarrer, 2015; Lange & Washburn, 2012). External attributions allow the actor to evade responsibility by blaming the misconduct on factors or circumstances beyond their control (Salancik & Meindl, 1984; Staw et al., 1983).

However, when situating a perpetrator within a broader group of organizations (i.e., bystanders), the "internal vs external" distinction is insufficient. Attribution processes also tend to be relational, where audiences try to discern whether others related to the perpetrator share the cause (Eberly et al., 2011; Lange & Washburn, 2012). This is why misconduct spillovers to bystanders, be they positive or negative, exist. When witnessing misconduct, audiences wonder to what extent other organizations are susceptible to similar problems, and therefore are also likely to engage in similar misconduct (Paruchuri & Misangyi, 2015). Thus, audiences are also motivated to assess whether the misconduct's cause is "isolated" to the perpetrator, or is part of a "systemic" problem among a larger group of actors (Desai, 2011).

We argue that attributions' "internal vs external" and "isolated vs systemic" dimensions reflect distinct continua. Whereas internal versus external distinctions are primarily relevant for assessing the *perpetrator's* culpability, the isolated versus systemic distinction is relevant for assessing *bystanders'* culpability – that is, for spillovers. For instance, a chemical spill resulting from a hurricane can lead to an external attribution, as it resulted from an uncontrollable force. Whether the event is isolated or systemic, however, depends on whether there are reasons to believe other firms are similarly susceptible (e.g., if other chemical plants were also located in the hurricane's path, but had built their facilities to higher standards, so that they were more able to withstand the hurricane and thus be less likely to experience a spill). Likewise, a financial fraud carried out by a rogue individual within a firm may lead to internal attributions, but whether they are isolated or systemic depends on whether audiences see the cause as unique to the firm (e.g., it has an idiosyncratic culture, or it hired a "bad egg"), or if they infer a more generalizable problem, such as perverted incentive structures or insufficient monitoring mechanisms that exist within firms across the corporate community, as occurred during the credit default swap frenzy preceding the great recession.

Although it may seem that the locus of attribution should be either isolated or systemic, we argue these attributions reflect the opposite ends of a single continuum, rather than two categorical outcomes. Audiences can vary in the certitude with which they make their attributions (Bundy & Pfarrer, 2015; Lange & Washburn, 2012). That is, while some misconduct incidents may clearly result from isolated or systemic causes, others require more speculation about the locus of attribution, influencing the spillover's likelihood and magnitude. In some cases, audiences may fail to form causal attributional judgments at all, leaving their implications for bystanders uncertain. Hence, approaching the ends of the continuum indicates more perceived certainty in making isolated or systemic attributions of responsibility, while the middle range represents a grayer area where audiences face more causal uncertainty, and thus are less confident in discerning the locus of attribution.

When stakeholders attribute misconduct to isolated causes, they also tend to assume that bystanders do not share the causes. However, when an organization's misconduct stimulates systemic attributions because they have seen other instances of firms engaging in the same behaviors, audiences come to doubt the belief and value systems shared across the broader set of organizations, reflected in their common ways of doing things (Desai, 2011; Greve et al., 2016; Han & Pollock, 2021). This facilitates generalizing culpability beyond the perpetrator (Paruchuri & Misangyi, 2015), initiating negative spillovers that can even lead to category delegitimation (Jonsson et al., 2009). On the other hand, what enables bystanders to gain from others' misconduct is the belief that the perpetrator has different intentions, and does things differently than the bystanders (Paruchuri et al., 2019; Piazza & Jourdan, 2018). For this to happen, audiences must first attribute the perpetrator's misconduct to isolated causes that do not apply to bystanders, making the perpetrator the attribution's sole target (Gomulya et al., 2019; Lange & Washburn, 2012), increasing the likelihood of positive spillovers.

We argue that this attribution process's influence supersedes common category membership in causing spillovers – the primary theoretical reasoning adopted by prior spillover studies – because whether audiences perceive two organizations as similar and/or distinct (initiating a negative or positive spillover) depends largely on whether they are primed to think about the perpetrator's and bystanders' similarities or differences (Naumovska & Zajac, 2022; Roehm & Tybout, 2006). That is, the extent to which audiences make isolated or systemic attributions of responsibility is the primary driver of spillovers' valence, although we also theorize how contextual factors can affect the attribution and spillover processes. Thus, as the first building block of our theoretical model we propose that:

> *P1a.* The clearer stakeholders are in making isolated attributions of responsibility for misconduct, the more likely the misconduct is to result in positive spillovers to bystanders.

> *P1b.* The clearer stakeholders are in making systemic attributions of responsibility for misconduct, the more likely the misconduct is to result in negative spillovers to bystanders.

Locus of Attribution Antecedents

Now that we have established the basic relationship between locus of attribution and spillover valence, we want to take a step back and further consider the factors that influence the extent to which a particular attribution locus dominates. We consider three factors that can influence these attributions: the misconduct's (1) nature, (2) prevalence within the perpetrator, and (3) prevalence among other firms.

Nature of the misconduct. We argue that the misconduct's nature can influence whether stakeholders make isolated or systemic attributions of responsibility. Research in social psychology and social evaluations has long identified capability – an actor's ability to perform – and integrity – an actor's adherence to accepted ethical, regulatory, and normative principles – as the fundamental dimensions through which humans evaluate others (Fiske et al., 2007; Mishina et al., 2012; Park & Rogan, 2019; Paruchuri et al., 2021; Wojciszke et al., 1998). Similarly, organizational misconduct typically takes two forms: *capability* failure, where an organization "falls short of technically proficient performance"; or *integrity* failure, where an organization's "motives, honesty, and/or character fall short" (Connelly et al., 2016, p. 2136). Chipotle's repeated *E. coli* problems, which appear to have resulted from their overly complex supply chain (Paruchuri et al., 2019), are an example of the former, and Wells Fargo's efforts to issue "sub-prime," no money down loans to people who clearly could not afford them so they could just be packaged and sold as securities is an example of the latter.

While stakeholders take both types of misconduct seriously, prior research has shown that, in general, integrity failures have a more profound influence than capability failures on stakeholders' post-misconduct evaluations of the perpetrator (Mishina et al., 2012; Paruchuri et al., 2021). This is because stakeholders treat indicators that the firm violated social norms and values as clear signs that the perpetrator intended to engage in misconduct. While failing to execute or perform activities can also result in misconduct, the misconduct may not have been the firm's intent (Paruchuri et al., 2021). That is, *motivation* plays a significant role in assessing, and determining the misconduct's consequences (Palmer et al., 2016).

We argue the differences in how stakeholders treat capability and integrity failures affect the spillover's valence, because these differences can affect how stakeholders perceive the locus of attribution. Stakeholders are more likely to assume firms will act with integrity than that they will perform capably (Mishina et al., 2012); thus integrity failures are particularly disruptive (Paruchuri et al., 2021), because they create powerful expectancy violations (Burgoon, 1978; Burgoon & Hale, 1988).

Interacting parties develop expectations about one another driven by social norms, actors' characteristics, and prior experience (Burgoon, 1978; Burgoon & Le Poire, 1993). When an actor deviates from these expectations they create an "expectancy violation."

> When behavior violates expectancies, people likely experience arousal and evaluate both the transgressor and transgression. These evaluations then guide the victim's behavioral response, as well as perceptions of the partner and relationship. (Bachman & Guerrero, 2006, p. 945)

Furthermore, both the expectations and violations are valenced; that is, an actor can have positive or negative expectations about the other's behavior, and the expectancy violations can be positive (exceeds expectations) or negative (fails to meet expectations). Experiencing negative expectancy violations when positive outcomes are expected – such as the expectancy violations created by integrity failures – often stimulate the largest negative reactions, diminishing stakeholders' subsequent assessments and expectations about future behaviors (Burgoon & Le Poire, 1993; Kim, 2014). Furthermore, scholars have also found that actors' reactions to negative expectancy violations are even greater when they learn the negative expectancy violation was intentional (Bachman & Guerrero, 2006).

Integrity-based expectancy violations lead to moral evaluations, which are frequently tied to organizational values and culture (Bundy & Pfarrer, 2015; Pollock et al., 2019). Furthermore, individuals are more like to perceive integrity violations as intentional, making reactions to the violations more intense (Bachman & Guerrero, 2006). Thus, stakeholders are more likely to question whether integrity failures reflect broader deficiencies in the norms and value system shared among the perpetrator's peers, since challenges to taken-for-granted norms often result in rapidly spreading fear and anxiety among audiences (Harmon, 2019). For example, once it became clear that some banks and mortgage lenders were making loans they knew had little chance of being repaid before the market meltdown of 2008, the public quickly began to wonder if *all* banks and lenders were engaging in these behaviors. Their doubts about one actor's morality spurred suspicions about the morality of others who share the same value system, increasing the likelihood stakeholders perceived a systemic locus of attribution.

Capability evaluations, in contrast, tend to be individuating – that is, targeted toward the evaluated actors themselves – and thus are usually less reflective of commonly-held traits. As a result, capability-based expectancy violations are more likely to result in stakeholders perceiving an isolated locus of attribution, as stakeholders are less likely to cast doubt on others' capabilities just because a single actor failed to meet an acceptable capability standard.[1] Thus, we argue that:

> *P2a*. Capability failures are more likely than integrity failures to lead to isolated attributions of responsibility for misconduct.

> *P2b*. Integrity failures are more likely than capability failures to lead to systemic attributions of responsibility for misconduct.

Misconduct prevalence within organizations. The extent to which misconduct is prevalent, or has been normalized, within the perpetrator organization can also affect the stakeholders' perceived locus of attribution (Vaughan, 1996, 1999). To the extent that the perpetrator has previously engaged in repeated misconduct – particularly if it went unnoticed or unpunished – the more likely the associated behaviors are to become "embedded in organizational routines," leading to the "institutionalization of deviance within organizational cultures" (Greve et al., 2010, p. 73). As a result, the organization's internal standards become skewed, which could eventually lead the entire system to fail (Starbuck & Milliken, 1988). Audiences are well-aware of this possibility and tend to react more negatively to repeated misconduct. Stakeholders are more likely to perceive the current incident as intentional, even if the repeated misconduct was due to errors or externally driven accidents, since the perpetrator has not taken steps to prevent the same misconduct (Pfarrer et al., 2008). Thus, the negative expectancy violation, whether it is because of a capability or integrity failure, will be more intense (Bachman & Guerrero, 2006).

The perceived normalization of misconduct in the perpetrator organization therefore increases perceptions of the perpetrator's intransigence and culpability – and its difference from other organizations – which can also increase the likelihood that stakeholders will perceive an isolating locus of attribution. Moreover, the fact that the perpetrator has managed to commit the same misconduct over and over could trigger doubts about the organization's ability to correct its behavior (Desai, 2011). In this case, audiences are likely to assume an implicit distinction between the perpetrator and bystanders, increasing the likelihood that they perceive the locus of attribution for the misconduct as isolated, and decreasing the likelihood they perceive it as systemic (Paruchuri & Misangyi, 2015).

This mechanism applies to both capability failures and integrity failures. As we argued above, stakeholders are more likely to attribute capability failures to isolating mechanisms, and misconduct due to perpetrators' repeated capability failures solidifies this attribution. In the case of integrity failures, audiences typically generalize the failure to value systems prevalent in the environment (i.e., if one firm's doing it, then they all are likely doing it); however, repeated misconduct due to integrity failures may also result in attributing the misconduct to isolated mechanisms, suggesting the firm may be a "bad apple" that is different from the rest of the firms in its industry – for example, the Catholic church's prevalence and handling of pedophile priests (Piazza & Jourdan, 2018). Although less common, this circumstance could still result in a positive spillover. Thus:

P3. Greater misconduct prevalence within the perpetrator will (a) increase the likelihood stakeholders make isolated attributions of responsibility for misconduct; and (b) decrease the likelihood stakeholders make systemic attributions of responsibility for misconduct.

Misconduct prevalence among organizations. The prior proposition focused on the perpetrator's repeated misconduct. However, the perpetrator does not exist in a vacuum; there are other firms engaging in a variety of actions, and some of them may also have engaged in the same misconduct in the past (or may be engaging in it concurrently and haven't been caught). This is why we refer to bystanders as "unimplicated" in the particular incident, rather than as "innocent." Thus, the extent to which other firms have engaged in the same misconduct can also affect attributions of how isolated or systemic the misconduct's causes are, and influence whether the perpetrator's current misconduct results in positive or negative spillovers.

Just as misconduct prevalence within the perpetrator focuses attention on the perpetrator's behavior and decreases attention to others' behavior, misconduct prevalence among other actors focuses attention on bystanders to the focal misconduct incident and places the perpetrator's actions within a broader social context. The prevalence of prior instances by others provides "social proof" (Cialdini, 2021; Pollock et al., 2008) that other firms share the same values, increasing perceptions that the perpetrator's misconduct reflects systemic problems, a process that is enhanced by individuals' tendencies to establish, or even force, patterns from repeated stimuli (Rindova et al., 2010). Depending on the misconduct's specific nature, these behaviors may be common to firms within a particular industry or category, such as cutting costs in ways that increase product recalls (Zavyalova et al., 2012), or they may be shared more broadly among firms in a variety of categories, such as data breaches or financial frauds (Dewan & Jensen, 2020). Regardless, the greater the prevalence of the same misconduct by other firms, the less differentiated the perpetrator seems from bystanders, and the more likely stakeholders are to attribute the misconduct to systemic, rather than isolated causes. We therefore propose:

P4. Greater misconduct prevalence among other organizations will (a) decrease the likelihood stakeholders make isolated attributions of responsibility for misconduct; and (b) increase the likelihood stakeholders make systemic attributions of responsibility for misconduct.

The Moderating Effects of Misconduct Prevalence

In addition to having a direct effect on the locus of attribution, we also argue that misconduct prevalence within the perpetrator and among other firms will affect the magnitude of the relationships between the isolated and systemic locus of attribution and spillover valence, although the moderating effects can differ from their main effects.

First, consistent with its positive main effect on isolated attributions, we expect that increasing misconduct prevalence within the perpetrator will strengthen the positive relationship between isolated attributions of responsibility for the misconduct and positive spillovers, increasing the spillover's magnitude. As we noted above, the strength of stakeholders' attributions is affected by both the misconduct's characteristics and contextual factors; thus, the strength of the attribution, and its effects on the spillover, can vary as a function of multiple mechanisms. However, we further argue that once an isolated attribution is made, for whatever reason, the misconduct prevalence within the firm will also influence the strength of the relationship between the attribution and the likelihood of positive spillover, because it can further influence perceptions of the difference between the perpetrator and the bystanders by affecting the magnitude of the expectancy violation (Bachman & Guerrero, 2006; Graffin et al., 2016; Pfarrer et al., 2010).

For example, if the perpetrator had a significant capability failure, but it was not a repeated failure, stakeholders may still attribute the misconduct to isolated causes. However, since the misconduct was not prevalent in the organization, the expectancy violation may not be as great because stakeholders can rationalize it as a "one-off" occurrence, and thus treat it as less intentional (Bachman & Guerrero, 2006). Stakeholders may not therefore differentiate the perpetrator as much from other firms (i.e., "yeah, they screwed up, but it could happen to anybody"), resulting in a weaker positive spillover. In contrast, if misconduct prevalence is high within the firm, the spillover's magnitude will likely be greater because of the intent reflected in the repeated misconduct (Bachman & Guerrero, 2006), increasing the perceived difference between the perpetrator and the bystanders, and strengthening the positive spillover effect. We therefore propose:

P5. The greater the misconduct prevalence within the perpetrator, the stronger the positive relationship between isolated attributions of responsibility for misconduct and positive spillovers.

Conversely, prevalent misconduct among other organizations in the environment can weaken the influence of a systemic locus of attribution on negative spillovers by reducing the distinctiveness and the magnitude of the expectancy violation it engenders. This is because, although misconduct prevalence among other firms increases the likelihood stakeholders will attribute the perpetrator's misconduct to systemic causes, it also diminishes the salience of the perpetrator's behavior and the degree to which it stands out. Prior research has demonstrated that there is a "safety in numbers" effect (Naumovska et al., 2021; Pollock et al., 2008; Zavyalova et al., 2012), because individuals are drawn to novel stimuli and perceive greater informational value in stimuli that stand out (Pfarrer et al., 2008; Pollock & Gulati, 2007; Zavyalova et al., 2012). When a behavior is prevalent, however, any one actor is less likely to be noticed, and thus is less likely to influence attributions about bystanders. Furthermore, because the misconduct is prevalent, it also influences expectations (Burgoon & Hale, 1988; Kim, 2014). If lots of other firms are engaging in the same misconduct, normalizing the behavior, it decreases expectations about other firms' behaviors, so the expectancy violation is smaller when the perpetrator reveals its misconduct. Thus, although misconduct prevalence among firms increases the likelihood stakeholders will attribute the misconduct to systemic causes, it also reduces the influence of a systemic locus of attribution on negative spillovers to bystanders. We therefore propose:

P6. The greater the misconduct prevalence among other organizations, the weaker the positive relationship between systemic attributions of responsibility for misconduct and negative spillovers.

DISCUSSION

In this paper, we developed a theoretical model predicting misconduct spillover valence, summarized in Fig. 1. Building on attribution and expectancy violations theory, we argued that audiences' locus of attribution – whether they perceive the cause to be isolated to the perpetrator or a part of a systemic problem – is at the center of their decision to punish or reward uninvolved bystanders. Isolated attributions of responsibility highlight the difference between the perpetrator and bystanders, which reduces concerns that others are engaged, or will also engage in the same misconduct (Paruchuri & Misangyi, 2015), and increases the likelihood of positive spillovers. In contrast, systemic attributions emphasize the perpetrator's similarities with bystanders based on shared common values, practices, or other characteristics, increasing concerns that others are also likely engaging in, or will engage in the misconduct, and thus increasing the likelihood of negative spillovers.

We further argued that the misconduct's nature (i.e., whether it resulted from capability or integrity failures) and the misconduct's prevalence within the perpetrator or among other firms affects the locus of attribution by influencing attributions about the motivation for the misconduct, and the magnitude of the expectancy violation. All else equal, capability failures are more likely to

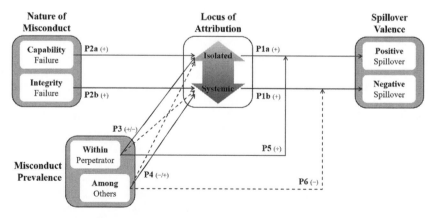

Fig. 1.   Conceptual Framework. *Note*: Solid lines represent positive/amplifying effects and dotted lines represent negative/attenuating effects.

increase the likelihood of isolated attributions because competence judgments tend to involve individuating perceptions, and may even be unintentional (Bundy & Pfarrer, 2015; Pollock et al., 2019), whereas integrity failures increase the likelihood of systemic attributions because audiences are more likely to associate morality and values-based failures with broader value systems (Paruchuri et al., 2021; Pollock et al., 2019).

We also considered how the prevalence of misconduct within and among firms affects the locus of attributions and the relationship between the locus of attribution and spillover valence. Repeated misconduct within the perpetrator increases perceptions that the firm intended to engage in the misconduct, and highlights its difference from other firms, enhancing the likelihood they will make isolated attributions (Pfarrer et al., 2008). In contrast, misconduct prevalence among other firms increases perceptions that the misconduct is widely engaged in, reducing differences and thus increasing systemic attributions. Finally, since the locus of attribution is influenced by multiple factors, we argue that misconduct prevalence within the perpetrator will strengthen the relationship between isolated attributions of responsibility and positive spillovers, but that greater misconduct prevalence among other firms provides safety in numbers that weakens the relationship between a systemic locus of attribution and negative spillovers. We believe our theory makes important contributions to the literature on misconduct spillovers and provides useful insights for future research.

Implications for Theory and Future Research

The misconduct spillovers literature faces two significant issues: (1) prior studies have paid disproportionate attention to negative spillovers, and (2) even the few studies on positive spillovers have largely attempted to explain positive spillovers using the same theoretical mechanisms – similarities in organizational characteristics – used to explain negative spillovers (Naumovska & Lavie, 2021; Paruchuri et al., 2019; Piazza & Jourdan, 2018). Some argue bystanders must share similar characteristics with the perpetrators to experience either type of spillover, but at the same time should be different in other aspects that differentiate them in desirable ways to experience positive spillovers (Paruchuri et al., 2021; Piazza & Jourdan, 2018). Others argue that some degree of similarity between bystanders and perpetrators leads to negative spillovers, but higher degrees of overlap and more fine-grained similarities, which result in more direct competition among the firms, lead to positive spillovers (Naumovska & Lavie, 2021). However, the problems of just how much similarity, and in what respects bystanders need to be (dis)similar from the perpetrators, remains.

Rather than developing endless – and inevitably context-specific – taxonomies of firm-specific characteristics, or developing categories that are so general they are empirically meaningless, we make our major theoretical contribution by moving away from attribute-based (dis)similarities as spillover valence's primary driver, and instead focus on the cognitive processes underlying attributions and expectancy violations, and how innate aspects of the misconduct itself and the context in which it occurs shapes audiences' attributions regarding the locus of the misconduct, and through it the spillover's valence. We believe our attribution-based approach is more useful in understanding misconduct spillovers' valences because the perceptions of (dis)similarities are far from absolute; rather, they tend to be malleable depending on situational factors and stakeholders' evaluative goals (Durand & Paolella, 2013; Naumovska & Zajac, 2022; Roehm & Tybout, 2006).

From this perspective, organizational similarities' confusing role in the literature does not result from improper theorization. Rather, it reflects the way attributions are actually made: the similarities can mean different things in different contexts. Moreover, our attribution-based approach does not require industry-based interorganizational similarities as a necessary condition for misconduct spillovers, increasing our ability to understand and explain "boundaryless" spillovers that are not related to the typical, industry-based similarities used in prior research. Considering that some of the most notable scandals – such as the Enron scandal, the options backdating scandal, the subprime mortgage scandal, and the Facebook-Cambridge Analytica data breach scandal – had ramifications well beyond any single industry (Dewan & Jensen, 2020; Paruchuri et al., 2021), theorizing based on product or industry-based attribute similarities as the primary antecedent to misconduct spillovers may be too restrictive.

Our theory also opens some interesting avenues for future research. Although we have conceptualized whether a perpetrator's misconduct results from a capability or integrity failure as a primary factor influencing the locus of attribution, this distinction is not always so clear. Thus, exploring situations where the two types of failures are intertwined (e.g., an integrity failure leads to a capability failure, as when cutting corners to increase profit margins leads to capability losses that result in misconduct) could yield additional insights into how mixed attributions are made, how they are likely to influence whether spillovers occur, and what their valence is. Additionally, wrongdoing could occur in different forms; some forms may map more directly onto capability or integrity failures, whereas others may not map as directly onto one particular failure type. Future research could theorize about the nuances in capability or integrity failure effects on isolated or systemic attributions based on these wrongdoing forms. We also recognize that the locus of attribution is a continuum where isolated and systemic attributions of responsibility represent the endpoints. For ease of theorizing, we have focused on the ends of the continuum in developing our propositions, but there is obviously a range of options in between. How these mixed attributions affect spillover valence, and the factors that influence these outcomes, are another interesting avenue for future research.

Our theory also considers contextual factors – specifically, the misconduct's prevalence within the perpetrator and among other firms – as important factors influencing the locus of attribution, and in creating boundary conditions influencing the likelihood that stakeholders' attributions result in positive and negative spillovers to bystanders. There has been an active debate on the effect of misconduct prevalence as a separate stream of research; for example, the safety in numbers effect primarily focuses on how a controversial act's prevalence among firms affects the outcomes for perpetrators (Naumovska et al., 2021; Pfarrer et al., 2008; Zavyalova et al., 2012). In addition to enriching this research stream by extending the theory to include bystanders' outcomes, our theory could provide potential answers regarding why we do not witness spillovers in every instance of misconduct. That is, while prior studies' primary goal has been to prove that misconduct spillovers exist (Jonsson et al., 2009; Paruchuri & Misangyi, 2015; Paruchuri et al., 2019; Piazza & Jourdan, 2018), whether and why spillovers do or do not occur following an actor's misconduct are important yet insufficiently addressed questions, and a promising avenue for future research. We therefore encourage researchers to explore additional factors that affect misconduct salience and how it is interpreted, and the ways they influence the relationship between the locus of attribution, whether it results in a spillover, and the spillover's valence.

Finally, as scholars expand our model by exploring a variety of additional relevant constructs, we recommend they consider perpetrators' and bystanders' social evaluations – or "socially constructed, collective perceptions of firms such as status, reputation, celebrity, and stigma" (Pollock et al., 2019, p. 444) – as a particularly fruitful extension. Scholars have long considered social evaluations an important factor shaping audiences' interpretation of and reaction to organizational misconduct, particularly due to their ability to provide audiences with cognitive heuristics that alleviate perceived uncertainty at the onset of misconduct (Bundy & Pfarrer, 2015; Chandler et al., 2020; Dewan & Jensen, 2020; Park & Rogan, 2019). These evaluations contain unique sociocognitive content that dictates audiences' idiosyncratic expectations (Pollock et al., 2019). Such expectations may have direct relevance for the attribution process and the expectancy violations stakeholders experience, as even the same behavior can be interpreted differently depending on the firms' social evaluations (Hubbard et al., 2018; Pfarrer et al., 2010). For instance, the same misconduct could trigger isolated attributions of responsibility for some perpetrators and systemic attributions for others if the sociocognitive content underlying the perpetrators' social evaluations induce stakeholders to perceive the perpetrator as distinct from, or representative of a broader group of firms.

CONCLUSION

The idea that misconduct's aftermath can reach beyond the perpetrators and affect uninvolved bystanders has long fascinated management and organizational researchers, perhaps even more so recently with the emerging evidence of positive spillovers. As one of the earliest attempts to simultaneously consider both positive and negative spillovers, we proposed that understanding how stakeholders make attributions is key to bringing both types of spillovers together in an integrated and generalizable theoretical framework. Perhaps it will also help you understand why you were blamed when another kid broke the neighbor's window, or why you always suffered when your younger brother or sister did something wrong, but they never seemed to share the blame when you were the perpetrator.

NOTE

1. This does not mean that integrity failures cannot result in an isolated locus of attribution, or that capability failures cannot be perceived as systemic; however, we do think that, on average, they will be more frequently associated with the locus of attribution we theorize. We use the terms "more/less likely" here and elsewhere to recognize the probabilistic nature of these relationships.

ACKNOWLEDGMENT

A pre-published version of this paper appeared on ResearchGate.

REFERENCES

Bachman, G., & Guerrero, L. (2006). An expectancy violations analysis of relational quality and communicative responses following hurtful events in dating relationships. *Journal of Social and Personal Relationships, 23*, 943–963.

Barnett, M. L., & King, A. A. (2008). Good fences make good neighbors: A longitudinal analysis of an industry self-regulatory institution. *Academy of Management Journal, 51*, 1150–1170.

Bednar, M. K., Love, E. G., & Kraatz, M. (2015). Paying the price? The impact of controversial governance practices on managerial reputation. *Academy of Management Journal, 58*, 1740–1760.

Bundy, J., & Pfarrer, M. D. (2015). A burden of responsibility: The role of social approval at the onset of a crisis. *Academy of Management Review, 40*, 345–369.

Burgoon, J. K. (1978). A communication model of personal space violations: Explication and an initial test. *Human Communication Research, 4*, 129–142.

Burgoon, J. K., & Hale, J. L. (1988). Nonverbal expectancy violations: Model elaboration and application to immediacy behaviors. *Communication Monographs, 55*, 58–79.

Burgoon, J. K., & Le Poire, B. A. (1993). Effects of communication expectancies, actual communication, and expectancy disconfirmation on evaluations of communicators and their communication behavior. *Human Communication Research, 20*, 67–96.

Chandler, D., Polidoro, F., & Yang, W. (2020). When is it good to be bad? Contrasting effects of multiple reputations for bad behavior on media coverage of serious organizational errors. *Academy of Management Journal, 63*, 1236–1265.

Cialdini, R. B. (2021). *Influence: The psychology of persuasion.* HarperCollins.

Connelly, B. L., Ketchen, D. J., Gangloff, K. A., & Shook, C. L. (2016). Investor perceptions of CEO successor selection in the wake of integrity and competence failures: A policy capturing study. *Strategic Management Journal, 37*, 2135–2151.

Desai, V. M. (2011). Mass media and massive failures: Determining organizational efforts to defend field legitimacy following crises. *Academy of Management Journal, 54*, 263–278.

Dewan, Y., & Jensen, M. (2020). Catching the big fish: The role of scandals in making status a liability. *Academy of Management Journal, 63*, 1652–1678.

Durand, R., & Paolella, L. (2013). Category stretching: Reorienting research on categories in strategy, entrepreneurship, and organization theory. *Journal of Management Studies, 50*, 1100–1123.

Eberly, M. B., Holley, E. C., Johnson, M. D., & Mitchell, T. R. (2011). Beyond internal and external: A dyadic theory of relational attributions. *Academy of Management Review, 36*, 731–753.

Elsbach, K. D. (2006). *Organizational perception management.* Lawrence Erlbaum.

Fiske, S. T., Cuddy, A. J. C., & Glick, P. (2007). Universal dimensions of social cognition: Warmth and competence. *Trends in Cognitive Sciences, 11*, 77–83.

Fiske, S. T., & Taylor, S. E. (1991). *Social cognition* (2nd ed.). McGraw-Hill.

Gomulya, D., Jin, K., Lee, P. M., & Pollock, T. G. (2019). Crossed wires: Endorsement signals and the effects of IPO firm delistings on venture capitalists' reputations. *Academy of Management Journal, 62*, 641–666.

Graffin, S. D., Haleblian, J., & Kiley, J. T. (2016). Ready, AIM, acquire; Impression offsetting and acquisitions. *Academy of Management Journal, 59*, 232–252.

Greve, H. R., Kim, J. Y., & Teh, D. (2016). Ripples of fear: The diffusion of a bank panic. *American Sociological Review, 81*, 396–420.

Greve, H. R., Palmer, D., & Pozner, J.-E. (2010). Organizations gone wild: The causes, processes, and consequences of organizational misconduct. *Academy of Management Annals, 4*, 53–107.

Han, J.-H., & Pollock, T. G. (2021). The two towers (or somewhere in between): The behavioral consequences of positional inconsistency across status hierarchies. *Academy of Management Journal, 64*, 562–586.

Harmon, D. J. (2019). When the Fed speaks: Arguments, emotions, and the microfoundations of institutions. *Administrative Science Quarterly, 64*, 542–575.

Heider, F. (1958). *The psychology of interpersonal relations*. Wiley.

Hubbard, T. D., Pollock, T. G., Pfarrer, M. D., & Rindova, V. P. (2018). Safe bets or hot hands? How status and celebrity influence strategic alliance formations by newly public firms. *Academy of Management Journal, 61*, 1976–1999.

Jonsson, S., Greve, H. R., & Fujiwara-Greve, T. (2009). Undeserved loss: The spread of legitimacy loss to innocent organizations in response to reported corporate deviance. *Administrative Science Quarterly, 54*, 195–228.

Kelley, H. H., & Michela, J. L. (1980). Attribution theory and research. *Annual Review of Psychology, 31*, 457–501.

Kim, S. (2014). The role of prior expectancies and relational satisfaction in crisis. *Journalism & Mass Communication Quarterly, 91*, 139–158.

Lange, D., & Washburn, N. T. (2012). Understanding attributions of corporate social irresponsibility. *Academy of Management Review, 37*, 300–326.

Love, E. G., & Kraatz, M. S. (2017). Failed stakeholder exchanges and corporate reputation: The case of earnings misses. *Academy of Management Journal, 60*, 880–903.

Martinko, M. J., Harvey, P., & Dasborough, M. T. (2011). Attribution theory in the organizational sciences: A case of unrealized potential. *Journal of Organizational Behavior*, 144–149.

Mishina, Y., Block, E. S., & Mannor, M. J. (2012). The path dependence of organizational reputation: How social judgment influences assessments of capability and character. *Strategic Management Journal, 33*, 459–477.

Naumovska, I., & Lavie, D. (2021). When an industry peer is accused of financial misconduct: Stigma versus competition effects on non-accused firms. *Administrative Science Quarterly, 66*(4), 1130–1172.

Naumovska, I., Zajac, E., & Lee, P. M. (2021). Strength and weakness in numbers? Unpacking the role of prevalence in the diffusion of reverse mergers. *Academy of Management Journal, 64*, 409–434.

Naumovska, I., & Zajac, E. J. (2022). How inductive and deductive generalization shape the guilt-by-association phenomenon among firms: Theory and evidence. *Organization Science, 33*, 373–392.

Palmer, D., Smith-Crowe, K., & Greenwood, R. (2016). The imbalances and limitations of theory and research on organizational wrongdoing. In D. Palmer, K. Smith-Crowe, & R. Greenwood (Eds.), *Organizational wrongdoing: Key perspectives and new directions* (pp. 1–13). Cambridge University Press.

Park, B., & Rogan, M. (2019). Capability reputation, character reputation, and exchange partners; reactions to adverse events. *Academy of Management Journal, 62*, 553–578.

Paruchuri, S., Han, J.-H., & Prakash, P. (2021). Salient expectations? Incongruence across capability and integrity signals and investor reactions to organizational misconduct. *Academy of Management Journal, 64*, 562–586.

Paruchuri, S., & Misangyi, V. F. (2015). Investor perceptions of financial misconduct: The heterogeneous contamination of bystander firms. *Academy of Management Journal, 58*, 169–194.

Paruchuri, S., Pollock, T. G., & Kumar, N. (2019). On the tip of the brain: Understanding when negative reputational events can have positive reputation spillovers, and for how long. *Strategic Management Journal, 40*, 1965–1983.

Pfarrer, M. D., DeCelles, K. A., Smith, K. G., & Taylor, M. S. (2008). After the fall: Reintegrating the corrupt organization. *Academy of Management Review, 33*, 730–749.

Pfarrer, M. D., Pollock, T. G., & Rindova, V. P. (2010). A tale of two assets: The effects of firm reputation and celebrity on earnings surprises and investors' reactions. *Academy of Management Journal, 53,* 1131–1152.

Piazza, A., & Jourdan, J. (2018). When the dust settles: The consequences of scandals for organizational competition. *Academy of Management Journal, 61,* 165–190.

Pollock, T. G., & Gulati, R. (2007). Standing out from the crowd: The availability enhancing effects of IPO-related signals on alliance formation by entrepreneurial firms. *Strategic Organization, 5,* 339–372.

Pollock, T. G., Lashley, K., Rindova, V. P., & Han, J.-H. (2019). Which of these things are not like the others? Comparing the rational, emotional and moral aspects of reputation, status, celebrity and stigma. *Academy of Management Annals, 13,* 444–478.

Pollock, T. G., Rindova, V. P., & Maggitti, P. G. (2008). Market watch: Information and availability cascades among the media and investors in the U.S. IPO market. *Academy of Management Journal, 51,* 335–358.

Pontikes, E., Negro, G., & Rao, H. (2010). Stained red: A study of stigma by association to blacklisted artists during the "red scare" in Hollywood, 1945 to 1960. *American Sociological Review, 75,* 456–478.

Rindova, V., Ferrier, W. J., & Wiltbank, R. (2010). Value from gestalt: How sequences of competitive actions create advantage for firms in nascent markets. *Strategic Management Journal, 31,* 1474–1497.

Roehm, M. L., & Tybout, A. M. (2006). When will a brand scandal spill over, and how should competitors respond? *Journal of Marketing Research, 43,* 366–373.

Salancik, G. R., & Meindl, J. R. (1984). Corporate attributions as strategic illusions of management control. *Administrative Science Quarterly, 29,* 238–254.

Starbuck, W. H., & Milliken, F. J. (1988). Challenger: Fine-tuning the odds until something breaks. *Journal of Management Studies, 25,* 319–340.

Staw, B., McKechnie, P., & Puffer, S. (1983). The justification of organizational performance. *Administrative Science Quarterly, 28,* 582–600.

Vaughan, D. (1996). *The challenger launch decision: Risky technology, culture, and deviance at NASA.* University of Chicago Press.

Vaughan, D. (1999). The dark side of organizations: Mistake, misconduct and disaster. *Annual Review of Sociology, 25,* 271–305.

Weick, K. E. (1995). *Sensemaking in organizations.* Sage.

Wojciszke, B., Bazinska, R., & Jaworski, M. (1998). On the dominance of moral categories in impression formation. *Personality and Social Psychology Bulletin, 24,* 1251–1263.

Zavyalova, A., Pfarrer, M. D., Reger, R. K., & Shapiro, D. L. (2012). Managing the message: The effects of firm actions and industry spillovers on media coverage following wrongdoing. *Academy of Management Journal, 55,* 1079–1101.

CHAPTER 3

"CROWD CONTAMINATION"? SPILLOVER EFFECTS IN THE CONTEXT OF MISCONDUCT ALLEGATIONS

Brigitte Wecker and Matthias Brauer

ABSTRACT

Misconduct allegations have been found to not only affect the alleged firm but also other, unalleged firms in form of reputational and financial spillover effects. It has remained unexplored, however, how the number of prior allegations against other firms matters for an individual firm currently facing an allegation. Building on behavioral decision theory, we argue that the relationship between allegation prevalence among other firms and investor reaction to a focal allegation is inverted U-shaped. The inverted U-shaped effect is theorized to emerge from the combination of two effects: In the absence of prior allegations against other firms, investors fail to anticipate the focal allegation, and hence react particularly negatively ("anticipation effect"). In the case of many prior allegations against other firms, investors also react particularly negatively because investors perceive the focal allegation as more warranted ("evaluation effect"). The multi-industry, empirical analysis of 8,802 misconduct allegations against US firms between 2007 and 2017 provides support for our predicted, inverted U-shaped effect. Our study complements recent misconduct research on spillover effects by highlighting that not only a current allegation against an individual firm can "contaminate" other, unalleged firms but that

Organizational Wrongdoing as the "Foundational" Grand Challenge: Consequences and Impact
Research in the Sociology of Organizations, Volume 85, 53–72
Published under exclusive licence by Emerald Publishing Limited
ISSN: 0733-558X/doi:10.1108/S0733-558X20230000085004

also prior allegations against other firms can "contaminate" investor reaction to a focal allegation against an individual firm.

Keywords: Corporate misconduct; allegation; spillover; investor reaction; anticipation; evaluation

INTRODUCTION

Prior misconduct research has generated valuable insights on investor reaction to allegations of corporate misconduct (e.g., Christensen, 2016; Godfrey et al., 2009; Karpoff et al., 2005). A key finding of this line of work has been that the decline in stock market value due to negative investor reaction to an allegation by far exceeds the sum of all regulatory and legal penalties which are imposed once an allegation is proven (e.g., Karpoff et al., 2008; Pierce, 2018). Against the backdrop of this main finding, negative investor reaction to misconduct allegations has been acknowledged as an important deterrent to corporate misconduct (Karpoff et al., 2008; Mariuzzo et al., 2020; Sampath et al., 2018).

Misconduct allegations, however, not only affect the alleged firm, as evidenced by a significantly negative investor reaction around the initial public announcement of an allegation, but also other, unalleged firms in form of reputational and financial spillover effects. Prior misconduct literature has mostly documented spillover effects for unalleged industry peers (e.g., Diestre & Rajagopalan, 2014; Naumovska & Lavie, 2021; Paruchuri & Misangyi, 2015). Some studies have also found spillover effects for unalleged firms other than industry peers (such as alliance partners, firms with board interlocks, or firms from the same country) (e.g., Chen, 2016; Galloway et al., 2021; Kang, 2008), and, very recently, even for firms "irrespective of [their] similarity to the offending firm" (Naumovska & Zajac, 2022, p. 373). Overall, prior studies have provided valuable insights on how a current allegation against an individual firm affects other, unalleged firms.

It has remained unexplored, however, how prior allegations against other firms matter for the individual firm currently facing an allegation. Hence, we make this the focus of our study and investigate how the number of prior allegations against other firms (i.e., allegation prevalence among other firms) influences investor reaction to a focal allegation. Building on behavioral decision theory (e.g., Poulton, 1994; Slovic et al., 1977; Takemura, 2014), we argue that investor reaction to a focal allegation is determined by two distinct effects: the "anticipation effect" and the "evaluation effect." Specifically, we theorize that the number of prior allegations against other firms increases both investors' anticipation of a focal allegation as well as their negative evaluation of it. The combination of these two effects suggests that the relationship between allegation prevalence among other firms and investor reaction to a focal allegation is inverted U-shaped, i.e., investors are expected to react most negatively to a focal allegation if there have been either few or many prior allegations against other firms. In the absence of prior allegations against other firms, investors have not anticipated the focal allegation and thus failed to price it into the firm's current stock price, leading to a pronounced negative reaction (anticipation effect) (e.g., Fama, 1970; Gande & Lewis, 2009; Kang, 2008). In case of many prior allegations against other firms, investors are also expected to react comparably negatively because they perceive the focal allegation as more warranted (evaluation effect) (e.g., Fama, 1970; Tversky & Kahneman, 1973, 1974). Our multi-industry, empirical analysis of 8,802 misconduct allegations against US firms between 2007 and 2017 provides support for the predicted, inverted U-shaped effect.

Overall, our study contributes to corporate misconduct literature by being first to examine how allegation prevalence among other firms influences investor reaction to a focal allegation. In particular, our findings complement recent research on spillover effects in the context of corporate misconduct by highlighting that not only a current allegation against an individual firm can "contaminate" other, unalleged firms but that also prior allegations against other firms can "contaminate" investor reaction to a focal allegation against an individual firm.

THEORY AND HYPOTHESIS

In this study, we investigate how the number of prior allegations against other firms influences investor reaction to a focal allegation. Unlike most prior studies on spillover effects in the context of corporate misconduct (e.g., Paruchuri & Misangyi, 2015; Zavyalova et al., 2012), we account not only for allegations against industry peers but consider a much wider population of firms. Our approach is in line with recent research arguing that industry membership as a traditional boundary for spillover effects is "porous in the eyes of audience members and can hardly act as artificial confines" to investor assessments (Aranda et al., 2020, p. 1901). Recent contributions on corporate misconduct indeed suggest that a wider population of firms than industry peers is affected by spillover effects (e.g., Chen, 2016; Galloway et al., 2021). Most recently, Naumovska and Zajac (2022) have found that even non-similar firms are subject to spillover effects. A key explanation for this finding is that even allegations against non-similar firms inform investors and hence influence their reaction. Therefore, in our theorizing we account for prior allegations against all other firms.

Building on behavioral decision theory (e.g., Poulton, 1994; Slovic et al., 1977; Takemura, 2014), we argue that investor reaction to a focal allegation is determined by two effects: first, the extent to which investors have anticipated the focal allegation (anticipation effect), and second, the extent to which investors perceive the focal allegation as warranted (evaluation effect). In the following, we lay out how allegation prevalence among other firms influences these two effects, and how their combination influences investor reaction to a focal allegation. To illustrate our theoretical reasoning, we use a practical example. Specifically, we outline anticipation, evaluation, and reaction to allegations against firms in the automotive industry after Volkswagen's alleged emission manipulation, which has recently been a popular context for misconduct research on spillover effects (e.g., Barth et al., 2022; Bouzzine & Lueg, 2020; Jacobs & Singhal, 2020).

Anticipation Effect

When Volkswagen (VW) was initially publicly alleged of emission manipulation in September 2015, the media and investment community labeled this allegation as "surprising" and "unexpected" (ABC News, 2015; Financial Times, 2015; Scientific American, 2015). Soon after the allegation against VW, however, the business press speculated that "it won't be surprising if this kind of thing happens more often in the future" and conjectured that "reports of another major carmaker having potentially been 'at it' would hardly come as a surprise" (CNBC., 2015; The Week, 2015). When further firms such as Suzuki, Fiat Chrysler, and Renault were later indeed also alleged of emission manipulations, these allegations were "no surprise" and had widely been anticipated by investors (e.g., BBC News, 2015; Financial Times, 2017; Fortune, 2017; Motoring Research, 2016). Collectively, this practical example from the automotive industry (cf. Fig. 1a) suggests that investors' and other stakeholders' anticipation of a focal allegation differs depending on allegation prevalence among other firms.

Behavioral decision theory (e.g., Poulton, 1994; Slovic et al., 1977; Takemura, 2014) suggests that anticipation is an important determinant of an actor's reaction to an event (Gavetti et al., 2012). The less anticipated an event the more pronounced usually an actor's reaction. For our research context, this suggests

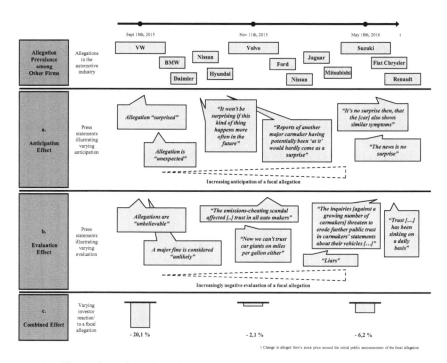

Fig. 1.   Illustration of Anticipation, Evaluation, and Reaction to Allegations in the Automotive Industry.

that investors react particularly negatively to a focal allegation which they have largely failed to anticipate due to the absence of prior allegations against other firms (e.g., Barnett, 2014; Fama, 1970; Malatesta & Thompson, 1985) (cf. Fig. 2a). In contrast and in line with our practical example, an increasing number of prior allegations against other firms increases investors' anticipation of a focal allegation (e.g., Kang, 2008; Naumovska & Lavie, 2021; Naumovska & Zajac, 2022) (cf. left axis of Fig. 2a). As a result, the focal allegation takes investors less by negative surprise and has to a larger extent already been "priced in" the focal firm's current stock price (e.g., Bromiley et al., 1988; Fama, 1970; McWilliams & Siegel, 1997). Investors' reaction to the focal allegation is thus less negative (e.g., Gande & Lewis, 2009; McWilliams & Siegel, 1997) (cf. right axis of Fig. 2a).

Importantly however, behavioral decision theory also suggests that not all prior allegations against other firms have the same informational value for investors (e.g., Gavetti et al., 2012; Slovic et al., 1977). Early allegations against other firms have the largest informational value for investors, warning them that further firms may be alleged in the future, and thus influence investors' anticipation most strongly (e.g., Gande & Lewis, 2009). In contrast, subsequent allegations against other firms have decreasing informational value for investors as the warning becomes redundant, and thus influence investor anticipation less and less (e.g., Bromiley et al., 1988) (cf. left axis of Fig. 2a). As there are limits to the informational value of additional prior allegations against other firms, investor anticipation of a focal allegation first increases rapidly and then flattens. Hence, investors' negative reaction to a focal allegation is expected to decrease non-linearly (cf. right axis of Fig. 2a).

Fig. 2a depicts the resulting non-linear relationship between allegation prevalence among other firms and investor reaction as a function of investor anticipation.

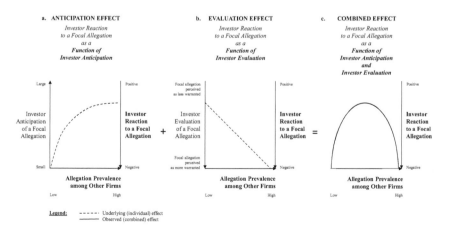

Fig. 2. Investor Reaction Explained by Investor Anticipation and Evaluation.

Evaluation Effect

As indicated at the outset of our theorizing, investor reaction to a focal allegation is not solely determined by the extent to which investors have anticipated the focal allegation (anticipation effect). Instead, behavioral decision theory proposes that the extent to which investors perceive the focal allegation as warranted (evaluation effect) is another crucial determinant of investor reaction to a focal allegation (Poulton, 1994; Slovic et al., 1977; Takemura, 2014).

Like the anticipation effect, the evaluation effect can be illustrated with reference to the allegations against firms in the automotive industry. When Volkswagen was initially publicly alleged of emission manipulation, the allegation seemed "unbelievable" (Mother Jones, 2015), and a major fine was thus considered "unlikely" (Autoblog, 2015). Soon however, the "emissions-cheating scandal affected [.] trust in all auto makers" (The Wall Street Journal, 2015). Hence, when further carmakers like Daimler and BMW were subsequently alleged of different misconduct, these allegations were evaluated against the backdrop of the prior allegation against Volkswagen. As a result, the allegations against Daimler and BMW were perceived as much more warranted as reflected, among others, in the media's reaction: "Now we can't trust car giants [Daimler and BMW] on miles per gallon either" (Daily Mail, 2015). Subsequent inquiries and allegations against numerous other automotive OEMs and their suppliers then further "eroded [.] public trust in carmakers' statements about their vehicles" (Financial Times, 2016), and made trust "sink[.] on a daily basis" (NY Times, 2017). As a result of this loss of trustworthiness, the media and investment community did not believe in the alleged firms' pledges of innocence, assuming they were "liars" (News Wheel, 2016). Allegations at that point in time, such as allegations against Suzuki, Fiat Chrysler, or Renault, were thus readily perceived as warranted (e.g., Financial Times, 2017). As illustrated by this practical example from the automotive industry (cf. Fig. 1b), investors' and other stakeholders' evaluation of a focal allegation differs depending on allegation prevalence among other firms.

Importantly, the initial public announcement of a focal allegation usually does not provide definite evidence of the alleged firm's actual offending, i.e., it is typically uncertain whether the focal allegation is warranted (e.g., Barnett, 2014; Dewan & Jensen, 2020; Karpoff et al., 2008; McDonnell & King, 2018; Pfarrer et al., 2008; Pierce, 2018). Due to this informational constraint, allegations, unlike proven violations, require evaluation. Behavioral decision theory suggests that investors use the number of prior allegations against other firms as an informational cue to evaluate whether the focal allegation seems warranted (e.g., Slovic et al., 1977; Tversky & Kahneman, 1974). This is in line with the notion that, under uncertainty, information about prior (in particular negative) behavior determines what is the most plausible interpretation for a focal event (Mishina et al., 2012; Paruchuri et al., 2021; Shu & Wong, 2018). In our research context, this means that in case of few prior allegations against other firms, investors may be willing to give an alleged firm the "benefit of the doubt" and perceive the focal allegation as less warranted (e.g., Barnett, 2014) (cf. left axis of Fig. 2b), which makes investors' reaction to a focal allegation less negative (e.g., Wei et al., 2017) (cf. right axis of Fig. 2b). Additional prior allegations against other firms however constantly increase the perception that the focal allegation is warranted (Tversky & Kahneman, 1973, 1974) such that investors perceive the focal allegation as more warranted in case of many prior allegations against other firms (cf. left axis of Fig. 2b). This perception makes investor reaction to a focal allegation more negative (e.g., Haslem et al., 2017; Pierce, 2018) (cf. right axis of Fig. 2b).

The resulting linear relationship between allegation prevalence among other firms and investor reaction as a function of investor evaluation is illustrated in Fig. 2b.

Combined Effect

While allegation prevalence among other firms for one thing *attenuates* negative investor reaction in a non-linear manner because an increasing number of prior allegations against other firms increases investors' anticipation of a focal allegation (cf. Fig. 2a), allegation prevalence among other firms also linearly *aggravates* negative investor reaction because an increasing number of prior allegations against other firms increases investors' perception that the focal allegation is warranted (cf. Fig. 2b). In isolation, investor anticipation and evaluation thus have a disparate effect on investor reaction to a focal allegation.

The observed investor reaction to a focal allegation is, however, determined by both the anticipation effect *and* the evaluation effect (combined effect). As shown by prior methodological research (Haans et al., 2016), this combination of a non-linear and a linear effect results in an inverted U-shaped relationship (cf. Fig. 2c). In our specific setting, the inverted U-shaped relationship emerges because the positive non-linear anticipation effect is offset by a linearly negative evaluation effect. Fig. 1c illustrates the resulting inverted U-shaped relationship with reference to the pattern of allegations in the automotive industry.

Hypothesis. The relationship between allegation prevalence among other firms and investor reaction to a focal allegation is inverted U-shaped, i.e., investor reaction is most negative in case of a low or high number of prior allegations against other firms.

METHODS

Sample

To identify the date when an allegation is initially publicly announced as well as to assess allegation prevalence among other firms, we draw on the RepRisk database provided by Wharton Research Data Services (WRDS) (RepRisk AG, 2017).[1] RepRisk systematically screens a broad range of news sources in over 20 major business languages on a daily basis to identify misconduct allegations of different type (e.g., corruption, tax evasion, discrimination, child labor, Organizational Health and Safety Act (OHSA) issues, pollution, or animal mistreatment) against publicly listed firms not limited to a certain industry or index (RepRisk, 2021). Due to its broad scope and detailed information, the database has been repeatedly used by corporate misconduct research (e.g., Breitinger & Bonardi, 2019; Gaganis et al., 2021; Kölbel et al., 2017; Schembera & Scherer, 2017). For our study, we include all allegations against US listed firms initially publicized between 2007 and 2017. Missing data and the exclusion of confounds lead to a final sample of 8,802 focal allegations.

Dependent Variable

Investor Reaction. To assess investor reaction, we use event study methodology (e.g., McWilliams & Siegel, 1997), which is well-established in the corporate misconduct literature (e.g., Cumming et al., 2015; Naumovska & Lavie, 2021; Paruchuri et al., 2021; Pierce, 2018). Event studies assess investor reaction to the announcement of a focal event by measuring the difference between a firm's observed and its expected stock market return during an observation period around the announcement date (i.e., cumulative abnormal return [CAR]) (e.g., Bromiley et al., 1988; McWilliams & Siegel, 1997). This means that event studies compare how a firm's observed stock market return (i.e., the focal event has taken place) deviates from its expected stock market return (i.e., if the focal event had not taken place). If a firm's observed stock market return is smaller than its expected stock market return, the CAR is negative. A negative CAR hence indicates that investors react negatively to a focal event. We follow prior research (e.g., Flammer, 2013; Godfrey et al., 2009; Karpoff et al., 2008; Shiu & Yang, 2017; Zeidan, 2013) and calculate CARs (in percent) using the market model, an estimation window of 120 days, and an $(-3, 3)$ event window. Data were obtained from Event Study by WRDS.

Explanatory Variable

Allegation Prevalence Among Other Firms. To assess allegation prevalence among other firms, we use the RepRisk database and count the number of allegations against all firms except the focal firm which have been announced in high reach news sources (such as *Wall Street Journal*, *Financial Times*, or *NY Times*) in the three years prior to the focal allegation (in thousands) (e.g., Flammer, 2013; Godfrey et al., 2009; Shiu & Yang, 2017). The use of the three-year time window assures that investors are still aware of the prior allegations despite their limited cognitive capacity (e.g., Barnett, 2014; Chandler et al., 2020; Paruchuri et al., 2019).

Control Variables

To account for alternative factors that could influence investor reaction to a focal allegation, we control for several characteristics of the alleged firm, the focal allegation, and its initial public announcement. Data for the control variables were obtained from Compustat, Datastream, IBES, Kinder Lydenberg and Domini (KLD), and RepRisk. All control variables are lagged by one period unless otherwise indicated.

With respect to the alleged firm, we control for its size (i.e., total assets), performance (i.e., return on assets), book-to-market ratio, risk (i.e., debt-to-equity ratio), analyst coverage, industry affiliation (i.e., historical two-digit SIC dummies), age (i.e., years since incorporation), prior good behavior (i.e., sum of KLD strengths in the three years prior to the focal allegation), and prior bad behavior (i.e., sum of KLD concerns in the three years prior to the focal allegation).

With respect to the focal allegation, we control for its type (i.e., type dummies), its severity (i.e., categorical variable [low, medium, high] as indicated by RepRisk), whether it is a transgression of a "codified line" (i.e., alleged violation of an international standard, alleged violation of a law dummies), and the country in which it occurred (i.e., country dummies).

With respect to the initial public announcement of the focal allegation, we control for the year of the announcement (i.e., year dummies), the reach of the news source (i.e., categorical variable (low, medium, high) as indicated by RepRisk), and the language of the news source (i.e., language dummies).

Method of Analysis

To test our hypothesis, we use a fixed effects model to account for any time-constant unobserved heterogeneity between firms that could otherwise lead to endogeneity (Wooldridge, 2010). We report cluster-robust standard errors because firms can face multiple allegations during the observation period (Rogers, 1993; Wooldridge, 2010).

RESULTS

Table 1 presents means, standard deviations, and correlation coefficients of our variables. On average, we find a small, but significantly negative investor reaction ($p = 0.00$) to a focal allegation, which is consistent with prior findings on corporate misconduct (e.g., Clemente, 2015; Haslem et al., 2017; Zeidan, 2013).

Table 2 depicts the regression results of our explanatory and control variables on investor reaction. As indicated by the F-test, all models are significant ($p = 0.00$). Furthermore, our results do not seem to be affected by multicollinearity as the variance inflation factors (VIFs) are below 2.66, and the mean VIF is 1.63 (O'Brien, 2007).

Our hypothesis suggests that the relationship between allegation prevalence among other firms and investor reaction to a focal allegation is inverted U-shaped. To test this hypothesis, we utilize an empirically rigorous three-step approach (Haans et al., 2016; Lind & Mehlum, 2010): We examine (1) the squared term of our explanatory variable, (2) the steepness of the slope at both ends of the data range, and (3) the location of the turning point. As shown in Model 2 of Table 2 (1) the coefficient of allegation prevalence among other firms squared is negative and significant ($b = -0.09$; $p = 0.00$). (2) The slope at the lower end of the data range is positive and significant ($p = 0.00$), *and* the slope at the higher end of the data range is negative and significant ($p = 0.00$). (3) The turning point, at which allegation prevalence among other firms evokes the most positive investor reaction, is located at 7.15.[2] Following the recommendations by Haans et al. (2016), we use the Fieller (1954) method to test whether the turning point is located well within the data range. Hence, we construct a confidence interval around the

Table 1. Descriptive Statistics and Correlations.

No.	Variable	Mean	SD	1	2	3	4	5	6	7	8	9	10	11	12	13	14	15
1.	Investor reaction	-0.18	4.61															
2.	Allegation prevalence among other firms	7.17	3.46	0.00														
3.	Firm size	9.71	1.67	0.04***	0.02*													
4.	Firm performance	0.05	0.08	0.05***	-0.05***	0.03*												
5.	Firm book-to-market ratio	7.36	81.91	0.00	0.04***	-0.02	0.08***											
6.	Firm risk	4.53	27.64	0.01	0.03*	0.03**	0.02*	0.78***										
7.	Firm analyst coverage	17.20	8.65	0.03**	0.08***	0.45***	0.17***	0.02	0.00									
8.	Firm age	43.18	33.43	0.02	-0.00	0.13***	0.09***	0.03*	-0.01	0.02								
9.	Firm prior good behavior	12.80	11.53	0.02	-0.13***	0.55***	0.18***	0.01	0.01	0.33***	0.31***							
10.	Firm prior bad behavior	8.56	8.33	-0.00	-0.50***	0.41***	0.08***	-0.03**	-0.01	0.11***	0.21***	0.51***						
11.	Allegation severity (low)	0.64	0.48	-0.02*	-0.02*	-0.02	0.02	-0.01	-0.01	0.05***	0.01	0.05***	0.03*					
12.	Allegation severity (medium)	0.34	0.48	0.02	0.04**	0.02	-0.02*	-0.00	0.01	-0.05***	-0.01	-0.05***	-0.03*	-0.98***				
13.	Alleged violation of an international standard	0.04	0.19	-0.01	-0.01	0.01	-0.01	-0.00	0.01	-0.01	-0.01	-0.01	-0.01	-0.19***	0.18***			
14.	Alleged violation of a law	0.39	0.49	-0.01	0.01	-0.04***	-0.01	-0.02	-0.01	-0.02	-0.04***	-0.07***	-0.04***	0.02	-0.02	0.01		
15.	News announcement source reach (low)	0.45	0.50	0.02	0.07***	-0.03***	-0.02*	-0.00	-0.00	-0.05***	0.03*	-0.04***	-0.06***	-0.22***	0.21***	0.14***	-0.17***	
16.	News announcement source reach (medium)	0.40	0.49	0.00	-0.12***	-0.01	0.01	0.01	0.00	-0.02	0.00	0.02*	0.08***	0.08***	-0.07***	-0.08***	0.10***	-0.73***

Notes: $N = 8,802$.

*$p < 0.05$; **$p < 0.01$; ***$p < 0.001$.

Table 2. Regression Results Predicting Investor Reaction to a Focal Allegation.

Variable	Model 1		Model 2	
Control variables				
Firm size	−0.11	(0.78)	−0.11	(0.78)
Firm performance	1.66	(0.24)	1.63	(0.25)
Firm book-to-market ratio	−0.00	(0.81)	−0.00	(0.91)
Firm risk	0.00	(0.29)	0.00	(0.33)
Firm analyst coverage	0.04*	(0.04)	0.04*	(0.04)
Firm age	0.03	(0.88)	−0.17	(0.68)
Firm prior good behavior	−0.01	(0.24)	−0.01	(0.22)
Firm prior bad behavior	0.01	(0.75)	0.01	(0.76)
Allegation severity (low)	−0.93†	(0.07)	−1.00*	(0.05)
Allegation severity (medium)	−0.85†	(0.08)	−0.92†	(0.06)
Alleged violation of an international standard	−0.30	(0.36)	−0.29	(0.37)
Alleged violation of a law	0.27*	(0.02)	0.27*	(0.02)
News announcement source reach (low)	0.25	(0.20)	0.23	(0.24)
News announcement source reach (medium)	0.34†	(0.06)	0.34†	(0.06)
Intercept	1.36	(0.88)	8.10	(0.62)
Explanatory variables				
Allegation prevalence among other firms			1.30**	(0.01)
Allegation prevalence among other firms squared			**−0.09****	**(0.00)**
Observations	8,802		8,802	
Within- R^2	0.06		0.06	
Firm fixed effects	yes		yes	
Firm industry dummies included	yes		yes	
Allegation type dummies included	yes		yes	
Allegation country dummies included	yes		yes	
News announcement year dummies included	yes		yes	
News announcement source language dummies included	yes		yes	

Notes: P-values are given in parentheses. Cluster-robust standard errors have been used.
†$p < 0.10$; *$p < 0.05$; **$p < 0.01$; ***$p < 0.001$.

turning point, which accounts for finite sample bias and biases caused by potential departure from normality. Both the lower and the upper end of the 95-per cent Fieller confidence interval [3.98; 9.71] are located well within the data range [0.91; 11.42]. This suggests that our results are not driven by outliers (Haans et al., 2016). Based on these tests (overall test of the presence of an inverted U-shape: $p = 0.00$) and the graphical illustration of the effect (cf. Fig. 3), we are confident that the relationship between allegation prevalence among other firms and investor reaction to a focal allegation indeed has an inverted U-shape, supporting our hypothesis.

Robustness Tests

To test the sensitivity of our empirical results, we also re-ran our analysis using alternative variable and model specifications.

First, we used alternative specifications of our dependent variable (investor reaction), applying (1) alternative event windows (i.e., (– 1, 0), (0, 0), and (– 2, 2)) and (2) an alternative estimation period (200 days). Our results remain consistent.[3]

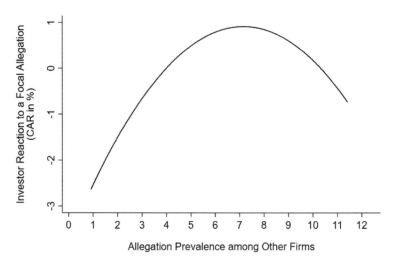

Fig. 3.   Influence of Allegation Prevalence Among Other Firms on Investor
Reaction to a Focal Allegation.

Second, we used alternative specifications of our explanatory variable (allegation prevalence among other firms). We accounted for (1) alternative time horizons (i.e., two, four, and five years prior to the focal allegation), (2) alternative reaches of the news source (i.e., news sources of at least medium reach, news sources of any reach), (3) alternative languages of the news source (i.e., only news sources in English language), (4) alternative types of prior allegations (i.e., only prior allegations of similar type, only prior allegations of the same type as the focal allegation), (5) alternative levels of severity of prior allegations (i.e., only prior allegations of at least medium severity, only prior allegations of high severity), (6) alternative transgressions of prior allegations (i.e., only prior alleged violations of at least an international standard, only prior alleged violations of a law), and (7) alternative countries of prior allegations (i.e., only prior US allegations). With regard to all of these alternative specifications of our explanatory variable, our results remain consistent. (8) We restricted the assessment of prior allegations to prior allegations against industry peers (two-digit NAICS code) and find that this changes the effect.[4] To investigate the within-industry effect further, we then examined whether the share of prior allegations against industry peers (i.e., prior allegations against industry peers/prior allegations against other firms) moderates our main relationship. We find that the share of prior allegations against industry peers significantly flattens the inverted U-shaped relationship.[5] This supplementary analysis suggests that as the share of prior allegations against industry peers increases, additional prior allegations against other firms have a more consistent informational value for investors (i.e., the anticipation effect becomes more linear). This is perfectly consistent with the notion that allegations against industry peers more strongly inform investors' anticipation of a focal allegation than allegations against other firms (e.g., Paruchuri &

Misangyi, 2015). The finding of a significant moderation effect is thus not only theoretically meaningful but also explains why considering prior allegations against other firms and prior allegations against industry peers leads to different results.

Third, we used an alternative specification of our control variable firm prior bad behavior. We operationalized it as the number of allegations against the focal firm which have been announced in high reach news sources in the three years prior to the focal allegation (as consistent with our measure of allegation prevalence among other firms). Again, our results remain consistent.

Additionally, we tested whether endogeneity biases our empirical results. In our research context, endogeneity is typically caused by omitted variables (Semadeni et al., 2014). To account for omitted variable bias, we ran our main model using a fixed effects model, which corrects for endogeneity caused by any omitted time-*constant* factors (Hamilton & Nickerson, 2003; Wooldridge, 2010). Furthermore, we applied an instrumental variables approach (with a 2SLS-estimator and cluster-robust standard errors), which corrects for endogeneity caused by any omitted time-*variant* factors (Bascle, 2008; Certo et al., 2016). As part of the 2SLS analysis, we used a firm's accumulated stress of failure (i.e., whether the firm's cash flow has been negative in the prior three years) and board independence as instruments as extant research has argued and found that these factors affect the likelihood that a particular firm is alleged of misconduct (e.g., Kassinis & Vafeas, 2002; Kesner et al., 1986; Schnatterly et al., 2018; Zheng & Chun, 2017). We also made sure that our instruments are valid (e.g., Bascle, 2008; Semadeni et al., 2014). Results from the 2SLS analysis support our initial findings. The coefficient of allegation prevalence among other firms is positive and significant ($b = 6.69$; $p = 0.03$) and the coefficient of allegation prevalence among other firms squared is negative and significant ($b = -0.29$; $p = 0.03$). Importantly, the test for endogeneity, i.e., a Durbin-Wu-Hausman test, is non-significant ($p = 0.58$). This suggests that allegation prevalence among other firms and allegation prevalence among other firms squared can be treated as exogenous, and that endogeneity does not materially affect our empirical results.

DISCUSSION AND IMPLICATIONS

Recent misconduct research has generated valuable insights into how a current allegation against an individual firm is associated with reputational and financial spillover effects for other, unalleged firms (e.g., Chen, 2016; Galloway et al., 2021; Jonsson et al., 2009; Naumovska & Lavie, 2021; Naumovska & Zajac, 2022). Our study complements and extends this vein of research by exploring whether prior allegations against other firms are associated with financial spillover effects for the individual firm currently facing an allegation.

In particular, our study raises awareness for the fact that not only the alleged firm's prior behavior (e.g., Christensen, 2016; Godfrey et al., 2009; Janney & Gove, 2011; Shiu & Yang, 2017) but also the prior behavior of other firms matters for investor reaction to a focal allegation. As highlighted by our practical example from the automotive industry and past studies on corporate misconduct (e.g., Bookman, 2008; Gabbioneta et al., 2013; Palmer, 2013; Wiersema & Zhang, 2013), consideration of prior allegations against other firms appears essential because a focal allegation is seldom an "isolated" event but is often situated in a series of allegations against other firms. As a result, investors do not react to the focal allegation in isolation but against the backdrop of these prior allegations. Collectively, our study's theorizing and findings suggest that allegation prevalence among other firms should be accounted for in future research studies to assure that misconduct research more accurately reflects practical reality and to assure that empirical analyses comprehensively explain investor reaction to corporate misconduct.

Moreover, our study's findings align with the recent notion that spillover effects in the context of corporate misconduct are not limited to industry peers (e.g., Naumovska & Zajac, 2022). Specifically, our findings suggest that prior allegations against a wide population of other firms have a marked influence on investor reaction to a focal allegation.

Finally, informed by behavioral decision theory (e.g., Poulton, 1994; Slovic et al., 1977; Takemura, 2014), our study further extends research on corporate misconduct by identifying the behavioral mechanisms that appear to determine investor reaction to a focal allegation. Specifically, we theorize that investor reaction results from the interplay of investor anticipation and investor evaluation. Our study thus contributes to a more nuanced understanding of investor reaction to corporate misconduct.

Limitations and Future Research

Like any other study, our study is subject to several limitations, which provide opportunities for future research. In this section, we jointly describe them.

First, in our study, we focus on the influence of allegation prevalence among other firms on investor reaction to a focal allegation. This specific focus on allegations is consistent with prior research on corporate misconduct and spillover effects (e.g., Chen, 2016; Goldman et al., 2012; Kang, 2008; Naumovska & Lavie, 2021; Naumovska & Zajac, 2022). However, we were unable to discern whether prior allegations against other firms were proven or not because secondary data providers such as RepRisk do not provide such detailed data. As our sample includes over 8,000 observations, manual coding was also not a feasible option. Future studies which rely on smaller sample sizes or qualitative research studies, however, could introduce this important distinction to shed light on whether it makes a material difference to investor reaction whether prior allegations against other firms turned out to be warranted or not. From a theoretical perspective, the predicted, inverted U-shaped effect can be expected to hold even if the share of proven, prior allegations against other firms is large. This is because proven, prior allegations against other firms are an even stronger indicator of prior misconduct than prior allegations against other firms (e.g., Pierce, 2018), which likely strengthens the theoretical mechanisms (i.e., investor anticipation and investor evaluation) underlying our predicted effect. The inverted U-shaped effect remains unaffected by this change or becomes even more pronounced (Haans et al., 2016).

Second, it should be noted that our key measure captures prior allegations against various types of other firms. This approach is in line with recent findings on spillover effects (Aranda et al., 2020; Naumovska & Zajac, 2022). We see, however, great merit in future research studies that build upon our study and examine the effect our study identifies more granularly. For instance, future research could assess the boundary conditions of our effect by examining how investor reaction to a focal allegation changes depending on the share of prior allegations against e.g., industry peers, alliance partners, suppliers, or firms with board interlocks. Theoretically, the share of prior allegations against a specific type of other firm may affect investors' anticipation of a focal allegation as well as their perception that the focal allegation is warranted, and hence moderates our effect.

Third, our practical example from the automotive industry, which we use to illustrate our theorizing, suggests that the media is another important constituent that influences investor reaction. In fact, corporate misconduct is not only socially situated but also socially constructed (e.g., Greve et al., 2010). In the process of social construction, the media plays an important role (Clemente et al., 2016). For example, the portrayal of allegations in the media is not a simple representation of facts, but the media may frame the same allegation differently, thereby shaping investors' reaction (e.g., Clemente et al., 2016; Clemente & Gabbioneta, 2017). Future research could thus examine how the portrayal of prior allegations against other firms across news announcements (e.g., positive/ negative tone, emotional tone, scandal frame used) as well as the extent of media attention to these allegations influence investor anticipation and evaluation of a focal allegation, and thus their reaction. Moreover, future research which investigates the extent to which the media directs attention toward prior allegations or toward previously alleged firms when reporting on a focal allegation could offer a valuable extension to our study.

Finally, as outlined in our introduction, assessing investor reaction to a focal allegation is critical to further our understanding of the costs and benefits associated with alleged corporate misconduct for firms. Regarding the latter, selected studies have found that investor reaction to corporate misconduct is sometimes positive (e.g., Pierce, 2018). Similarly, we find that investor reaction to a focal allegation is positive in case of a moderate number of prior allegations against other firms. This may be the case because some investors have previously anticipated a more significant focal allegation than actually occurs (e.g., Gande & Lewis, 2009). To more accurately explain positive investor reaction to allegations, we see merit in future qualitative research studies. Furthermore, to provide for a more comprehensive understanding of how firms are penalized for their alleged misconduct, we also see great value in studies that examine the reaction of key firm stakeholders other than investors. Our study offers the novel insight that a relatively low and a relatively high number of prior allegations against other firms are associated with the most negative investor reaction. Consequently, it would be interesting to study to which extent the reaction of customers, employees, creditors, and other stakeholders differs from the reaction of investors.

NOTES

1. Empirically, our focus on the date when allegations are initially publicly announced is in line with prior research on investor reaction to corporate misconduct (e.g., Christensen, 2016; Godfrey et al., 2009; Karpoff et al., 2005; Murphy et al., 2009) as well as the methodological literature on assessing investor reaction (e.g., Bromiley et al., 1988; McWilliams & Siegel, 1997).

2. Predicted investor reaction to a focal allegation is statistically significantly positive ($CAR = 0.91$; $p = 0.01$) for allegation prevalence among other firms at 7.15 (i.e., the turning point). Graphical inspection of the 95-per cent confidence bounds indicates that predicted investor reaction to a focal allegation is also statistically significantly positive for values of allegation prevalence among other firms right around the turning point.

3. With respect to all robustness tests, additional analyses are available from the authors upon request.

4. The coefficient of allegation prevalence among industry peers squared is insignificant ($p = 0.31$).

5. The coefficient of the interaction term between the share of prior allegations against industry peers and allegation prevalence among other firms squared is positive and significant ($b = 0.39$; $p = 0.04$).

REFERENCES

ABC News. (2015, September 22). How Volkswagen fooled regulators around the world. https://abcnews.go.com/Business/volkswagen-fooled-regulators-world/story?id=33944234

Aranda, A. M., Conti, R., & Wezel, F. C. (2020). Distinct but not apart? Stigma reduction and cross-industry evaluative spillovers: The case of medical marijuana legalization. *Academy of Management Journal*, 64(6), 1901–1926.

Autoblog. (2015, September 18). VW air rule violation allegations 'stunning,' $18B fine unlikely. https://www.autoblog.com/2015/09/18/vw-air-rule-violation-allegations-stunning-18b-fine-unlikely/

Barnett, M. L. (2014). Why stakeholders ignore firm misconduct: A cognitive view. *Journal of Management*, 40(3), 676–702.

Barth, F., Eckert, C., Gatzert, N., & Scholz, H. (2022). Spillover effects from the Volkswagen emissions scandal: An analysis of stock and corporate bond markets. *Schmalenbach Journal of Business Research*, 74(1), 37–76.

Bascle, G. (2008). Controlling for endogeneity with instrumental variables in strategic management research. *Strategic Organization*, 6(3), 285–327.

BBC News. (2015, October 12). Volkswagen: The scandal explained. https://www.bbc.com/news/business-34324772

Bookman, Z. (2008). Convergences and omissions in reporting corporate and white collar crime. *DePaul Business & Commercial Law Journal*, 6(3), 347–392.

Bouzzine, Y. D., & Lueg, R. (2020). The contagion effect of environmental violations: The case of Dieselgate in Germany. *Business Strategy and the Environment*, 29(8), 3187–3202.

Breitinger, D., & Bonardi, J.-P. (2019). Firms, breach of norms, and reputation damage. *Business & Society*, 58(6), 1143–1176.

Bromiley, P., Govekar, M., & Marcus, A. (1988). On using event-study methodology in strategic management research. *Technovation*, 8(1–3), 25–42.

Certo, S. T., Busenbark, J. R., Woo, H., & Semadeni, M. (2016). Sample selection bias and Heckman models in strategic management research. *Strategic Management Journal*, 37(13), 2639–2657.

Chandler, D., Polidoro, F., & Yang, W. (2020). When is it good to be bad? Contrasting effects of multiple reputations for bad behavior on media coverage of serious organizational errors. *Academy of Management Journal*, 63(4), 1236–1265.

Chen, L. (2016). Local institutions, audit quality, and corporate scandals of US-listed foreign firms. *Journal of Business Ethics*, 133(2), 351–373.

Christensen, D. M. (2016). Corporate accountability reporting and high-profile misconduct. *Accounting Review*, 91(2), 377–399.

Clemente, M. (2015). What is the share price reaction to organizational social misconduct? *Academy of Management Annual Meeting Proceedings*, https://doi.org/10.5465/ambpp.2015.15988abstract.

Clemente, M., Durand, R., & Porac, J. (2016). Organizational wrongdoing and media bias. In D. Palmer, K. Smith-Crowe, & R. Greenwood (Eds.), *Organizational wrongdoing: Key perspectives and new directions* (pp. 435–473). Cambridge University Press.

Clemente, M., & Gabbioneta, C. (2017). How does the media frame corporate scandals? The case of German newspapers and the Volkswagen diesel scandal. *Journal of Management Inquiry, 26*(3), 287–302.

CNBC. (2015, September 24). Europe's carmakers caught up in VW storm. https://www.cnbc.com/2015/09/24/bmw-shares-slip-on-report-of-high-emission-levels.html

Cumming, D., Leung, T. Y., & Rui, O. (2015). Gender diversity and securities fraud. *Academy of Management Journal, 58*(5), 1572–1593.

Daily Mail. (2015, September 28). Now we can't trust car giants on miles per gallon either: After VW scandal, Mercedes and BMW accused over fuel efficiency. http://www.dailymail.co.uk/news/article-3252717/Now-t-trust-car-giants-mpg-VW-scandal-Mercedes-BMW-accused-fuel-efficiency.html

Dewan, Y., & Jensen, M. (2020). Catching the big fish: The role of scandals in making status a liability. *Academy of Management Journal, 63*(5), 1652–1678.

Diestre, L., & Rajagopalan, N. (2014). Toward an input-based perspective on categorization: Investor reactions to chemical accidents. *Academy of Management Journal, 57*(4), 1130–1153.

Fama, E. F. (1970). Efficient capital markets: A review of theory and empirical work. *Journal of Finance, 25*(2), 383–417.

Fieller, E. C. (1954). Some problems in interval estimation. *Journal of the Royal Statistical Society. Series B (Methodological), 16*(2), 175–185.

Financial Times. (2015, September 24). EPA surprised by scale of Volkswagen's deceit. https://www.ft.com/content/bbd61c58-62d7-11e5-9846-de406ccb37f2

Financial Times. (2016, June 20). European diesel car sales hit by VW scandal. https://www.ft.com/content/94c56a30-3476-11e6-bda0-04585c31b153

Financial Times. (2017, January 12). Fiat Chrysler accused by US regulator of emissions cheating. https://www.ft.com/content/dc7794a0-d8e2-11e6-944b-e7eb37a6aa8e

Flammer, C. (2013). Corporate social responsibility and shareholder reaction: The environmental awareness of investors. *Academy of Management Journal, 56*(3), 758–781.

Fortune. (2017, January 13). Were they all at it? France cranks up probe into Renault diesels. https://fortune.com/2017/01/13/france-renault-diesel-emissions/

Gabbioneta, C., Greenwood, R., Mazzola, P., & Minoja, M. (2013). The influence of the institutional context on corporate illegality. *Accounting, Organizations and Society, 38*(6–7), 484–504.

Gaganis, C., Papadimitri, P., Pasiouras, F., & Ventouri, A. (2021). Informal institutions and corporate reputational exposure: The role of public environmental perceptions. *British Journal of Management, 32*(4), 1027–1061.

Galloway, T. L., Miller, D. R., & Liu, K. (2021). Guilty by association: Spillover of regulative violations and repair efforts to alliance partners. *Journal of Business Ethics.* Advance online publication.

Gande, A., & Lewis, C. M. (2009). Shareholder-initiated class action lawsuits: Shareholder wealth effects and industry spillovers. *Journal of Financial & Quantitative Analysis, 44*(4), 823–850.

Gavetti, G., Greve, H. R., Levinthal, D. A., & Ocasio, W. (2012). The behavioral theory of the firm: Assessment and prospects. *Academy of Management Annals, 6*(1), 1–40.

Godfrey, P. C., Merrill, C. B., & Hansen, J. M. (2009). The relationship between corporate social responsibility and shareholder value: An empirical test of the risk management hypothesis. *Strategic Management Journal, 30*(4), 425–445.

Goldman, E., Peyer, U., & Stefanescu, I. (2012). Financial misrepresentation and its impact on rivals. *Financial Management, 41*(4), 915–945.

Greve, H. R., Palmer, D., & Pozner, J.-E. (2010). Organizations gone wild: The causes, processes, and consequences of organizational misconduct. *Academy of Management Annals, 4*(1), 53–107.

Haans, R. F. J., Pieters, C., & He, Z.-L. (2016). Thinking about U: Theorizing and testing U- and inverted U-shaped relationships in strategy research. *Strategic Management Journal, 37*(7), 1177–1195.

Hamilton, B. H., & Nickerson, J. A. (2003). Correcting for endogeneity in strategic management research. *Strategic Organization, 1*(1), 51–78.

Haslem, B., Hutton, I., & Smith, A. H. (2017). How much do corporate defendants really lose? A new verdict on the reputation loss induced by corporate litigation. *Financial Management*, *46*(2), 323–358.

Jacobs, B. W., & Singhal, V. R. (2020). Shareholder value effects of the Volkswagen emissions scandal on the automotive ecosystem. *Production & Operations Management*, *29*(10), 2230–2251.

Janney, J. J., & Gove, S. (2011). Reputation and corporate social responsibility aberrations, trends, and hypocrisy: Reactions to firm choices in the stock option backdating scandal. *Journal of Management Studies*, *48*(7), 1562–1585.

Jonsson, S., Greve, H. R., & Fujiwara-Greve, T. (2009). Undeserved loss: The spread of legitimacy loss to innocent organizations in response to reported corporate deviance. *Administrative Science Quarterly*, *54*(2), 195–228.

Kang, E. (2008). Director interlocks and spillover effects of reputational penalties from financial reporting fraud. *Academy of Management Journal*, *51*(3), 537–555.

Karpoff, J. M., Lee, D. S., & Martin, G. S. (2008). The cost to firms of cooking the books. *Journal of Financial & Quantitative Analysis*, *43*(3), 581–611.

Karpoff, J. M., Lott, J. R., Jr., & Wehrly, E. W. (2005). The reputational penalties for environmental violations: Empirical evidence. *Journal of Law & Economics*, *48*(2), 653–675.

Kassinis, G., & Vafeas, N. (2002). Corporate boards and outside stakeholders as determinants of environmental litigation. *Strategic Management Journal*, *23*(5), 399–415.

Kesner, I. F., Victor, B., & Lamont, B. T. (1986). Research notes: Board composition and the commission of illegal acts: An investigation of Fortune 500 companies. *Academy of Management Journal*, *29*(4), 789–799.

Kölbel, J. F., Busch, T., & Jancso, L. M. (2017). How media coverage of corporate social irresponsibility increases financial risk. *Strategic Management Journal*, *38*(11), 2266–2284.

Lind, J. T., & Mehlum, H. (2010). With or without U? The appropriate test for a U-shaped relationship. *Oxford Bulletin of Economics and Statistics*, *72*(1), 109–118.

Malatesta, P. H., & Thompson, R. (1985). Partially anticipated events: A model of stock price reactions with an application to corporate acquisitions. *Journal of Financial Economics*, *14*(2), 237–250.

Mariuzzo, F., Ormosi, P. L., & Majied, Z. (2020). Fines and reputational sanctions: The case of cartels. *International Journal of Industrial Organization*, *69*©, 102584.

McDonnell, M.-H., & King, B. G. (2018). Order in the court: How firm status and reputation shape the outcomes of employment discrimination suits. *American Sociological Review*, *83*(1), 61–87.

McWilliams, A., & Siegel, D. (1997). Event studies in management research: Theoretical and empirical issues. *Academy of Management Journal*, *40*(3), 626–657.

Mishina, Y., Block, E. S., & Mannor, M. J. (2012). The path dependence of organizational reputation: How social judgment influences assessments of capability and character. *Strategic Management Journal*, *33*(5), 459–477.

Mother Jones. (2015, September 18). The Feds just accused Volkswagen of an unbelievable scheme to evade pollution laws. https://www.motherjones.com/politics/2015/09/obama-volkswagen-clean-air-emissions-citation-epa/

Motoring Research. (2016, June 14). It's not just VW: 30 dirty diesels accused of emissions cheating. https://www.motoringresearch.com/car-news/not-just-vw-30-dirty-diesels-accused-emissions-cheating/

Naumovska, I., & Lavie, D. (2021). When an industry peer is accused of financial misconduct: Stigma versus competition effects on non-accused firms. *Administrative Science Quarterly*, *66*(4), 1130–1172.

Naumovska, I., & Zajac, E. J. (2022). How inductive and deductive generalization shape the guilt-by-association phenomenon among firms: Theory and evidence. *Organization Science*, *33*(1), 373–392.

News Wheel. (2016, April 20). Mitsubishi Motors cheats in fuel economy testing: Joins VW on list of liars. https://thenewswheel.com/mitsubishi-motors-cheats-in-fuel-economy-testing-joins-vw-on-list-of-liars/

NY Times. (2017, July 22). German carmakers face potential new scandal over antitrust issues. https://www.nytimes.com/2017/07/22/business/german-carmakers-antitrust.html

O'Brien, R. M. (2007). A caution regarding rules of thumb for variance inflation factors. *Quality & Quantity*, *41*(5), 673–690.

Palmer, D. (2013). The new perspective on organizational wrongdoing. *California Management Review*, *56*(1), 5–23.

Paruchuri, S., Han, J.-H., & Prakash, P. (2021). Salient expectations? Incongruence across capability and integrity signals and investor reactions to organizational misconduct. *Academy of Management Journal*, *64*(2), 562–586.

Paruchuri, S., & Misangyi, V. F. (2015). Investor perceptions of financial misconduct: The heterogeneous contamination of bystander firms. *Academy of Management Journal*, *58*(1), 169–194.

Paruchuri, S., Pollock, T. G., & Kumar, N. (2019). On the tip of the brain: Understanding when negative reputational events can have positive reputation spillovers, and for how long. *Strategic Management Journal*, *40*(12), 1965–1983.

Pfarrer, M. D., Decelles, K. A., Smith, K. G., & Taylor, M. S. (2008). After the fall: Reintegrating the corrupt organization. *Academy of Management Review*, *33*(3), 730–749.

Pierce, J. R. (2018). Reexamining the cost of corporate criminal prosecutions. *Journal of Management*, *44*(3), 892–918.

Poulton, E. C. (1994). *Behavioral decision theory: A new approach*. Cambridge University Press.

RepRisk AG. (2017). *RepRisk: Datasets, methodology, and data elements for WRDS subscribers*.

RepRisk. (2021). Approach. https://www.reprisk.com/approach

Rogers, W. H. (1993). Regression standard errors in clustered samples. *Stata Technical Bulletin*, *3*(13), 19–23.

Sampath, V. S., Gardberg, N. A., & Rahman, N. (2018). Corporate reputation's invisible hand: Bribery, rational choice, and market penalties. *Journal of Business Ethics*, *151*(3), 743–760.

Schembera, S., & Scherer, A. G. (2017). Organizational strategies in the context of legitimacy loss: Radical versus gradual responses to disclosed corruption. *Strategic Organization*, *15*(3), 301–337.

Schnatterly, K., Gangloff, K. A., & Tuschke, A. (2018). CEO wrongdoing: A review of pressure, opportunity, and rationalization. *Journal of Management*, *44*(6), 2405–2432.

Scientific American. (2015, September 24). How a U.S. clean air NGO caught Volkswagen cheating. https://www.scientificamerican.com/article/how-a-u-s-clean-air-ngo-caught-volkswagen-cheating/

Semadeni, M., Withers, M. C., & Certo, S. T. (2014). The perils of endogeneity and instrumental variables in strategy research: Understanding through simulations. *Strategic Management Journal*, *35*(7), 1070–1079.

Shiu, Y.-M., & Yang, S.-L. (2017). Does engagement in corporate social responsibility provide strategic insurance-like effects? *Strategic Management Journal*, *38*(2), 455–470.

Shu, H., & Wong, S. M.-L. (2018). When a sinner does a good deed: The path-dependence of reputation repair. *Journal of Management Studies*, *55*(5), 770–808.

Slovic, P., Fischhoff, B., & Lichtenstein, S. (1977). Behavioral decision theory. *Annual Review of Psychology*, *28*(1), 1–39.

Takemura, K. (2014). *Behavioral decision theory: Psychological and mathematical descriptions of human choice behavior*. Springer.

The Wall Street Journal. (2015, October 9). Volkswagen U.S. CEO says he didn't know in 2014 of emissions defeat devices. https://www.wsj.com/articles/volkswagen-u-s-ceo-says-he-didnt-know-in-2014-of-emissions-defeat-devices-1444316371

The Week. (2015, September 24). Volkwagen's unethical emissions scam is partly the government's fault. https://theweek.com/articles/578725/volkwagens-unethical-emissions-scam-partly-governments-fault

Tversky, A., & Kahneman, D. (1973). Availability: A heuristic for judging frequency and probability. *Cognitive Psychology*, *5*(2), 207–232.

Tversky, A., & Kahneman, D. (1974). Judgment under uncertainty: Heuristics and biases. *Science*, *185*(4157), 1124–1131.

Wei, J., Ouyang, Z., & Chen, H. (2017). Well-known or well-liked? The effects of corporate reputation on firm value at the onset of a corporate crisis. *Strategic Management Journal*, *38*(10), 2103–2120.

Wiersema, M. F., & Zhang, Y. (2013). Executive turnover in the stock option backdating wave: The impact of social context. *Strategic Management Journal*, *34*(5), 590–609.

Wooldridge, J. M. (2010). *Econometric analysis of cross section and panel data* (2nd ed.). The MIT Press.

Zavyalova, A., Pfarrer, M. D., Reger, R. K., & Shapiro, D. L. (2012). Managing the message: The effects of firm actions and industry spillovers on media coverage following wrongdoing. *Academy of Management Journal, 55*(5), 1079–1101.

Zeidan, M. J. (2013). Effects of illegal behavior on the financial performance of US banking institutions. *Journal of Business Ethics, 112*(2), 313–324.

Zheng, Q., & Chun, R. (2017). Corporate recidivism in emerging economies. *Business Ethics: A European Review, 26*(1), 63–79.

CHAPTER 4

PEERS: POWERFUL OR NEGLIGIBLE? A SYSTEMATIC REVIEW ON PEER FACTORS AND INTERNAL WHISTLEBLOWING

Behnud Mir Djawadi, Sabrina Plaß and Sabrina Schäfers

ABSTRACT

When reporting wrongdoing internally, whistleblowers are confronted with the dilemma of weighing up their loyalty toward the organization (e.g., ethical standards) and their co-workers (e.g., the social norm of not snitching on peers). However, the role played by peers in the whistleblowing decision process and in the aftermath has rarely been addressed in existing reviews. We therefore perform a systematic review that identifies seven thematic clusters of peer factors, offering researchers an informative overview of (a) the peer factors that have been examined to influence the whistleblowing decision, and (b) the extent to which the whistleblower experiences adverse consequences from peers in the aftermath of whistleblowing. As peer factors seem to be important to explain and predict internal whistleblowing, researchers are encouraged to address in future works the research gaps our review unraveled.

Keywords: Whistleblowing; peer factors; co-workers; systematic review; whistleblowing antecedents; whistleblowing consequences

Organizational Wrongdoing as the "Foundational" Grand Challenge: Consequences and Impact
Research in the Sociology of Organizations, Volume 85, 73–100
ISSN: 0733-558X/doi:10.1108/S0733-558X20230000085005

INTRODUCTION

One way of mitigating wrongdoing in organizations is to encourage employees to blow the whistle on observed unethical behavior (e.g., Keenan, 2000). We define whistleblowing as

> the disclosure by organization members (former or current) of illegal, immoral, or illegitimate practices under the control of their employers, to persons or organizations that may be able to effect action. (Near & Miceli, 1985, p. 4)

Regulators and managers have increasingly become aware of the benefits of wrong-doing being reported internally before it is publicly exposed. In contrast to reporting observed wrongdoing through external channels, internal whistleblowing enables organizations to address and correct wrongdoing themselves and minimizes reputational damage (Lee & Xiao, 2018). Whistleblowing has thus become an accepted part of the regulatory environment of organizations, to ensure legal compliance and ethical business practice (Vandekerckhove et al., 2014). As such, organizations increasingly adopt and establish whistleblowing programs as part of their formal compliance systems, which include, e.g., policies and reporting channels to structure and facilitate the reporting process and make the organization's commitment to whistleblowing more transparent (Dixon, 2016; Hassink et al., 2007).

However, to engage in internal whistleblowing, employees must be willing to report on organizational members with whom they stand in a direct or indirect professional and/or personal relationship (Trevino & Victor, 1992). Especially given the growing trend whereby organizations invest in team building and set up working groups (Oh et al., 2004), the potential whistleblower would have to consider turning on colleagues, which would cause a dilemma and threaten the strong social ties that organizations try so hard to foster. Hence, whistleblowing scholarship has seen a shift in the way internal whistleblowing is framed: it is no longer merely an act of ethical resistance aimed at changing corporate or governmental behavior and, in the process, being met with crude antagonism by the organization (Glazer & Glazer, 1989). Rather, whistleblowing is recognized more as a complex social phenomenon, due to whistleblowers having to weigh up their loyalty toward the organization and its ethical standards against their relationship with co-workers (e.g., by conforming to the prevailing social norm by not snitching on peers). In this regard, the role of peers in the process and in the aftermath of the whistleblowing decision has more recently become a non-trivial dimension in whistleblowing research (Khan & Howe, 2021; Mayer et al., 2013).

Moreover, studies based on different theories, such as social identity theory (e.g., Anvari et al., 2019) and social information processing (e.g., Gundlach et al., 2003; Near & Miceli, 1995), stress the importance of the immediate workgroup for a whistleblower to assess the observed situation as wrongdoing, and its reporting as a reasonable action. Due to their direct proximity, peers are particularly salient and satisfy individuals' social needs (Greenberger et al., 1987), and hence may have a formative impact on a whistleblower's decision. McLain and Keenan (1999) even pose the theoretical argument that in a perceived conflict over whistleblowing between the organization's response and co-workers' responses, employees are more likely to behave in a way that pleases the peers rather than the organization. Muehlheusser and Roider (2008) similarly propose that peers place social loyalty over integrity, resulting in a wall of silence, where peers will not be reported, despite an organization's policy promoting the reporting of misconduct. As these theoretical studies demonstrate, over-prioritizing the relationship with peers in one's immediate working environment might hamper the attempt to blow the whistle on observed wrongdoing (Dungan et al., 2019).

Therefore, this paper asks how different peer factors are related to internal whistleblowing. We hereby complement existing reviews (e.g., Culiberg & Mihelič, 2017; Mesmer-Magnus & Viswesvaran, 2005), which have focused on individual, situational, and organizational factors of whistleblowing. Performing a systematic literature review allows us to identify which peer factors have already been investigated and which have potential for further research (Rousseau et al., 2008; Tranfield et al., 2003). We consider this method appropriate because the role of peers in the context of whistleblowing has already been investigated in studies based on different constructs and with specific foci. However, the studies are fragmented and disconnected, notably because they evolved in different contexts, such as academia, accounting, business, the military, or nursing.

Our review makes several contributions. First, we provide a framework that structures and categorizes the existing literature on peer factors and internal whistleblowing into two main strands: (a) the peer factors that have been examined to influence the whistleblowing decision, and (b) the extent to which the whistleblower experiences adverse consequences from peers in the aftermath. While the effect of peers has often been simplified in one variable, such as co-worker support, we find that peer factors are far more multifaceted. Our framework groups peer factors thematically into seven further clusters, offering researchers an informative overview of the factors studied within each category along with their (mixed) empirical findings. Second, we suggest that peer factors interact with other types of variables (i.e., moderating effects), so that specific relationships might only persist under particular social conditions. Third, we identify that further research is needed in order to unravel how and why peer factors influence the whistleblowing decision, and whether peer factors can explain relationships between previously investigated variables and whistleblowing (i.e., mediating effects). Lastly, by better understanding the different patterns of negative consequences for whistleblowers, researchers will be able to differentiate formal organizational variables (e.g., work-related retaliation) from informal peer variables (e.g., peer ostracism) which, in turn, could help managers develop more fine-grained programs for the prevention of these consequences and the promotion of whistleblowing.

SHORTCOMINGS OF PEER FACTOR STUDIES IN PREVIOUS WHISTLEBLOWING LITERATURE REVIEWS

Similar to Near and Miceli (1995), we refer to peers as co-workers or colleagues in the immediate workgroup with whom potential whistleblowers share at least a professional relationship. Peer factors are by and large intangible, hard to observe, and only indirectly controllable by the organization. They refer to, for example, the informal social norms, implicit agreements, and informal relationships. Peer factors, then, form the set of variables in the immediate relational and social context of potential whistleblowers, and can be assigned to the informal social structure of the organization, i.e., to each respective working group (Murphy, 2021).

Although theoretical work suggests that peer factors serve as valid antecedents for whistleblowing and affect the whistleblower in the aftermath, peer factors as set of variables have rarely been addressed in existing whistleblowing reviews. Over a decade ago, a meta-analysis of whistleblowing factors conducted by Mesmer-Magnus and Viswesvaran (2005) provided an essential momentum for whistleblowing research.[1] Their review examined 26 empirical studies identifying the personal, situational, and contextual predictors for the internal and external whistleblowing intention, for actual whistleblowing behavior, and retaliation. However, the authors mainly treat the influence by peers as a composite variable for organizational retaliation. We argue that responses by peers differ from work-related retaliation. While the former manifest in the form of informal social sanctions (e.g., ostracism), mostly by co-workers (Williams, 2001), work-related retaliation takes the form of poor performance reviews, relocation, or suspension from the job. Yet, as Hollinger and Clark (1982) show, employees are far more susceptible to – and more likely to be deterred by – the fear of social threats and sanctions emanating from co-workers, than by the organization's formal sanctions.

Likewise, subsequent literature reviews that built on this seminal meta-analysis did not focus on peer factors either. Vadera et al. (2009), for example, reveal that situational and contextual determinants predict whistleblowing outcomes more consistently than personality factors. Culiberg and Mihelič (2017) identify further research gaps by developing a framework that captures a comprehensive set of variables concerning who the whistleblower is, how, and why they report the wrongdoing, and to whom. Gao and Brink (2017) use the model proposed by Near and Miceli (1995) to review whistleblowing studies in the context of accounting-related misconduct. The authors cluster the determinants of whistleblowing intentions, reviewing the relevant empirical findings for each determinant. Lee and Xiao (2018) expand the scope of determinants (e.g., whistleblowing legislation) in the context of accounting-related misconduct and show that predictors for internal and external whistleblowing intentions differ.

Variables on the group level, such as group cohesiveness that cannot be assigned to either organizational or individual factors, have not been addressed in any of these reviews. While some reviews (e.g., Vadera et al., 2009) partly examine the influence of the organizational climate – by exploring employees' perception of the organization's ethical standards – they do not capture the attitude of peers. This aggregated categorization may stem from the assumption that the ethos underpinning the organizational response to whistleblowing is shared equally among the whistleblower's peers. As such, variables pertaining to the whole organization are assumed to be conceptually equivalent to variables on the group level. However, as discussed in several studies (e.g., Tenbrunsel et al., 2003), an organizational climate can fundamentally differ from the norms developed and established informally in a working group. To the best of our knowledge, the only review that explicitly mentions peer factors (as "social factors") as further determinants is that by Nicholls et al. (2021), who connect different literature strands (e.g., in an accounting and a non-accounting context) and extend the group of potential determinants of whistleblowing intentions. However, because their review comprises seven other sets of variables related to the whistleblowing intention (e.g., cost-benefit motives, expectation of whistleblowing consequences), the number of identified peer factors is quite limited (mainly, norms, group structure, and support for the whistleblower). Furthermore, their review includes studies that refer to the whole organization rather than to workgroups of peers (e.g., studies about whistleblower support).

In contrast to the published reviews, our systematic review focuses on variables on the peer level. Hence, we refer to whistleblowing as a social phenomenon, with the whistleblower firmly located in a network of non-trivial relationships, in which they consider the consequences of their decision for various parties, and weigh up the often competing interests such as those of the organization, superiors, or peers (Khan & Howe, 2021). With our review, we seek to complement the research on organizational, situational, and individual determinants to advance the understanding of the factors that enhance or hinder internal whistleblowing.

METHOD

We guided our systematic literature review along the three main stages exemplified by Tranfield et al. (2003), and Thorpe et al. (2005), namely, review planning, conducting, and reporting and dissemination of findings.

Using Scopus, Web of Science, and EBSCOhost as a database we identified a total of 788 articles for the keywords whistle* AND peer* OR cowork* OR co-work* OR team* OR colleague. In a first screening, we removed 200 duplicates, before performing several rounds with exclusion criteria excluding further in total 479 studies. We only proceeded with peer-reviewed journal articles that used primary empirical research (i.e., excluding handbook chapters). After a detailed review, we excluded further 83 studies that did not fit the peer variable or the underlying whistleblowing definition as defined for this review. Note that we count peer reporting as a sub-category of whistleblowing following the conceptualization of peer reporting as a type of whistleblowing by Trevino and Victor (1992). Additionally, we included seven articles that fit the criteria and that were mentioned as a reference in the reviewed papers. This resulted in a total of 33 studies.

REVIEW RESULTS

To analyze the 33 retained studies, we identified two overarching categories under which we clustered the results, namely, whether peer factors are described as an influence over (=antecedent) or as a consequence of (=aftermath) the whistleblowing decision. Within these overarching categories, we assigned all identified factors to a second level of thematic categories (see Fig. 1), but only for structuring purposes, as they do not represent a theoretically-based categorization, and are overlapping.[2]

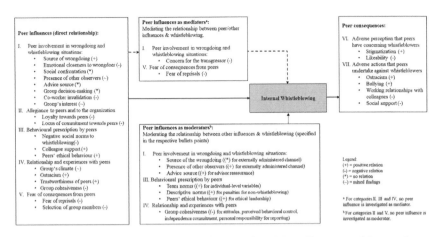

Fig. 1.   Framework with Seven Subcategories of Peer Factors and Internal
Whistleblowing (Influences & Consequences).

PEER INFLUENCES ON WHISTLEBLOWING

The study characteristics and findings on peer influences are summarized in Table 1. In total, this category comprises 26 studies conducted in diverse countries and cultures (e.g., western and Asian). Moreover, the underlying contexts and samples vary greatly, including, for example, athletes, military personnel, auditors, students, and employees. Sample sizes range between 15 and 10,850. Twenty-two articles used quantitative methods, three employed qualitative methods, and one article used both. Half of the studies examined the direct relationship between the corresponding peer variable and whistleblowing. Of these, the majority (17) investigate whistleblowing *intentions*, 7 analyze actual whistleblowing *behavior*, and 2 consider both intentions and actual behavior.

In the context of peer influences, we found five categories to which we assigned the identified peer factors: (I) peer involvement in wrongdoing and whistleblowing situations, (II) allegiance to peers and the organization, (III) behavioral prescription by peers, (IV) relationship and experiences with peers, and (V) fear of consequences from peers (see Fig. 1).

Peer Involvement in Wrongdoing and Whistleblowing Situations

The first category, *peer involvement in wrongdoing and whistleblowing situations,* synthesizes studies investigating factors that relate to peers directly involved in either the wrongdoing or the whistleblowing situation.

Three studies on peer involvement in wrongdoing situations focused on whether the *source of the wrongdoing* influences the whistleblowing decision (Gao et al., 2015; McIntosh et al., 2019; Taylor & Curtis, 2013), that is, whether the wrongdoing is committed by a peer or by a superior. All three studies consistently find that intentions for whistleblowing are more likely if the perpetrator is a peer rather than a supervisor. While reporting a peer might be perceived as less of a

Table 1. Identified Articles About Peer Influences on Internal Whistleblowing.

Author(s) (year)	Context	Country	Sample	Sample Size	Method	Peer Factor(s)	Category	Direct relationship / mediator/ moderator	Intention or Behavior	Main Results
Afe et al. (2019)	Wrongdoing in Organizations	Turkey	Academic personnel	250	Questionnaire (quant.)	Mobbing	Relationship and experiences with peers	Direct	Intention	Persons who perceive mobbing by peers are more willing to blow the whistle on their peers' unethical act informally (no effect for formal whistleblowing)
Alleyne et al. (2019)	Fraud in organizations	Barbados	Auditors	226	Survey, scenario (quant.)	Group cohesiveness	Relationship and experiences with peers	Moderator	Intention	Strong group cohesion negatively interacts with predictors of whistleblowing
Barkoukis et al. (2021)	Doping in sports	Cyprus	Sport athletes, coaches, sport directors	15	Structured interviews (qual.)	Perceived social norms toward whistleblowing	Behavioral prescription by peers	Direct	Intention	Perceived social norms toward whistleblowing as a deterrent for whistleblowing; Especially in small community, people attribute negative connotations to whistleblowing
Boo et al. (2021)	Fraud in organizations	Singapore	Senior auditors	69	Scenario experiment, questionnaire (quant.)	Advice source	Peer involvement in wrongdoing and whistleblowing situations	Direct, moderator	Intention	Whistleblowing intention does not differ depending on whether advice on the whistleblowing situation comes from the technical department as an authoritative source or from a colleague as a non-authoritative source; No significant interaction with advisor reassurance
Chang et al. (2017)	Corruption in organizations	South Korea	Government employees	5,706	Survey (quant.)	Colleague support	Behavioral prescription by peers	Direct	Intention	Positive relationship between perceptions about colleague support and whistleblowing intentions
Chen et al. (2017)	/	/	Students	147	Laboratory experiment (quant.)	Descriptive norms	Behavioral prescription by peers	Moderator	Behavior	Interaction between incentive framing and descriptive norms: penalties lead to a greater increase in whistleblowing (compared to rewards) when descriptive norms supporting whistleblowing are strong than when descriptive norms supporting whistle-blowing are weak

(*continued*)

Table 1. (Continued)

Author(s) (year)	Context	Country	Sample	Sample Size	Method	Peer Factor(s)	Category	Direct relationship / mediator/ moderator	Intention or Behavior	Main Results
Curphy et al. (1998)	Violation of honor code	USA	Military employees	365	Scenarios (quant.)	Emotional closeness to wrongdoer; Presence of other witnesses	Peer involvement in wrongdoing and whistleblowing situations	Emotional closeness to wrongdoer: direct Presence of other witnesses: direct	Intention	Emotional closeness to wrongdoer: wrongdoing committed by peers who are close friends is less likely reported than wrongdoing committed by peers who are relative strangers Presence of other witnesses: higher reporting intentions when others also observed the wrongdoing
Gao et al. (2015)	Fraud in organizations	USA	Students	369	Scenario experiment (quant.)	Bystander effect (presence of bystanders); Wrongdoer (superior vs. co-worker)	Peer involvement in wrongdoing and whistleblowing situations	Bystander effect: direct, moderator; Wrongdoer (superior vs. co-worker): direct, moderator	Intention	Bystander effect that negatively impacts whistleblowing intentions in one scenario and a positive impact in the other scenario An individual's whistleblowing intention is significantly lower when the wrongdoer is a supervisor than when s/he is a co-worker The source of wrongdoing does not significantly influence the positive relationship between an externally administered reporting channel and whistleblowing The presence of other bystanders positively influences the positive relationship between an externally administered reporting channel and whistleblowing
Goddiksen et al. (2021)	Academic cheating	Denmark Hungary Ireland	Students	72	Qualitative interviews, scenarios (qual.)	Loyalty toward peers; Fear of negative responses from peers	Loyalty toward peers: Allegiance to peers and the organization Fear of negative responses from peers: Fear of consequences from peers	Direct	Intention	Loyalty leads to direct, personal confrontation with wrongdoer (not whistleblowing) Negative reactions from peers

Reference	Context	Country	Sample	N	Method	Independent variable	Operationalization	Role	DV	Findings
Iwai et al. (2021)	Academic cheating	Brazil	Students	947	Questionnaire, scenarios (quant.)	Peer ethical behavior; Fear of reprisal from one's peers	Peer ethical behavior: Behavioral prescription by peers; Fear of reprisal from one's peers: Fear of consequences from peers	Peer ethical behavior: direct; Fear of reprisal from one's peers: mediator	Intention	Effects of peer ethical behavior on whistleblowing intentions are mediated by fear of retaliation. Fear of retaliation from peers as mediator: peer ethical behavior has negative effect on fear of retaliation.
Kaplan et al. (2010)	Fraud in organizations	/	Students	96	Scenario experiment (quant.)	Unsuccessful social confrontation	Peer involvement in wrongdoing and whistleblowing situations	Direct	Intention	After unsuccessful meeting with the transgressor, intentions to report the wrongdoing to the wrongdoer's supervisor are significantly higher than reporting intentions to an internal auditor; reporting intentions do not differ concerning the types of recipients without social confrontation; unsuccessful social confrontation does not generally affect reporting intentions
Khan and Howe (2021)	Fraud in organizations	USA	Study 1: students; Study 2: MTurk participants	Study 1: 187; Study 2: 375	Scenario experiments (quant.)	Group cohesiveness; Concern for transgressor	Group cohesiveness: Relationship and experiences with peers; Concern for transgressor: Peer involvement in wrongdoing and whistleblowing situations	Group cohesiveness: direct; Concern for transgressor: mediator	Intention	High group cohesiveness increases concern for the wrongdoer and consequently reduces the likelihood of whistleblowing. Increased concern for the wrongdoer decreased the likelihood of reporting
Latan et al. (2018)	Fraud in organizations	Indonesia	Public accountants	256	Questionnaire, scenarios (quant.)	Team norms	Behavioral prescription by peers	Moderator	Intention	Team norms partially moderate relationship of individual-level variables (attitudes toward whistleblowing, perceived behavioral control, independence commitment, personal responsibility for reporting, and personal cost of reporting) with (internal and external) whistleblowing intentions
Mayer et al. (2013)	Unethical behavior in organizations	USA	Employees	197	Questionnaire, field study, experiment (quant.)	Co-workers' ethical behavior	Behavioral prescription by peers	Moderator	Intention / Behavior	Interaction between supervisory ethical leadership and co-worker ethical behavior on internal whistleblowing

(continued)

Table 1. (Continued)

Author(s) (year)	Context	Country	Sample	Sample Size	Method	Peer Factor(s)	Category	Direct relationship / mediator / moderator	Intention or Behavior	Main Results
McIntosh et al. (2019)	Wrongdoing in Organizations	USA	Students	534	Scenario (quant.)	Source of unethical behavior (peer or advisor)	Peer involvement in wrongdoing and whistleblowing situations	Direct	Intention	Participants less likely to report the observed misconduct of an advisor compared to a peer
Miceli et al. (1991)	Academic misconduct	USA	Students	295	Field experiment (quant.)	Number of observers of wrongdoing	Peer involvement in wrongdoing and whistleblowing situations	Direct	Behavior	Observers of wrongdoing more likely to blow the whistle when more, rather than fewer, other observers were present
Miceli et al. (2012)	Wrongdoing in Organizations	USA	Military and civilian employees	3,288	Questionnaire (quant.)	Co-worker invalidation	Peer involvement in wrongdoing and whistleblowing situations	Direct	Behavior	Less perceived invalidation of whistleblowing by co-workers predicted whistleblowing
Pershing (2002)	Violation of honor code	USA	Military employees	Survey: 527 Interviews: 40	Survey, semi-structured interviews (qual.)	Loyalty	Allegiance to peers and the organization	Direct	Behavior	Peer loyalty results into non-reporting for occupational misconduct; "code of silence" impedes direct reporting even with an Honor Concept in place, and forms of counseling the perpetrators are chosen to uphold both loyalties
Rennie and Crosby (2002)	Academic misconduct	Scotland	Students	676	Questionnaire (quant.), focus groups (qual.)	Fear of negative reactions from peers	Fear of consequences from peers	Direct	Intention	Fear of negative reactions from peers negatively relate to whistleblowing
Reuben and Stephenson (2013)	/	/	/	68	Laboratory experiment (quant.)	(Anticipation of) group in- & exclusion (selection)	Fear of consequences from peers	Direct	Behavior	Option that peers can select who is included in a group for future cooperation reduces probability of reporting wrongdoing
Rothwell and Baldwin (2007)	Violations of rules	USA	Police officers; civilian employees	382	Survey, vignettes (quant.)	Friendship or team climate	Relationship and experiences with peers	Direct	Intention / Behavior	Team climate positively related to whistleblowing intentions but unrelated to whistleblowing behavior
Spoelma et al. (2021)	Unethical behavior in organizations	USA	Study 1: Employees Study 2: Students	Study 1: 109 Study 2: 108	Surveys, experiment (quant.)	Ostracism	Relationship and experiences with peers	Direct	Behavior	Ostracism has a positive effect on whistleblowing

Study	Context	Country	Sample	N	Method	Variable	Mediator/Relationship	Effect	Outcome	Finding
Taylor (2018)	Wrongdoing in organizations	Australia	Employees	10,850	Australian government data (quant.)	Trustworthiness of co-workers	Relationship and experiences with peers	Direct	Behavior	Internal whistle-blowing is positively related to perceptions of trustworthy co-workers
Taylor and Curtis (2010)	Fraud in organizations	/	Senior auditors	120	Vignette scenarios (quant.)	Locus of Commitment (organization vs. co-workers)	Allegiance to peers and the organization	Direct	Intention	As an individual's commitment moves toward the organization and away from colleagues, likelihood of reporting and perseverance increase
Taylor and Curtis (2013)	Fraud in organizations	USA	Senior auditors	106	Vignette (quant.)	Reporting peer vs. supervisor	Peer involvement in wrongdoing and whistleblowing situations	Direct	Intention	Positive relationship to whistleblowing intention when wrongdoer is a peer rather than a supervisor
Trevino and Victor (1992)	Academic cheating; theft at workplace	USA	Study 1 & 2: students Study 3: employees	Study 1/2/3: 478/115/128	Scenarios, field study (quant.)	Group members' interests	Peer involvement in wrongdoing an whistleblowing situations	Direct	Intention	If group members are negatively affected by the wrongdoing, the inclination to blow the whistle increases

threat, the anticipated consequences of reporting an influential advisor tend to be higher (McIntosh et al., 2019). Examined as moderator, the source of wrongdoing does not significantly influence the positive relationship between an externally administered reporting channel and whistleblowing (Gao et al., 2015).

Among peers who commit the wrongdoing, Curphy et al. (1998) investigate the relationship between *emotional closeness to the wrongdoer* and the whistleblowing intention with a sample of cadets from the US Air Force Academy. They find that, if the wrongdoers are close friends, they are less likely to be reported than if they are relative strangers, even though cadets are expected to follow the Academy's honor code (a formalized norm for reporting) (Curphy et al., 1998).

Kaplan et al. (2010) set up an experiment with students to examine how an unsuccessful *social confrontation* with the wrongdoer influences to whom a potential whistleblower will report, finding that, after an unsuccessful meeting with the transgressor to discuss the wrongdoing, the whistleblower is more likely to report to the wrongdoer's supervisor than to an internal auditor. Drawing on power theories, the authors state that an unsuccessful confrontation increases the inclination to report to a powerful recipient (i.e., the wrongdoer's supervisor). By contrast, when a social confrontation does not take place, reporting intentions do not differ in terms of the choice of the recipient. Moreover, unsuccessful social confrontation does not generally affect reporting intentions.

Lastly, Khan and Howe (2021) elaborate on how a whistleblower is affected by their *concern for the transgressor (wrongdoer)*. In their experiment with students, participants who are asked to imagine a wrongdoing committed by a close group member report significantly greater concern for the transgressor, and, more specifically, for their potential suffering as a consequence of the whistleblowing. This increased concern for the transgressor decreases the likelihood of reporting them. Thus, the concern for the transgressor is identified as a mediating variable of the relationship between group cohesiveness and whistleblowing.

In the following, we consider studies where peers may influence the whistleblowing decision by their sheer presence or by affecting the potential whistleblower's decision-making process. Three studies address the *presence of other observers* of the wrongdoing (Curphy et al., 1998; Gao et al., 2015; Miceli et al., 1991). The results seem inconsistent. Curphy et al. (1998) find that reporting intentions are more likely when the wrongdoing is also observed by others. Miceli et al. (1991) further indicate that whistleblowing increases with the number of observers. By contrast, in one of their scenarios, Gao et al. (2015) provide indication for the bystander effect: when more than one person observes the wrongdoing, whistleblowing by any of the individual observers becomes less likely due to the diffusion of responsibility. The bystander effect is only apparent, however, if the reporting channel is administered internally, rather than externally. The presence of other bystanders enhances the positive relationship between an externally administered reporting channel and whistleblowing. In another scenario, the same authors (Gao et al., 2015) find that the presence of another observer impacts whistleblowing intentions positively.

O'Leary and Pangemanan (2007) analyze *whether individual or group decision-making* leads to ethical behavior in the form of whistleblowing. The study finds that groups are more likely to come to a neutral decision, i.e., ignoring an observed wrongdoing, whereas individuals make more extreme decisions either in the unethical direction of participating in the wrongdoing or in the ethical direction of reporting it.

Miceli et al. (2012) investigate, among others, the influence on whistleblowing exerted by a potential whistleblower's perception of how their co-workers perceive the wrongdoing and whether it should be reported. Their results reveal that the perceived *co-worker invalidation* is negatively associated with whistleblowing. This provides empirical evidence for the crucial influence of co-workers on whistleblowers, and on how whistleblowers justify their decision to report, or not. In three separate studies, Trevino and Victor (1992) examine the situation when the *group's interests* are negatively affected by the wrongdoing. In two of their studies (one in an academic context and the other in a fast-food restaurant), they observe that the inclination to blow the whistle increases if group members are negatively affected by the wrongdoing. They find no support for this relationship in their third study (also a fast-food restaurant context).

Finally, there is no support for whether the type of *advice source* is of particular importance. In an experiment with participants from the "Big 4" firms (e.g., KPMG), Boo et al. (2021) show that the whistleblowing intention does not depend on whether advice on the whistleblowing situation comes from the technical department, as an authoritative source, or from a colleague, as a nonauthoritative source. Furthermore, the interaction between advice source and advisory reassurance is statistically insignificant.

To summarize, the evidence in the category *peer involvement in wrongdoing and whistleblowing situation* is mixed: while the reviewed studies provide support for reporting a peer rather than a superior, the impact of the presence of observers varies. A potential reason for the inconsistency of these findings might be the different study settings and designs. While Curphy et al. (1998) examined these effects in a military institution, where an honor code guides cadets' behaviors, both Miceli et al. (1991) and Gao et al. (2015) ran a student experiment. The validity of the findings from these studies, e.g., *emotional closeness, concern for the transgressor* or *social confrontation,* would benefit from being replicated.

Allegiance to Peers and to the Organization

The second category, *allegiance to peers and to the organization*, spans studies that investigate factors relating to potential whistleblowers' allegiance to peers and/or to their organization.

Goddiksen et al. (2021) identify that *loyalty* considerations toward peers are an important reason for their reluctance to report. However, rather than leading to inaction, loyalty considerations are more likely to lead to a direct, personal confrontation with the wrongdoer. The influence of peer loyalty was also highlighted by Pershing (2002), who linked the non-reporting of occupational misconduct to a "code of silence", which forms a central part of the culture of the Naval Academy, and impedes the reporting even when an Honor Concept is in place. Confronting the perpetrator in private is the preferred option as it upholds loyalty both to the organization and to the peer.

Similar to the concept of loyalty, Taylor and Curtis (2010) deal with the relationship between *locus of commitment* and whistleblowing. In this context, the authors distinguish between commitment to the organization and to colleagues. Organizational commitment refers to the "strength of employees' identification with and involvement in a particular organization, a strong belief in organizational goals and values, and a willingness to exert considerable effort on behalf of the organization" (Taylor & Curtis, 2010, p. 24). Colleague commitment involves "a sense of responsibility, reliability, and readiness to support colleagues within an organization" (Taylor & Curtis, 2010, p. 24). They find that, the stronger the employee is committed to the organization – rather than to colleagues – the greater the likelihood of whistleblowing, hence linking commitment to colleagues negatively to the reporting of wrongdoing.

It becomes apparent, then, that all three outlined studies support the notion that peer loyalty and commitment inhibit whistleblowing, and, the stronger one's allegiance to peers, as opposed to the organization, the less likely whistleblowing becomes.

Behavioral Prescription by Peers

In the category *behavioral prescription by peers*, we summarize studies dealing with factors of how (perceived) expectations and behaviors by peers influence a potential whistleblower.

Three studies focus on the role of norms conveyed by peers. Latan et al. (2018) refer to *team norms* as rules that are informally adopted within groups to regulate the behavior of group members. They find that team norms partially moderate the relationship between several individual-level variables (e.g., attitude toward whistleblowing and perceived behavioral control) with internal and external whistleblowing intentions. Barkoukis et al. (2021) conduct interviews with stakeholders in the sports sector and find that, especially in small communities – where misconduct might be more easily identified and suspected, but reporting perceived as snitching – negative *perceived social norms to whistleblowing* can act as a deterrent for whistleblowing. Chen et al. (2017) address the question of how *descriptive norms* –an individual's perception of the behavior of others in a certain situation – influence whistleblowing. The authors reveal that descriptive norms interact with incentives for whistleblowing, i.e., when the descriptive norms for whistleblowing are strong rather than weak, sanctions are more effective than rewards in increasing whistleblowing.

Peers' ethical behavior and *support from colleagues* may likewise influence a whistleblower's perception on whether reporting will be endorsed or disapproved of. Two of the three studies analyzed in this regard investigate the relationship between *peers' ethical behavior* and whistleblowing (Iwai et al., 2021; Mayer et al., 2013). Mayer et al. (2013) operationalize this as the perception of the extent to which peers set an example by following ethical standards and behavior, and find that peers' ethical behavior and supervisory ethical leadership positively interact in explaining internal whistleblowing. Iwai et al. (2019) support the positive relationship between peers' ethical behavior and whistleblowing in an academic context. Another form of signaling whistleblowing as the appropriate behavior is *colleague support*. In a large survey ($n = 5,706$) with governmental employees in South Korea on corruption in organizations, Chang et al. (2017) find a positive relationship between the perceptions that arise from colleagues' positive responses after previous whistleblowing incidents and subsequent whistleblowing intentions.

In summary, the reviewed studies consistently indicate that potential whistleblowers are influenced by their perception of norms conveyed by peers, as well as by their behavior.

Relationship and Experiences with Peers

The fourth category, *relationship and experiences with peers,* refers to the social ties with peers and perceptions about important similarities and experiences with the other members of the social group.

Two studies examine the influence of the *group's climate* that has been developed through long-term interaction with peers. Rothwell and Baldwin (2007) show in their study with police officers that a team climate, which is expressed by showing concern for the well-being of others, is positively related to whistleblowing *intentions* but unrelated to whistleblowing *behavior*. A negative team experience is created by, for example, the climate of mobbing in the organization. Afe et al. (2019) examine the impact of such a climate on whistleblowing in an academic context, where they find that students who think they are more likely to be mobbed by peers are more willing to blow the whistle on them. However, this relationship is only observed when peers can blow the whistle informally (e.g., reporting to a close associate who may take further action) rather than formally (e.g., through formal procedures and communication lines for whistleblowing).

Spoelma et al. (2021) focus on the negative experience of *ostracism* – which they define as an individual's perception of being ignored or excluded by peers. Peers that have previously been excluded from the group are more willing to blow the whistle on their former group members than those who still feel that they belong to the group. The whistleblowing motives of the excluded peers tend to be driven by negative reciprocity for perceived bad treatment, rather than by altruistic or moral reasons. By contrast, Taylor (2018) examines how the *trustworthiness of peers*, which she conceptualizes as consisting of the ability, benevolence, and integrity attributed to co-workers, influences the whistleblowing decision. This study reveals that perceptions of trustworthy co-workers are positively linked to internal acts of whistleblowing, but trustworthy senior managers even more so than trustworthy co-workers and supervisors.

Lastly, according to Alleyne et al. (2019), *group cohesiveness* reflects the tendency of group members to form social bonds, creating a sense of group belonging. The authors use group cohesiveness as a moderator variable for the relationships between a set of predictors derived from the theory of planned behavior (Ajzen, 1991) and whistleblowing intentions on fraud in accounting. In almost all cases, group cohesiveness moderated the relationship between predictor variables and whistleblowing. These relationships prevailed only in groups with low cohesiveness, while they were not apparent in groups with high cohesiveness. Similarly, Khan and Howe (2021) find that high group cohesiveness (group unity) reduces the likelihood of whistleblowing, as long as the wrongdoer is part of the group.

In summary, the described studies show that whistleblowing is influenced by both social ties and by experiences with peers, whether these are positive or negative. Overall, the less attached to the peer group an individual is, the more willing they are to report the wrongdoing.

Fear of Consequences from Peers

The final category, *fear of consequences from peers*, deals with four studies that explicitly examine the potential negative responses of peers toward the whistleblower.

Three studies focus on the *fear of reprisals* or negative responses from peers in general. Goddiksen et al. (2021), Iwai et al. (2021), and Rennie and Crosby (2002) examine this relationship in an academic context, and identify that the fear of retaliation from fellow students negatively relates to the willingness to report on academic fraud. In addition, the fear of reprisals mediates the relationship between peer ethical behavior and whistleblowing intentions: even in a social environment where peers are perceived as being committed to ethical values, higher fear of reprisals reduces the willingness to report (Iwai et al., 2021).

In the fourth study, Reuben and Stephenson (2013) examine the relationship between the *selection of group members* and actual whistleblowing behavior where reporting has real monetary consequences for the peers. In their experimental laboratory study, they find that, when there is an option for peers to select who is included in a group for future cooperation, the probability of reporting wrongdoing decreases. However, as in this study, the potential whistleblower is seen more of a "rat" who reports others for individual gain, this may explain why peers anticipate that group members would not welcome whistleblowers into their group.

In summary, the reviewed studies show the tendency that fear of peer reprisal matters and that these responses may not only affect whistleblowing intentions but actual whistleblowing behavior.

PEER CONSEQUENCES AFTER WHISTLEBLOWING

Table 2 summarizes the characteristics and findings of studies examining actual peer responses toward the whistleblower in the aftermath of their reporting. The nine identified studies rely on different types of samples (e.g., employees, nurses, or social workers) and sample sizes, ranging from 2 to 83,214 observations. Four of these studies used qualitative, and five used quantitative methods. We divide the factors in these studies into the following two categories: (VI) adverse perception that peers have concerning whistleblowers, comprising stigmatization

Table 2. Identified Articles About Peer Consequences After Internal Whistleblowing.

Author(s), (year)	Context	Country	Sample	Sample Size	Method	Peer Factor(s)	Category	Main Results
Björkelo et al. (2011)	Workplace	Norway	Employees	2,539	Questionnaire (quant.)	Exposure to bullying	Adverse actions that peers undertake against whistleblowers	Whistleblowers reported significantly more workplace bullying than non-whistleblowers
Curtis et al. (2021)	Fraud in organizations	USA	MTurk participants	Study 1: 256; Study 2: 222	Scenario experiments (quant.)	Ostracism	Adverse actions that peers undertake against whistleblowers	Intentions to ostracize the whistleblower were significantly higher than intentions to ostracize the wrongdoer
De Maria and Jan (1997)	Fraud in organizations	Australia	Whistle-blowers, superiors	83,214	Survey (quant.)	Ostracism	Adverse actions that peers undertake against whistleblowers	Most whistleblowers experience unofficial reprisals from peers after whistleblowing; most frequent form of unofficial reprisals is ostracism by peers
Jackson et al. (2010)	Workplace	/	Nurses	18	Qualitative narrative inquiry design (qual.)	Working relationships	Adverse actions that peers undertake against whistleblowers	Whistleblowing had a profound and overwhelmingly negative effect on working relationships; Findings clustered into four themes: (1) Leaving and returning to work, (2) Spoiled collegial relationships, (3) Bullying and excluding, (4) Damaged inter-professional relationships
McGlynn and Richardson (2014)	Academic & financial misconduct, violating rules, rape cover-up	USA	Coaches, faculty members, university staff	13	In-depth interviews (qual.)	Social support	Adverse actions that peers undertake against whistleblowers	Whistleblowers experience reduced social support after whistleblowing; even though peers might express social support in private settings, they avoid doing so in public contexts; whistleblowers' support networks decrease

(continued)

Table 2. (Continued)

Author(s), (year)	Context	Country	Sample	Sample Size	Method	Peer Factor(s)	Category	Main Results
Raymond et al. (2017)	Unethical behavior in organizations	New Zealand	Social workers	10	Interviews (qual.)	Social support, isolation, ostracism	Adverse actions that peers undertake against whistleblowers	Participants report distressing experience of reduced social support, feeling isolated and being ostracized after whistleblowing
Reuben and Stephenson (2013)	/	/	/	68	Laboratory experiment (quant.)	Group in- & exclusion (selection)	Adverse actions that peers undertake against whistleblowers	Participants who previously reported wrongdoing are significantly less likely to be included by the group
Trevino and Victor (1992)	Academic cheating; theft at workplace	USA	Study 1 & 2: students Study 3: employees	Study 1: 478 Study 2: 115 Study 3: 128	Scenarios, field study (quant.)	Likeability	Adverse perception that peers have concerning whistleblowers	Influence of the extent to which misconduct threatens other group members' interests and to which whistleblowing is an individual group member's responsibility on the evaluation of whistleblowers (i.e., acceptability of whistleblowing, ethicality and likeability of peer reporter) differs across three studies; in scenario 2, participants have less negative emotional reactions to whistleblowing, marginally higher acceptability of whistleblowing and likeability of the whistleblower, when group interests are threatened
Van Portfliet (2020)	Sexual harassment; fraud in organizations	/	PhD, senior manager (whistle-blowers)	2	Semi-structured interviews (qual.)	Stigmatization	Adverse perception that peers have concerning whistleblowers	Whistleblowers experience stigmatization by colleagues, but differently respond to stigmatization as the identity "whistleblower" can be temporary and revisable

and likeability, and (VII) adverse actions that peers undertake, such as unofficial reprisals, ostracism, bullying, and the relationship with and social support for whistleblowers (see Fig. 1).

Adverse Perception That Peers Have Concerning Whistleblowers

Based on two case studies, Van Portfliet (2020) concludes that whistleblowers often experience *stigmatization* by friends and colleagues – where an individual is deemed to possess an attribute that sets them apart from others and is devalued as a person. However, Van Portfliet finds that whistleblowers may respond differently to stigmatization: some accept their fate of being labeled as a whistleblower and treated as such by their peers for the rest of their working life, whereas others hold the identity "whistleblower" only temporarily and regard themselves as regular employees after some time, and expecting conventional treatment by their peers.

Trevino and Victor (1992) focus on the evaluation and *likeability* of whistleblowers in the aftermath (i.e., acceptability of whistleblowing, ethicality and likeability of the peer reporter). Across their three studies, they find a differing degree of influence concerning the extent to which misconduct threatens the interests of other group members and whether whistleblowing is seen as the responsibility of each individual group member. In both the context of a scenario experiment in an academic setting and in a field survey in a fast-food restaurant, they find that such responsibility positively influences the evaluation of peer reporting as more acceptable and the reporter as less ethical but also more likable. In a third study (a scenario study in a fast-food context), where group interests are at stake, negative emotional reactions to whistleblowing are less negative, and thus the whistleblowing is marginally more acceptable and the whistleblower more likeable in the eyes of peers.

Adverse Actions That Peers Undertake Against Whistleblowers

De Maria and Jan (1997) provide empirical evidence that most whistleblowers experience unofficial reprisals from peers after whistleblowing, most frequently in the form of *ostracism*. Curtis et al. (2021) specifically focus on whether whistleblowers experience *ostracism* as a consequence. They refer to ostracism as the social exclusion or ignorance by peers, and provide empirical support that intentions to ostracize the whistleblower are significantly higher than intentions to ostracize the wrongdoer. These results chime with those of Reuben and Stephenson (2013) where peers select their group members for future cooperation. Those who have previously reported wrongdoing are significantly less likely to be included in the group.

Björkelo et al. (2011) refer to *bullying* as including actions such as harassment, badgering, niggling, freezing out, or offensive teasing, that happen regularly, in which the affected person finds it difficult to defend themselves. In their study, whistleblowers indicate significantly more workplace bullying than non-whistleblowers. Moreover, interviews with whistleblowers conducted by Jackson et al. (2010) revealed the negative effects on *working relationships with other colleagues* as a consequence of whistleblowing. They divide these consequences into four categories: being asked to leave the workplace, damaged collegial relationships (such as barriers created between a whistleblower and their colleagues), bullying and exclusion, and deteriorated inter-professional relationships (e.g., loss of trust).

McGlynn and Richardson (2014) focus on *social support* throughout and in the aftermath of the whistleblowing process. Referring to Goldsmith (2004, p. 13), they define social support as "what individuals say and do to help one another." They conclude that whistleblowers experience reduced social support in the aftermath. Even though peers might express social support in a private setting, they avoid doing so in a public context. Participants in an interview study in the context of social workers, conducted by Raymond et al. (2017), reported on their distressing experience of receiving reduced social support, and even experiencing isolation.

In conclusion, all the reviewed studies indicate that whistleblowers experience a range of adverse consequences from peers after reporting, whether in the form of being perceived more negatively or through active adverse responses by peers. The results may show the relevance of addressing more proactively the treatment and value of whistleblowing in the organizational culture to improve the reputation of whistleblowers.

DISCUSSION

Our systematic literature review complements the existing reviews on whistleblowing by answering the question of how different peer factors relate to whistleblowing. We organize the 27 identified distinct peer factors into a classification of antecedents and consequences (and seven subcategories) of whistleblowing and identify which peer factors have been investigated as moderators and mediators, as summarized in our framework in Fig. 1. This framework systematically illustrates that peer factors are diverse and cannot be simplified to one variable, such as the degree of co-worker support. It has to be noted that our framework does not claim to represent a theoretically sound model. Rather, scholars can use our framework in future research to detect categories where empirical results have been mixed and findings worth being replicated in other contexts. Moreover, they may identify and map further peer variables not yet studied, or introduce entirely new categories.

Our findings allow us to derive three main implications and propose future research topics regarding peer influences and consequences (see Table 3, which provides an overview of future research gaps, research paths and exemplary research questions[3]). First, the reviewed studies show that peer factors as moderators, can significantly intensify or weaken the relationship between the main independent variable and whistleblowing. This observation indicates that peer factors interact with further variables. Therefore, investigating whether peer factors can explain previously inconsistent findings on some variables and whether the hypothesized effect only appears under specific social conditions is promising

Table 3. List of Proposed Research Gaps, Research Paths & Exemplary Research Questions.

Research Gaps	Research Paths	Exemplary Research Questions
Interaction of peer factors with other variables	Interaction of individual and peer factors	• How do peer factors moderate the relationship between personal morality and whistleblowing? • Do peers influence individuals at certain stages of moral development differently? • Do peer factors influence whether individuals with different levels of self-esteem blow the whistle?
	Interaction of situational and peer factors	• How does group cohesiveness toward peers affect the relationship between the severity of the wrongdoing and whistleblowing? • How does emotional closeness to the wrongdoer affect the relationship between the severity of the wrongdoing and whistleblowing?
	Interaction of organizational and peer factors	• How do peer factors moderate the relationship between the organizational climate and whistleblowing? • How does the loyalty to peers moderate the relationship between formal programs and whistleblowing? • Do formal measures (e.g., codes of conducts) or informal signals about expected behavior by peers have a stronger influence on peers?
	Interaction of different peer factors	• How do antithetical prescriptions of peers affect the whistleblowing decision? • Does trustworthiness of peers influence the relationship of peers' ethical behavior and whistleblowing? • Does emotional closeness to the wrongdoer influence the relationship of advice source and whistleblowing?
Underlying mechanisms of how and why peer factors affect the whistleblowing decision	Peer factors as explanation for relationship	• How do reprisals from peers mediate the relationship between a whistleblowing policy and whistleblowing? • How does group climate mediate the relationship between organizational climate and whistleblowing?
	Understanding psychological foundations by which peer factors affect the whistleblowing decision	• Does information on peers' behavior induce concerns about social conformity or social comparison with regard to whistleblowing behavior? • How do peer factors affect the different step(s) in the whistleblowing process? • Does a peer's behavior influence the awareness about the wrongdoing and/or the motivation to report? • Do social norms in the immediate work group affect the whistleblowing decision through ethical considerations (e.g., personal norms) or cost-benefit considerations (e.g., by violating the social norm)?
Prevention of negative peer consequences	Promoting whistleblowing	• How can organizations best communicate the benefits of whistleblowing to all organizational members? • How can organizations link whistleblowing to more positive values? • How can organizations guide peers toward a welcoming whistleblowing attitude?
	Changing the image of whistleblowing	• How can organizations change the stigma attached to whistleblowing? • How do training and best practices change the image of whistleblowing? • How do employees judge whistleblowers if whistleblowing becomes a duty?

for future research. For instance, in their meta-analysis, Mesmer-Magnus and Viswesvaran (2005) specify that the organizational climate for whistleblowing is less strongly related to actual whistleblowing behavior than to intentions to blow the whistle. Controlling for peer factors that may significantly influence the relationship with actual reporting might explain this observation. Moreover, combining informal peer factors with the field of formal measures is of particular interest: Accounting for the network of relationships by including loyalty to peers when assessing the effectiveness of increasingly formalized whistleblowing programs (and other formal measures) may provide a more comprehensive understanding. In the course of this, it is of interest whether formal specifications on the part of the organization (e.g., codes of conduct) or informal signals about expected behavior of peers have a stronger influence on whistleblowing. Another aspect that seems worth pursuing is the interaction between individual and peer factors since it is often assumed that individual factors predict whistleblowing less consistently than organizational or situational factors (e.g., Mesmer-Magnus & Viswesvaran, 2005; Vadera et al., 2009). For instance, studies on the relationship between whistleblowing and personal morality, often conceptualized by the level of moral development (Kohlberg, 1964; Rest et al., 1999), found mixed support (Vadera et al., 2009). As the concept of moral development is based partly on perceptions of social norms and expectations about one's role, future research could examine whether individuals at certain stages of moral development are particularly influenced by their peers.

Second, the reviewed studies are to some extent not corroborated by a distinct theoretical foundation that explains the results. This indicates that the underlying mechanisms of how and why peer factors affect the whistleblowing decision might require further investigation, i.e., in the form of mediator analyses. On the one hand, we consider this investigation important because peer factors might explain relationships between other variables and whistleblowing. For instance, the anticipation of reprisals from peers could mediate the relationship between a whistleblowing policy (usually prohibiting reprisals) and actual whistleblowing, thereby contributing to a better understanding of how organizations should design policies and which parts to focus on. On the other hand, mediator analyses could advance the understanding of the psychological foundations by which peer factors affect the whistleblowing decision. Theories commonly applied to explain social influences on behavior such as social identity theory (Tajfel & Turner, 2004), social learning theory (Bandura, 1971), or social comparison theory (Festinger, 1954) might contribute to guiding future research by pointing toward variables that could be considered as mediators. For instance, scholars could ask whether information on peers' behavior induces concerns about social conformity or social comparison. How do peer factors affect the different step(s) in the whistleblowing process? Does colleagues' behavior influence the awareness about the wrongdoing and/or the motivation to report? Do social norms in the immediate work group affect the whistleblowing decision through ethical considerations (e.g., personal norms) or cost-benefit considerations (e.g., by violating the social norm)?

Third, even though peer consequences are relatively less investigated in the reviewed studies than peer influences, we emphasize their importance, because in all reviewed studies, whistleblowers only experience adverse consequences. Therefore, apart from research on how to prevent work-related retaliation, scholars should also focus on preventing negative peer responses. For instance, as proposed by Lewis (2022), the image of whistleblowers should be changed from being seen as acting against the norms of the group to being decent employees following a duty. However, this may entail that employees will be held liable for ethics at work, which eliminates individual responsibility and moral autonomy (Tsahuridu & Vandekerckhove, 2008). Future research may therefore examine whether and how policies that regard non-reporting of wrongdoing as a violation can increase internal whistleblowing, or whether this kind of policy backfires because employees are perceived to be treated unfairly as long as whistleblowing is still regarded as an act that requires moral courage above average standards. Scholars could also investigate how organizations can communicate the benefits of whistleblowing to all organizational members and link whistleblowing to more positive values, such as organizational citizenship behavior (Organ, 1988) or in- and extra-role behavior[4] (Bjørkelo & Macko, 2012). Stressing the benefits and improvements of an organization's service, products or processes achieved through whistleblowing might provide a first step in transforming the image of whistleblowing (Bjørkelo & Macko, 2012). However, stigma cannot only be transformed by merely changing the image, because reactions can also be triggered by underlying beliefs, which need to be transformed accordingly. Changing these beliefs is not easy or straightforward, however, due to deeply rooted social norms (e.g., not snitching on a colleague).

From a methodological point of view, the reviewed studies have examined whistleblowing intentions mainly through surveys involving self-reporting and hypothetical contexts. This may be problematic as predictors of intentions are often distinct from predictors of actual whistleblowing (Mesmer-Magnus & Viswesvaran, 2005). Likewise, interviews with actual whistleblowers may be restricted in their validity due to potential selection effects and the lack of control groups. Hence, complementing empirical approaches with observational field data and behavioral experiments would be helpful. Although scholars should place emphasis on observing and describing first-hand actual behavior in organizations, behavioral experiments in the laboratory or in the field are still noteworthy for several reasons. Systematically studying peer-related whistleblowing with observational field data may be challenging because both witnessing and reporting wrongdoing tend to be rare and are often confounded by other factors. For example, it would be extremely difficult to examine, in a field setting, the causal relationship between policies and whistleblowing behavior, because this causality can potentially be affected by the fear of ostracism.[5] By contrast, by exercising tight control over confounding variables and the decision environment (Hauser et al., 2017), laboratory experiments provide a more suitable empirical test environment for examining and clearly identifying causal relationships derived from theories. This might be of particular relevance when theories and social relationships are not tied to special organizational structures, circumstances and commodities that can be simplified and simulated in a more abstract decision environment. Concerning the examination of the potential research question stated above, laboratory experiments thus allow creating controlled conditions with and with-out the fear of ostracism, hence investigating the moderating effects of ostracism on the relationship between policies and whistleblowing. Likewise, in respect of the important study of mediator analyses, researchers are usually interested in the interaction of a few, specific variables. Thus, to detect the underlying mechanisms of a potential outcome and the interdependence of the independent variables, it is more important to control for possible social interactions, ties and group dynam-ics, as well as their controlled, exogenous variation (in the laboratory more than in the field). Research on interaction effects can also be conducted using observa-tional field data. However, longitudinal data on group variables such as dynam-ics may not be available or cross-sectional data may not be able to duplicate the controls that are necessary for mechanism testing.

The review is based on two reviewers who independently decided upon the inclusion and exclusion criteria and the cluster of categories following the given review methodology. Results were synthesized after each step with the purpose to structure the results. A potential limitation is that we only included studies published in peer-reviewed journals, and do not assess the quality of the reviewed studies in terms of, for example, their differing empirical value, the nature and size of the sample, or the strength of the findings. An additional difficulty arises from the different publication contexts (e.g., business, nursing, sports), which renders uniform weighting of the quality of studies more difficult.

Nevertheless, our review seeks to raise awareness about the conflicting loyalties that potential whistleblowers experience in the organization and which impact their willingness to report wrongdoing. Further research on how to resolve such conflicting interests by addressing peer factors alongside and combined with individual, situational and organizational determinants would seem to be ben-eficial in helping organizations achieve their goal of guarding themselves against wrongdoing.

NOTES

1. Whistleblowing research includes a vast array of studies. Different theoretical models address the question of the stages in the decision-making process that potential whistle-blowers go through to decide whether to report wrongdoing (e.g., Miceli & Near, 1992). Other studies examine how individual characteristics such as demographic features or moral personality traits distinguish potential whistleblowers from silent observers (e.g., Liyanarachchi & Newdick, 2009). Researchers investigate how the characteristics of the wrongdoing (i.e., type and seriousness), of the wrongdoer, or the fear of retaliation affect the whistleblowing decision (e.g., Cassematis & Wortley, 2013), often referred to as situ-ational factors. Studies on organizational factors examine how the characteristics of organ-izations (e.g., organizational climate), (ethical) leadership and changes in organizations' policies to protect whistleblowers and facilitate the reporting process can either increase or hamper the willingness of whistleblowing (e.g., Kaptein, 2011).

2. Some of the studies investigating a range of peer variables can be assigned to more than one category or overarching theme (e.g., two studies have variables on influences and consequences). Moreover, a peer factor is often only one of several variables examined in these studies.

3. While we discuss some of the most salient research issues in the main text, we sketch further research questions in Table 3.

4. While in-role behaviour is a requirement and part of the duties an employee has to fulfil, extra-role behaviour describes discretional behaviour beyond the daily expectations of employees (Bjørkelo & Macko, 2012).

5. Analysing this causal relationship with field data could be difficult because the decision of the organization in favour of a policy is not the result of an exogenous and randomized process, but a deliberate decision (i.e., self-selection). Furthermore, information about the prevalence, severity and form of ostracism is seldom reported and may not even be known.

REFERENCES

We marked references that are part of the literature review with an asterisk (*).

*Afe, C. E. I., Abodohoui, A., Mebounou, T. G. C., & Karuranga, E. (2019). Perceived organizational climate and whistleblowing intention in academic organizations: Evidence from Selçuk University (Turkey). *Eurasian Business Review, 9*(3), 1–20. https://doi.org/10.1007/s40821-018-0110-3

Ajzen, I. (1991). The theory of planned behavior. *Organizational Behavior and Human Decision Processes, 50*(2), 179–211.

*Alleyne, P., Haniffa, R., & Hudaib, M. (2019). Does group cohesion moderate auditors' whistleblowing intentions? *Journal of International Accounting, Auditing and Taxation, 34.* https://doi.org/10.1016/j.intaccaudtax.2019.02.004

Anvari, F., Wenzel, M., Woodyatt, L., & Haslam, S. A. (2019). The social psychology of whistleblowing: An integrated model. *Organizational Psychology Review, 9*(1), 41–67. https://doi.org/10.1177/2041386619849085

Bandura, A. (1971). *Social learning theory.* General Learning Press.

*Barkoukis, V., Petrou, M., Lazuras, L., & Ourda, D. (2021). An empirical investigation of sport stakeholders' beliefs about whistleblowing against doping behaviour. *International Journal of Sport and Exercise Psychology, 0*(0), 1–18. https://doi.org/10.1080/1612197X.2021.1948585

Bjørkelo, B., & Macko, M. (2012). The stigma of reporting wrongdoing at work: When doing right is perceived as wrong. *Polish Psychological Bulletin, 43*(2), 70–75.

*Björkelo, B., Einarsen, S., Nielsen, M. B., & Matthiesen, S. B. (2011). Silence is golden? characteristics and experiences of self-reported whistleblowers. *European Journal of Work and Organizational Psychology, 20*(2), 206–238. https://doi.org/10.1080/13594320903338884

*Boo, E., Ng, T., & Shankar, P. G. (2021). Effects of Advice on Auditor Whistleblowing Propensity: Do Advice Source and Advisor Reassurance Matter? *Journal of Business Ethics, 174*(2), 387–402. https://doi.org/10.1007/s10551-020-04615-0

Cassematis, P. G., & Wortley, R. (2013). Prediction of whistleblowing or non-reporting observation: The role of personal and situational factors. *Journal of Business Ethics, 117*(3), 615–634. https://doi.org/10.1007/s10551-012-1548-3

*Chang, Y., Wilding, M., & Shin, M. C. (2017). Determinants of whistleblowing intention: Evidence from the South Korean Government. *Public Performance and Management Review, 40*(4), 676–700. https://doi.org/10.1080/15309576.2017.1318761

*Chen, C. X., Nichol, J. E., & Zhou, F. H. (2017). The effect of incentive framing and descriptive norms on internal whistleblowing. *Contemporary Accounting Research, 34*(4), 1757–1778. https://doi.org/10.1111/1911-3846.12325

Culiberg, B., & Mihelič, K. K. (2017). The evolution of whistleblowing studies: A critical review and research agenda. *Journal of Business Ethics, 146*(4), 787–803. https://doi.org/10.1007/s10551-016-3237-0

*Curphy, G. J., Gibson, F. W., Macomber, G., Calhoun, C. J., Wilbanks, L. A., & Burger, M. J. (1998). Situational factors affecting peer reporting intentions at the U.S. Air Force Academy: A scenario-based investigation. *Military Psychology, 10*(1), 27–43. https://doi.org/10.1207/s15327876mp1001_3

*Curtis, M. B., Robertson, J. C., Cockrell, R. C., & Fayard, L. D. (2021). Peer ostracism as a sanction against wrongdoers and whistleblowers. *Journal of Business Ethics*, *174*(2), 333–354. https://doi.org/10.1007/s10551-020-04596-0

*De Maria, W., & Jan, C. (1997). Ealing its own: The whistleblower' s organization in. *Australien Journal of Social Issues*, *32*(1), 37–59.

Dixon, O. (2016). Honest Y Without Fear? Whistleblower anti-retaliation protections in corporate code of conduct. *Melbourne University Law Review*, *40*(1), 168–206.

Dungan, J. A., Young, L., & Waytz, A. (2019). The power of moral concerns in predicting whistleblowing decisions. *Journal of Experimental Social Psychology*, *85*(September 2018), 103848. https://doi.org/10.1016/j.jesp.2019.103848

Festinger, L. (1954). A theory of social comparison processes. *Human Relations*, *7*, 117–140.

Gao, L., & Brink, A. G. (2017). Whistleblowing studies in accounting research: A review of experimental studies on the determinants of whistleblowing. *Journal of Accounting Literature*, *38*(May), 1–13. https://doi.org/10.1016/j.acclit.2017.05.001

*Gao, J., Greenberg, R., & Wong-On-Wing, B. (2015). Whistleblowing intentions of lower-level employees: The effect of reporting channel, bystanders, and wrongdoer power status. *Journal of Business Ethics*, *126*(1), 85–99. https://doi.org/10.1007/s10551-013-2008-4

Glazer, M. P., & Glazer, A. P. (1989). *The whistleblowers: Exposing corruption in government and industry*. Basic Books.

*Goddiksen, M. P., Quinn, U., Kovács, N., Lund, T. B., Sandøe, P., Varga, O., & Willum Johansen, M. (2021). Good friend or good student? An interview study of perceived conflicts between personal and academic integrity among students in three European countries. *Accountability in Research*, *28*(4), 247–264. https://doi.org/10.1080/08989621.2020.1826319

Goldsmith, D. J. (2004). *Communicating social support*. Cambridge University Press.

Greenberger, D. B., Miceli, M. P., & Cohen, D. J. (1987). Oppositionists and group norms: The reciprocal influence of whistle-blowers and co-workers. *Journal of Business Ethics*, *6*(7), 527–542. https://doi.org/10.1007/BF00383744

Gundlach, M. J., Douglas, S. C., & Martinko, M. J. (2003). The decision to blow the whistle: A social information processing framework. *Academy of Management Review*, *28*(1), 107–123.

Hassink, H., De Vries, M., & Bollen, L. (2007). A content analysis of whistleblowing policies of leading European companies. *Journal of Business Ethics*, *75*(1), 25–44. https://doi.org/10.1007/s10551-006-9236-9

Hauser, O. P., Linos, E., & Rogers, T. (2017). Innovation with field experiments: Studying organizational behaviors in actual organizations. *Research in Organizational Behavior*, *37*, 185–198. https://doi.org/10.1016/j.riob.2017.10.004

Hollinger, R. C., & Clark, J. P. (1982). Formal and informal social controls of employee deviance linked references are available on JSTOR for this article: Formal and informal social controls of employee deviance. *Sociological Quarterly*, *23*(3), 333–343.

*Iwai, T., Yeung, L., & Artes, R. (2021). Voice or silence: Antecedents of whistleblowing intentions. *RAUSP Management Journal*, *56*(2), 186–201. https://doi.org/10.1108/RAUSP-06-2020-0126

*Jackson, D., Peters, K., Andrew, S., Edenborough, M., Luck, L., Salamonson, Y., … Wilkes, L. (2010). Trial and retribution: A qualitative study of whistleblowing and workplace relationships in nursing. *Contemporary Nurse*, *36*(1–2), 34–44. https://doi.org/10.5172/conu.2010.36.1-2.034

*Kaplan, S. E., Pope, K. R., & Samuels, J. A. (2010). The effect of social confrontation on individuals' intentions to internally report fraud. *Behavioral Research in Accounting*, *22*(2), 51–67. https://doi.org/10.2308/bria.2010.22.2.51

Kaptein, M. (2011). Toward effective codes: Testing the relationship with unethical behavior. *Journal of Business Ethics*, *99*(2), 233–251. https://doi.org/10.1007/s10551-010-0652-5

Keenan, J. P. (2000). Blowing the whistle on less serious forms of fraud: A study of executives and managers *Employee Responsibilities and Rights Journal*, *12*(4), 199–217.

*Khan, S. R., & Howe, L. C. (2021). Concern for the transgressor's consequences: An explanation for why wrongdoing remains unreported. *Journal of Business Ethics*, *173*(2), 325–344. https://doi.org/10.1007/s10551-020-04568-4

Kohlberg, L. (1964). Development of moral character and moral ideology. In M. L. Hoffman & L. W. Hoffman (Eds.), *Review of child development research* (pp. 383–431). Russell Sage Foundation.

*Latan, H., Ringle, C. M., & Jabbour, C. J. C. (2018). Whistleblowing intentions among public accountants in Indonesia: Testing for the moderation effects. *Journal of Business Ethics, 152*(2), 573–588. https://doi.org/10.1007/s10551-016-3318-0

Lee, G., & Xiao, X. (2018). Whistleblowing on accounting-related misconduct: A synthesis of the literature. *Journal of Accounting Literature, 41*, 22–46.

Lewis, D. (2022). Stigma and whistleblowing: Should punitive damages be available in retaliation cases? *Industrial Law Journal, 51*(1), 62–83. https://doi.org/10.1093/indlaw/dwaa032

Liyanarachchi, G., & Newdick, C. (2009). The impact of moral reasoning and retaliation on whistleblowing: New Zealand evidence. *Journal of Business Ethics, 89*(1), 37–57. https://doi.org/10.1007/s10551-008-9983-x

*Mayer, D. M., Nurmohamed, S., Treviño, L. K., Shapiro, D. L., & Schminke, M. (2013). Encouraging employees to report unethical conduct internally: It takes a village. *Organizational Behavior and Human Decision Processes, 121*(1), 89–103. https://doi.org/10.1016/j.obhdp.2013.01.002

*McGlynn, J., & Richardson, B. K. (2014). Private support, public alienation: Whistle-blowers and the paradox of social support. *Western Journal of Communication, 78*(2), 213–237. https://doi.org/10.1080/10570314.2013.807436

*McIntosh, T., Higgs, C., Turner, M., Partlow, P., Steele, L., MacDougall, A. E., … Mumford, M. D. (2019). To whistleblow or not to whistleblow: Affective and cognitive differences in reporting peers and advisors. *Science and Engineering Ethics, 25*(1), 171–210. https://doi.org/10.1007/s11948-017-9974-3

McLain, D. L., & Keenan, J. P. (1999). Risk, information, and the decision about response to wrongdoing in an organization. *Journal of Business Ethics, 19*(3), 255–271. https://doi.org/10.1023/A:1006168301995

Mesmer-Magnus, J. R., & Viswesvaran, C. (2005). Whistleblowing in organizations: An examination of correlates of whistleblowing intentions, actions, and retaliation. *Journal of Business Ethics, 62*(3), 277–297. https://doi.org/10.1007/s10551-005-0849-1

*Miceli, M. P., Dozier, J. B., & Near, J. P. (1991). Blowing the whistle on data fudging: A controlled field experiment. *Journal of Applied Social Psychology, 21*(4), 271–295.

Miceli, M. P., & Near, J. P. (1992). *Blowing the whistle: The organizational and legal implications for companies and employees.* Lexington Books.

*Miceli, M. P., Near, J. P., Rehg, M. T., & van Scotter, J. R. (2012). Predicting employee reactions to perceived organizational wrongdoing: Demoralization, justice, proactive personality, and whistle-blowing. *Human Relations, 65*. https://doi.org/10.1177/0018726712447004

Muehlheusser, G., & Roider, A. (2008). Black sheep and walls of silence. *Journal of Economic Behavior and Organization, 65*(3–4), 387–408.

Murphy, A. R. (2021). *Conscience and community.* Penn State University Press.

Near, J. P., & Miceli, M. P. (1985). Organizational dissidence: The case of whistle-blowing. *Journal of Business Ethics, 4*(1), 1–16.

Near, J. P., & Miceli, M. P. (1995). Effective whistle-blowing. *The Academy of Management Review, 20*(3), 679–708.

Nicholls, A. R., Fairs, L. R. W., Toner, J., Jones, L., Mantis, C., Barkoukis, V., … Schomöller, A. (2021). Snitches get stitches and end up in ditches: A systematic review of the factors associated with whistleblowing intentions. *Frontiers in Psychology, 12*(October). https://doi.org/10.3389/fpsyg.2021.631538

*O'Leary, C., & Pangemanan, G. (2007). The effect of groupwork on ethical decision-making of accountancy students. *Journal of Business Ethics, 75*(3), 215–228. https://doi.org/10.1007/s10551-006-9248-5

Oh, H., Chung, M. H. O., & Labianca, G. (2004). Group social capital and group effectiveness: The role of informal socializing ties. *Academy of Management Journal, 47*(6), 860–875. https://doi.org/10.5465/20159627

Organ, D. W. (1988). *Organizational citizenship behavior: The good soldier syndrome.* Lexington Books.

*Pershing, J. L. (2002). Whom to betray? Self-regulation of occupational misconduct at the United States Naval Academy. *Deviant Behavior, 23*(2), 149–175. https://doi.org/10.1080/016396202753424538

*Raymond, S., Beddoe, L., & Staniforth, B. (2017). Social workers' experiences with whistleblowing: To speak or not to speak? *Aotearoa New Zealand Social Work*, *29*(3), 17–29. https://doi.org/10.11157/anzswj-vol29iss3id305

*Rennie, S. C., & Crosby, J. R. (2002). Students' perceptions of whistle blowing: Implications for self-regulation. A questionnaire and focus group survey. *Medical Education*, *36*(2), 173–179. https://doi.org/10.1046/j.1365-2923.2002.01137.x

Rest, J. R., Narvaez, D., Thoma, S. J., & Bebeau, M. J. (1999). *Postconventional moral thinking: A Neo-Kohlbergian approach*. Psychology Press.

*Reuben, E., & Stephenson, M. (2013). Nobody likes a rat: On the willingness to report lies and the consequences thereof. *Journal of Economic Behavior and Organization*, *93*, 384–391. https://doi.org/10.1016/j.jebo.2013.03.028

*Rothwell, G. R., & Baldwin, J. N. (2007). Ethical climate theory, whistle-blowing, and the code of silence in police agencies in the State of Georgia. *Journal of Business Ethics*, *70*(4), 341–361. https://doi.org/10.1007/s10551-006-9114-5

Rousseau, D., Manning, J., & Denyer, D. (2008). Science: Assembling the field's full weight of scientific knowledge through syntheses. *AIM Research Working Paper Series*, *67*(8), 1–78.

*Spoelma, T. M., Chawla, N., & Ellis, A. P. J. (2021). If You Can't Join 'Em, Report 'Em: A model of ostracism and whistleblowing in teams. *Journal of Business Ethics*, *173*(2), 345–363. https://doi.org/10.1007/s10551-020-04563-9

Tajfel, H., & Turner, J. C. (2004). The social identity theory of intergroup behavior. In J. T. Jost & J. Sidanius (Eds.), *Political psychology: Key readings* (pp. 276–293). Psychology Press.

*Taylor, J. (2018). Internal whistle-blowing in the public service: A matter of trust. *Public Administration Review*, *78*(5), 717–726. https://doi.org/10.1111/puar.12946

*Taylor, E. Z., & Curtis, M. B. (2010). An examination of the layers of workplace influences in ethical judgments: Whistleblowing likelihood and perseverance in public accounting. *Journal of Business Ethics*, *93*(1), 21–37. https://doi.org/10.1007/s10551-009-0179-9

*Taylor, E. Z., & Curtis, M. B. (2013). Whistleblowing in audit firms: Organizational response and power distance. *Behavioral Research in Accounting*, *25*(2), 21–43. https://doi.org/10.2308/bria-50415

Tenbrunsel, A. E., Smith-Crowe, K., & Umphress, E. E. (2003). Building houses on rocks: The role of the ethical infrastructure in organizations. *Social Justice Research*, *16*(3), 285–307. https://doi.org/10.1023/A:1025992813613

Thorpe, R., Holt, R., Macpherson, A., & Pittaway, L. (2005). Using knowledge within small and medium-sized firms: A systematic review of the evidence. *International Journal of Management Reviews*, *7*(4), 257–281. https://doi.org/10.1111/j.1468-2370.2005.00116.x

Tranfield, D., Denyer, D., & Smart, P. (2003). Towards a methodology for developing evidence-informed management knowledge by means of systematic review. *British Journal of Management*, *14*(3), 207–222. https://doi.org/10.1111/1467-8551.00375

*Trevino, L. K., & Victor, B. (1992). Peer reporting of unethical behavior: A social context perspective. *The Academy of Management Journal*, *35*(1), 38–64.

Tsahuridu, E. E., & Vandekerckhove, W. (2008). Organisational whistleblowing policies: Making employees responsible or liable? *Journal of Business Ethics*, *82*(1), 107–118. https://doi.org/10.1007/s10551-007-9565-3

Vadera, A. K., Aguilera, R. V., & Caza, B. B. (2009). Making sense of whistle-blowing's antecedents: Learning from research on identity and ethics programs. *Business Ethics Quarterly*, *19*(4), 553–586. https://doi.org/10.5840/beq200919432

*Van Portfliet, M. (2020). Resistance will be futile? The stigmatization (or not) of whistleblowers. *Journal of Business Ethics*, *175*(3), 451–464. https://doi.org/10.1007/s10551-020-04673-4

Vandekerckhove, W., Brown, A. J., & Tsahuridu, E. (2014). Managerial responsiveness to whistle-blowing: Expanding the research horizon. In *International handbook on whistleblowing research*. https://doi.org/10.4337/9781781006795.00021

Williams, K. D. (2001). *Ostracism: The power of silence*. Guilford Press.

CHAPTER 5

I REPORT IF THEY REPORT: THE ROLE OF MEDIA IN WHISTLEBLOWING INTENTIONS ON FRAUD AND CORRUPTION

Sebastian Oelrich

ABSTRACT

Researchers and practitioners recognize whistleblowers and the media as disparate control agents to uncover fraud and corruption in and by organizations. However, whistleblowing is mainly studied in relation to individual and organizational antecedents. Social norms and in particular the media as a form of social norm influence or norm conveyer on whistleblowing are largely unexplored. In this paper, I study the influence of perceived critical media coverage (i.e., whether media are perceived as criticizing fraud and corruption) on whistleblowing intentions (WBI) on fraud and corruption. I draw on norm activation theory to develop a moderation-mediation model of whistleblowing to highlight how the media can convey social norms influencing WBI. Using a cross-national survey of employees from China, Germany, and Russia (n = 1,159), I hypothesize and find that media directly influence employee attitudes toward fraud and corruption as well as the likelihood to whistle blow. Critical media coverage also reduces the influence of descriptive norms by co-worker misconduct on attitudes and the negative influence of fear of retaliation on WBI. This paper is the first to highlight the importance of critical mass media on whistleblowing decisions. My findings suggest that the media influence potential whistleblowers in a way that can be described along the lines of "I report if they report."

Keywords: Whistleblowing; media; social norm; corruption; fraud; survey

Organizational Wrongdoing as the "Foundational" Grand Challenge: Consequences and Impact
Research in the Sociology of Organizations, Volume 85, 101–120
Copyright © 2023 by Sebastian Oelrich
Published under exclusive licence by Emerald Publishing Limited
ISSN: 0733-558X/doi:10.1108/S0733-558X20230000085006

1. INTRODUCTION

Fraud and corruption are severe threats to democracy, prosperity, and economic development. However, uncovering corruption in organizations has proven difficult, especially when such practices are institutionalized (Gabbioneta et al., 2013). Instead of relying on traditional corporate governance actors, whistleblowers[1] have taken center stage as an effective (Call et al., 2018) and frequent (ACFE, 2020; Dyck et al., 2010) means to uncover fraud and corruption, including some of the largest scandals, such as Enron, WorldCom, or Wirecard. Research so far has focused on individual, situational, or organizational aspects that influence intentions to whistle blow, largely ignoring social norm influences (Bushnell, 2020; Culiberg & Mihelič, 2017; Nicholls et al., 2021). Media can be seen as one such social norm influence or conveyor of norms: Selecting, depicting, and constructing events that influence public opinion (Greve et al., 2010; Kepplinger et al., 2012; McCombs & Shaw, 1972). In this paper, I address the current lack of research on social norm influences on WBI by asking *how* perceived media coverage on fraud and corruption (i.e., whether employees perceive media to criticize fraud and corruption) affects employees' attitudes toward and their likelihood to blow the whistle on such misconduct.

I draw on social norm activation theory (Bicchieri, 2005), which argues that implicit social norms can be activated by making norms salient. One such way could be through extensive media coverage that fraud and corruption are not tolerated or detrimental to society. When made salient, social norms may also override problematic descriptive norms at work. I argue that if employees perceive media to criticize fraud and corruption openly (perceived critical media coverage), this leads to a decrease in positive attitudes toward such misconduct, increases the likelihood that employees blow the whistle, and even reduces the influence of corrupt descriptive norms in their workplace.

I test and find empirical evidence for these relationships using a survey of Chinese, German, and Russian employees ($n = 1,159$). In particular, I document three main mechanisms through which the media as social control agent can operate: (1) through a direct influence on WBI; (2) indirectly through attitudes toward fraud and corruption, which, when framed as misconduct, influence employee WBI; (3) the media as norm activator, who, by making social norms salient, reduce the effect of (adverse) descriptive norms (co-worker behavior and retaliation) in the workplace.

This paper contributes to whistleblowing and fraud literature in several ways. First, whistleblowing literature is mainly concerned with individual, situational, or organizational level perspectives (Culiberg & Mihelič, 2017; Nicholls et al., 2021). I extend this view by arguing that WBI are formed within complex social dynamics and norms beyond the workplace. This also opens a new perspective on social influences beyond mere cultural differences (Oelrich & Erlebach, 2021; Park et al., 2008).

Second, I show that the media can be one such source of social norms, whereas prior whistleblowing research has understood media primarily as another source of whistleblowing (e.g., Dyck et al., 2008, 2010). The media can be interpreted as conveying social norms to employees through their reporting behavior. By framing behaviors as misconduct, the media can directly stimulate employees to report on observed fraud cases within their firms and influence their attitudes on workplace behaviors. This builds on and extends prior whistleblowing studies that looked at the role of attitudes and WBI (e.g., Brown et al., 2016; Park & Blenkinsopp, 2009) regarding how these attitudes are formed.

Third, my findings show that descriptive workplace norms, i.e., unethical co-worker behaviors and retaliation, can deter WBI, in line with prior research documenting the spread of fraud in organizations (Davis & Pesch, 2013; Free & Murphy 2015; Gabbioneta et al., 2013) and retaliation against whistleblowers (e.g., Cassematis & Wortley, 2013; Park et al., 2020). However, I give a way out as I show that activation of social norms can reduce the effect of harmful workplace norms and that the media can be a means to make such social norms salient.

Fourth, this paper answers research calls to study how the media as social control agent can impact fraud and corruption (Greve et al., 2010) by documenting their connection to deterrence and detection mechanisms, i.e., whistleblowing: If an employee notices that the media criticize fraud and corruption as harmful, this positively influences employees' WBI, and they would then be more likely to speak up when observing misconduct in their organizations.

In the next section, I review prior literature and, drawing on norm activation theory, develop hypotheses on a moderation-mediation model of media and WBI. I then used a diverse survey sample of employees from China, Germany, and Russia to test my hypotheses. My findings suggest the influence of media on WBI can be described from the employee perspective as "I report if they report," suggesting that when employees perceive the media as criticizing fraud and corruption, they are encouraged to blow the whistle when confronted with corrupt and fraudulent behaviors at work. I close the paper with a discussion and implication of my findings for further research.

2. BACKGROUND AND HYPOTHESIS DEVELOPMENT

2.1. Basic Whistleblowing Model

An extensive body of research exists on how potential whistleblowers are influenced and how WBI on misconduct are formed (for recent reviews, see Culiberg & Mihelič, 2017; Nicholls et al., 2021). Here, attitudes, co-workers, and retaliation fears have been depicted as central influences on WBI, which form the base of this study.

First, according to Ajzen (1991), attitudes influence intentions. When attitudes toward corruption are positive (negative), whistleblowing becomes more unlikely (likely) because people blow the whistle on behavior they view as harmful or illegitimate (Brown et al., 2016; Bushnell, 2020; Park & Blenkinsopp, 2009).

Second, employees learn norms from behavior they observe within their group (Dannals et al., 2020; Mayer et al., 2013). Corrupt co-worker behavior has been found to influence corrupt and fraudulent behaviors of other employees

(Courtois & Gendron, 2017; Kish-Gephart et al., 2010), whereas ethical co-worker behavior can directly increase WBI and actual whistleblowing (Mayer et al., 2013). In addition to their effect on behavior and intention, these in-group norms can also influence attitudes. In a simulation study, Davis and Pesch (2013) showed how corruption attitudes spread within organizations, normalizing deviance in certain groups. Free and Murphy (2015) give detailed qualitative insights into the collusion in fraud, highlighting how attitudes disperse, co-workers become complicit, and corruption is "normalized." Thus, colleague behavior can be an (opposing) norm within the organization that influences WBI and corrupt attitudes.

A third significant influence – and another expression of workplace norms – is how voice behaviors are addressed, for example, through (in)formal reward and sanctioning processes. Retaliation against whistleblowers is well documented and can range from informal means such as ostracism over bullying to more formal responses such as demotion or dismissal (Bussmann et al., 2021; Kenny et al., 2019; Park et al., 2020). Prior research on fraud and corruption in accounting and management has highlighted the pivotal role of retaliation in forming WBI[2] (e.g., Brown et al., 2016; Cassematis & Wortley, 2013; Kenny et al., 2019; Oelrich, 2019; Park et al., 2020).

So far, studies at the intersection of whistleblowing and media are mainly concerned with either how whistleblowers *are* portrayed in the media or *ought* to be portrayed (e.g., Stolowy et al., 2019; van Es & Smit, 2003), *which* whistleblowers use the media to blow the whistle (e.g., Callahan & Dworkin, 1994), or the media *as* a whistleblower to uncover fraud (e.g., Dyck et al., 2008, 2010). Yet, *how* media depiction of wrongdoing influences WBI is largely absent. I draw on norm activation theory (Bicchieri, 2005) to add to this literature by asking how media influence WBI, extending the basic model above.

2.2. Social Norms, Media, and Whistleblowing

The influence of social norms is acknowledged in several social science theories (e.g., Ajzen, 1991; Bicchieri, 2005). Norms about desired behaviors are learned in many social contexts and have been shown to influence attitudes and ultimately WBI and actions (Butler et al., 2020; Watts & Buckley, 2017). While the co-workers discussed above can be interpreted as socialization agents from inside the organization, employees also learn norms from behavior outside the organization. Mass media (e.g., newspapers or daily news shows) can be one such way to convey and influence social norms. In communications literature, media have been shown to play a central role in the framing of events (e.g., Kepplinger et al., 2012; Semetko & Valkenburg, 2000) and to actively influence public debate and opinions (Carroll & McCombs, 2003; Gamson & Modigliani, 1989; McCombs & Shaw, 1972).

This role of media as a way to influence intentions and actions is also recently acknowledged in research on fraud and corruption in the organizational and management literature. Here, Greve et al. (2010, p. 57) note that "the media has the ability to frame behaviors as misconduct and put pressure on social-control agents." Media coverage on fraud and corruption plays a vital role in conveying images of organizational misconduct to the public (e.g., Clemente & Gabbioneta, 2017; Daudigeos et al., 2020; Roulet, 2019). Such coverage has been shown to negatively affect corporate governance violations (Dong et al., 2018; Dyck et al., 2008), accounting frauds (Miller, 2006), and even spark social change initiatives in the context of tax avoidance (Neu et al., 2019).

The media thus play an important role as a socialization agent that calls out norm deviations and desired behavior in its broader context within a society or group. Suppose mass media are perceived as criticizing fraud and corruption. In that case, they communicate a social norm that not only asks not to engage in fraud but also to engage in actions that may hinder the spread of fraud, e.g., whistleblowing.

In addition to this effect on WBI and actions, social norms can influence people's perceptions of or attitudes toward certain behaviors. In terms of fraud and corruption, take, for example, the practice of *guanxi*, extensive gift-giving in China to enable business transactions: Bribery may be viewed as an enabling, constructive behavior (Bian & Zhang, 2014). Yet, media reports that criticize guanxi as a corrupt practice have been shown to change its perception (Dong et al., 2018). Here, media as a socialization agent introduced a social norm that changed attitudes. Drawing on these findings, I hypothesize that if mass media criticize fraud and corruption as problematic and non-desirable behavior, they influence intentions as well as attitudes toward these behaviors in a broader sense.

H1. Stronger perceived critical media coverage increases WBI.

H2. Stronger perceived critical media coverage reduces positive attitudes toward fraud and corruption.

2.3. Norm Salience and the Moderating Role of Critical Media Coverage

These organizational and societal level norms can be at odds, and employees can be part of several, sometimes conflicting, moral systems. Which norm system dominates depends on the situation and the salience of each system. Norm activation theory (Bicchieri, 2005) argues that descriptive norms developed in the workplace (e.g., corrupt colleague behavior or retaliation) can be dominated by social norms when the latter are made salient. However, activation of a particular norm is "possible only when a norm is recognized as such within a given culture" (p. 70). Media could provide such a priming effect by "covering violations of social norms" (Kepplinger et al., 2012, p. 659) and establishing what are (perceived) prevalent social norms (Kepplinger et al., 2012; McCombs & Shaw, 1972).

This "salience" can empirically be understood as a moderator which increases the relevance of certain social norms and reduces the influence of contradicting norms. The latter can be descriptive norms in the workplace, such as co-worker behavior. But also expressions of acceptance and rejection of behaviors through reward and sanctioning processes, i.e., retaliation on whistleblowing. Courtois and Gendron (2017) give a negative example in the context of deviant personalities: They show how deviance is adopted and normalized when contradicting social norms are not prevalent. That is when they are not "activated" and made salient.

In the context of whistleblowing and media, critical media reports that condemn fraud and corruption can thus "activate" corresponding social norms and superimpose descriptive norms by co-workers to the contrary, rendering them less salient or relevant in forming attitudes toward the behavior. Similarly, when critical media coverage of corruption highlights social norms that condemn fraudulent behaviors, employees would be more inclined to report misconduct, despite fearing retaliation by their employer. Knowing that society condemns corrupt behaviors would reduce the influence of retaliatory fears, as whistleblowing is seen as a legitimate course of action that should be pursued. Bushnell (2020) implicitly speaks to this moderation when she argues that "blowing the whistle is an action in response to our larger understanding of behaviour that is harmful to the public" (p. 2).

H3. Perceived media coverage affects the influence of corrupt colleague behavior on positive attitudes toward fraud and corruption. That is, stronger perceived critical media coverage reduces the positive influence of corrupt colleague behavior on positive attitudes toward fraud and corruption.

H4. Perceived media coverage affects the influence of fear of retaliation on WBI. That is, stronger perceived critical media coverage reduces the negative influence of fear of retaliation on WBI.

The full moderation-mediation model is given in Fig. 1. The basic whistleblowing model (dotted lines) based on prior findings is extended by the hypothesized relationships regarding the role of media (straight lines). The model argues

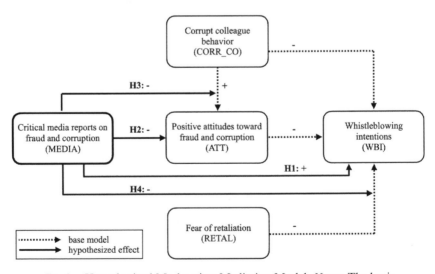

Fig. 1. Hypothesized Moderation-Mediation Model. *Notes*: The basic whistleblowing intention model is derived from prior literature (dotted lines). It is extended by the variable of interest, critical media reports on fraud and corruption (MEDIA) and its hypothesized influences (straight lines).

for three key effects of media in the context of whistleblowing: First, a direct effect with media as a socialization agent, conveying social norms that influence employees in their attitudes and intentions to act (*H1* and *H2*). Second, such norms also indirectly influence intentions through the mediation of attitudes. And third, media as a norm activation mechanism that makes norms salient and overrides (conflicting) descriptive norms in the workplace (*H3* and *H4*).

3. SAMPLE AND MEASURES

3.1. Sample

Levels of corruption differ by country, region, and even industry. In *Transparency International's 2020 Corruption Perception Index*,[3] China ranks 78 out of 180 countries (rank 1 represents the lowest level of corruption), Germany ranks 9, and Russia 129. In the study used for this paper, these countries were chosen for their differences to get the needed variation across responses. The study and data used in this paper are part of a larger research project on fraud and corruption. A random computer-assisted telephone survey design was employed and carried out by local survey institutes. Respondents were assured anonymity throughout the questionnaire. In China and Russia, metropolitan regions were contacted. In Germany, an equal distribution across country states was achieved. An advantage of this approach, particularly compared to online surveys, is that early-late response biases are not an issue. It also ensures a diverse set of respondent socio-demographics, gives more control over the target audience, and helps eliminate ambiguity in question understanding, as respondents can check on the question again. Investigators can ask again on non-response items. An initial pre-test led to minor changes in the survey structure and questions. Pre-test data were excluded.

The questionnaire was translated back-to-back in the respective languages, consisted of several parts, and took about 20 minutes for respondents to complete. I only use responses that were given a hypothetical case on whistleblowing.[4] The sample size after non-response correction is 1,159, with China $n = 382$, Germany $n = 398$, and Russia $n = 379$.

46 per cent of respondents identified as female. They were on average in the range of 30 to 39 years and held a master's degree or equivalent (see Table 1 for other descriptive statistics). Demographic characteristics align with actual demographics in the respective country, ensuring a somewhat representative sample. All respondents were employed in an organization of more than 100 employees and at least 22 years old at the time of the interview.

3.2. Measures

Dependent variable WBI. WBI were elicited using a hypothetical vignette question. Respondents were given a case of fraudulent behavior they observed during their everyday work at the company. They were then asked whether they would report their observation or not on a scale of 1 (very unlikely) to 5 (very likely), measuring WBI.

Table 1. Correlation Matrix.

	M	SD	WBI	ATT	COR_CO	RETAL	MEDIA	AGE	GNDR	SIZE
WBI	3.35	1.14	–							
ATT	2.22	0.77	-0.206***	–						
CORR_CO	2.38	0.91	-0.193***	0.336***	–					
RETAL	3.31	1.16	-0.084*	-0.080*	-0.082**	–				
MEDIA	3.40	1.25	0.130***	-0.237***	-0.326***	0.149***	–			
AGE	4.41	1.18	0.122***	-0.153***	0.016	-0.115***	0.012	–		
GNDR	1.48	0.50	0.013	0.095**	0.078**	0.052	-0.096**	-0.097**	–	
SIZE	3.46	1.43	0.028	-0.027	-0.012	-0.088**	-0.007	-0.017	-0.035	–
C_CHN	0.34	0.48	-0.048	0.303***	0.116***	0.054	-0.026	-0.174***	0.145***	-0.187***
C_GER	0.33	0.47	0.193***	-0.275***	0.034	-0.005	0.056	0.299***	-0.081**	0.053
C_RUS	0.33	0.47	-0.155***	-0.024	-0.152***	-0.049	-0.030	-0.127***	-0.063*	0.133***

Notes: Pearson correlation coefficient and significance values in brackets. **WBI** = whistleblowing intentions (1 = very unlikely, 5 = very likely), **ATT** = positive attitudes toward fraud and corruption (1 = very low, 5 = very high), **CORR_CO** = corrupt successful colleague behavior (1 = very low, 5 = very high), **FEAR** = fear of retaliation (1 = very low, 5 = very high), **MEDIA** = critical media reporting perception (1 = very low, 5 = very high), **AGE** = age category (1 = 21 or younger, 2 = 22–25, 3 = 26–29, 4 = 30–39, 5 = 40–49, 6 = 50–59, 7 = 60+), **GNDR** = self-identified gender (1 = male, 2 = female), **SIZE** = company size measured as employees within the respective company (1 = less than 100, 2 = 101–250, 3 = 251–499, 4 = 500–999, 5 = 1,000–4,999, 6 = 5,000–10,000, 7 = 10,000+), **C_CHN** = country dummy for China (1 = China, 0 = otherwise), **C_GER** = country dummy for Germany (1 = Germany, 0 = otherwise), **C_RUS** = country dummy for Russia (1 = Russia, 0 = otherwise), *M* = mean, SD = standard deviation.
* p < 0.05; ** p < 0.01; *** p < 0.001.

Critical media coverage (MEDIA). The idea of how the respondents perceive mass media coverage is inherently subjective. Some respondents may regard only certain media outlets or do interpret the news coverage as more or less critical, as media frames are altered by the recipient (Kepplinger et al., 2012; Roulet, 2019). Thus, instead of looking at actual media coverage, respondents were asked whether they thought that media were criticizing bribery, corruption, and fraud on a scale from 1 (strongly disagree) to 5 (strongly agree). Fig. 2 gives some credence to this perception approach, rather than using an "objective" variable for actual media coverage. I split the sample by country and within each country by region surveyed. Mean values (triangles) differ across countries and strongly within countries between areas, and variance within areas (circles) is also pronounced. Thus, two people from the same area may not experience the same media sources or interpret the same news differently.

Positive attitudes toward fraud and corruption (ATT). Participants were also asked several questions on what they thought about controversial actions (fraud and corruption). This was preceded by a statement that there are different opinions about fraud and corruption in society and that the topic had many facets. This was done to reduce a social desirability bias and present corrupt practices as a neutral activity from the interviewee's point of view. They were asked whether they agreed or disagreed with several statements on a 5-point scale from 1 (strongly disagree) to 5 (strongly agree). Example statements are "Corruption is the only way to obtain some contracts" or "Corruption distorts competition" (reverse coded). Cronbach's $\alpha = 0.452$ is relatively low. However, alternative construct reliability measures such as composite reliability ($CR = 0.703$) or rho_A ($rho\_A = 0.746$) show very good construct fit (Hair et al., 2017).

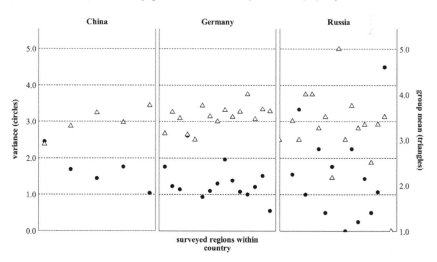

Fig. 2. Perceived Media Coverage of Fraud and Corruption Overview.
Notes: Perceived media coverage of fraud and corruption (MEDIA) by country and within-country by area. Circles are variance within-group, and triangles represent group means for the variable.

Corrupt colleague behavior (CORR_CO). Fraudulent colleague behavior was elicited by asking respondents to think of their current company. They were asked which statements would characterize successful co-workers from 1 (strongly disagree) to 5 (strongly agree). Example questions are "Disregard company guidelines if it will help to do a job well" or "Deal with business partners honestly and sincerely" (reverse coded). Construct fit indices are well above the recommended thresholds with Cronbach's $\alpha = 0.782$, $CR = 0.859$.

Fear of retaliation (RETAL). Retaliatory actions can take many forms (Kenny et al., 2019; Park et al., 2020). Employees were asked what they thought how likely several retaliatory measures would be to occur if they blew the whistle and what they feared might happen in the course of their report from 1 (very unlikely/strongly disagree) to 5 (very likely/strongly agree). They were asked for setbacks to their career, lack of confidentiality or anonymity, and doubts regarding whether their suspicion would be thoroughly investigated (similar items are used by Cassematis & Wortley, 2013; Oelrich, 2019; Park et al., 2008). Cronbach's $\alpha = 0.812$ and $CR = 0.888$ show very good construct fit.

Control variables. Several control variables were elicited, in particular sociodemographic variables such as age (AGE), gender (GNDR), and company size (SIZE). Due to the research design, country variables (C_CHN, C_GER, C_RUS) may be used as a proxy for cultural and institutional differences across the three sub-samples.[5] I use these country dummies for additional control regressions. However, this research focuses on media as a social institutional influence rather than individual or societal differences that affect WBI.

4. RESULTS

The theoretical model can be described as moderation-mediation model, for which structural equation modeling (SEM) is well suited (Hair et al. 2017; Hair et al., 2018). I use a partial-least-squares approach (PLS), which utilizes bootstrapping to generate confidence intervals and significance values. All latent variables are modeled as reflective constructs, interactions (moderation terms) are generated with a two-stage procedure, product terms are standardized and mean-centered, and missing data is replaced by sample means (Hair et al., 2017).[6] Discriminant validity is assumed, as all heterotrait-monotrait ratios are well below the recommended threshold of 0.85 (0.03 to 0.52, Hair et al., 2018, p. 61). Collinearity issues cannot be assumed based on the variance inflation factors, which are all below 5 (1.00 to 2.12, Hair et al., 2018, pp. 56, 62). Correlations and descriptive statistics are shown in Table 1, and structural equation model results are given in Table 2.

Based on prior whistleblowing studies, I derived a basic model of whistleblowing. Table 2 shows that the proposed relationships are also present in this study: The negative effect of positive attitudes toward corruption on whistleblowing intentions (ATT → WBI, $\beta = -0.081$, $p = 0.029$); The negative correlation between perceived corrupt colleague behavior and WBI (CORR_CO → WBI,

Table 2. PLS SEM Results of Moderation-Mediation Analysis.

Structural Path		β	SD	*p*-value	CI [2.5%,97.5%]
A. Direct effects on WBI					
MEDIA	→ WBI	0.071*	0.033	0.033	[0.005, 0.135]
CORR_CO	→ WBI	−0.138***	0.034	<0.000	[−0.203, −0.070]
ATT	→ WBI	−0.081*	0.037	0.029	[−0.152, −0.10]
RETAL	→ WBI	−0.104**	0.031	0.001	[−0.170, −0.051]
B. Direct effects on ATT (mediation)					
MEDIA	→ ATT	−0.165***	0.031	<0.000	[−0.226, −0.105]
CORR_CO	→ ATT	0.245***	0.031	<0.000	[0.189, 0.309]
C. Moderation effects					
MEDIA × CORR_CO	→ ATT	−0.176***	0.029	<0.000	[−0.227, −0.115]
MEDIA × RETAL	→ WBI	0.064*	0.030	0.032	[0.003, 0.120]

Notes: For variable descriptions, see Table 1. SD = standard deviation, CI = confidence interval. PLS SEM results with bootstrap $n = 5,000$ and path weighting scheme. All variables are standardized. The overall model is significant with $p < 0.000$, and dependent variable ATT $R^2 = 0.226$ (*adj.* $R^2 = 0.224$) and WBI with $R^2 = 0.057$ (*adj.* $R^2 = 0.053$).
* $p < 0.05$; ** $p < 0.01$; *** $p < 0.001$.

$\beta = -0.138, p < 0.000$) and the positive relationship between perceived corrupt colleague behavior and positive attitudes toward fraud and corruption (CORR_ CO → ATT, $\beta = 0.245, p < 0.000$); And the negative effect of fear of retaliation on WBI (RETAL → WBI, $\beta = -0.104, p = 0.001$).

Critical media coverage (MEDIA) extends this model. *H1* and *H2* posited that stronger perceived critical media coverage increases WBI and decreases positive attitudes toward fraud and corruption, respectively. Results in Table 2 support these relationships as they indicate that **MEDIA** positively correlates with the dependent variable WBI ($\beta = 0.071, p = 0.033$) and negatively with ATT ($\beta = -0.165, p < 0.000$).

H3 assumed a moderation effect of critical media coverage on the relationship between colleague behavior and corruption attitudes and is supported by the interaction effect of *MEDIA* × *CORR_CO*, which is significant and negative with $\beta = -0.176, p < 0.000$. Fig. 3 shows this moderation in a spotlight analysis graphically: When media are perceived to rarely critically assess corruption (dotted line, $-1SD$), then high prevalence of corruption in the company strongly influences attitudes toward fraud and corruption, represented by the steep slope ($\beta = 0.421$, $p < 0.000$). However, when employees perceive the media to report critically about corruption (straight line, $+1SD$), this relationship becomes weaker ($\beta = 0.069, p = 0.029$).

H4 posited that this relationship would be moderated by perceived critical media coverage, so that stronger perceived critical media coverage reduces the negative influence of fear of retaliation on WBI. This relationship is supported

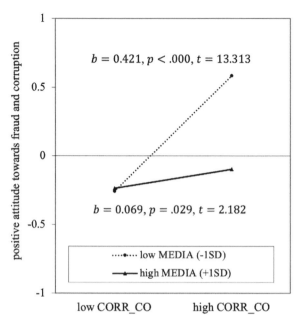

Fig. 3.   Moderation MEDIA × CORR_CO. *Notes*: Moderation interaction of
critical media perception (MEDIA) and prevalence of corrupt colleague behavior
(CORR_CO) in the company on positive attitudes toward fraud and corruption
(ATT). Variables are standardized and mean-centered. Slope coefficients and
significance values for −1/+1 standard deviation (SD) spotlight analysis.

by the significant and positive interaction effect of *MEDIA* × *RETAL*, with
$\beta = 0.064$, $p = 0.032$. A spotlight analysis in Fig. 4 indicates that the influence
is strong when media reports are perceived to be less critical and rare (dotted
line, $-1SD$, $\beta = -0.168$, $p < 0.000$), whereas when employees perceive media
to strongly criticize corruption (straight line, $+1SD$), fear of retaliation no
longer significantly influences their intentions to blow the whistle ($\beta = -0.040$,
$p = 0.206$).

I used OLS regression analyses (Table 3) to corroborate my results by adding
additional control variables. First, I replicated the model with WBI and positive
attitudes toward fraud and corruption as dependent variables (Table 3, models 1
and 3). I then added sociodemographic variables to the models (Table 3, models 2
and 4). In a third step, I added country control dummies to the models (Table 3,
models 3 and 6) with Germany as the base country. Interpretation of all effects
remains essentially unchanged. The only relevant difference is in model 3, where
MEDIA's direct effect on WBI is significant only at $p < 0.10$ with all control
variables added.

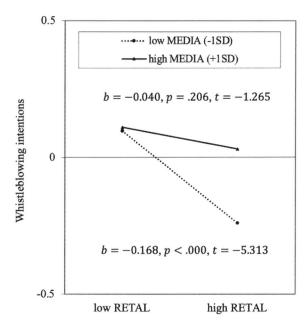

Fig. 4. Moderation MEDIA × RETAL. *Notes*: Moderation interaction of critical media perception (MEDIA) and fear of retaliation (RETAL) on WBI. Variables are standardized and mean-centered. Slope coefficients and significance values for $-1/+1$ standard deviation (SD) spotlight analysis.

Regarding controls, age seems to be positively correlated to WBI and negatively to ATT, while female employees seem to have higher WBI. Country effects indicate that Chinese and Russian employees are generally less likely to blow the whistle than German employees. However, the influencing factors are similar, which may be attributed to country or culture-specific differences.

Table 3. OLS Regressions with Sociodemographic and Country Dummy Controls.

	(1) WBI		(2) WBI		(3) WBI		(4) ATT		(5) ATT		(6) ATT	
	B	SE	B	SE	B	SE	B	SE	B	SE	B	SE
constant	4.431***	0.221	3.729***	0.315	4.211***	0.321	1.933***	0.102	2.316***	0.157	1.822***	0.162
MEDIA	0.062*	0.031	0.067*	0.031	0.052+	0.031	-0.089***	0.018	-0.085***	0.018	-0.081***	0.017
CORR_CO	-0.170***	0.044	-0.184***	0.044	-0.230***	0.044	0.250***	0.025	0.250***	0.025	0.241***	0.024
ATT	-0.230***	0.050	-0.208***	0.051	-0.175***	0.052						
RETAL	-0.115***	0.032	-0.108***	0.033	-0.114***	0.032						
AGE			0.083**	0.031	0.038	0.032			-0.103***	0.018	-0.052**	0.018
GNDR			0.150*	0.073	0.148*	0.072			0.077+	0.043	0.032	0.041
SIZE			0.018	0.025	0.032	0.025			-0.017	0.015	0.005	0.015
C_CHN					-0.192*	0.094					0.544***	0.052
C_RUS					-0.519***	0.091					0.274***	0.052
df	4		7		9		2		5		7	
F	18.936***		12.455***		13.701***		86.504***		43.376		49.423	
R^2	0.077		0.088		0.120		0.133		0.162		0.235	
adj. R^2	0.073		0.080		0.111		0.131		0.158		0.231	
N	916		916		916		1131		1131		1131	

Notes: For variable descriptions, see Table 1. SE = standard error. The number of observations is smaller than the initial reported 1,159 observations due to missing value exclusion instead of mean replacement. Results remain interpretatively unchanged if missing values are replaced by means. $+ p < 0.1$; $* p < 0.05$; $** p < 0.01$; $*** p < 0.001$.

5. DISCUSSION

Whistleblowing is an important source to uncover fraud and corruption in and by organizations. And while research on the topic is extensive, Watts and Buckley (2017, p. 679) note that "empirical research examining the influence of external influences on the whistleblowing process remains limited." Whistleblowing is mostly studied from individual, situational, or organizational level perspectives (Nicholls et al., 2021), neglecting that whistleblowing is situated within complex social dynamics and norms beyond the workplace (e.g., Bushnell, 2020; Butler et al., 2020; Watts & Buckley, 2017). My findings suggest that WBI are influenced by external social norms, which opens a new perspective on social influences beyond cultural differences, as advanced by prior research (Oelrich & Erlebach, 2021; Park et al., 2008).

In this study, I look at one such possible external influence on WBI: The media as an important social control agent in fraud contexts (Greve et al., 2010). In whistleblowing research, media have so far been mostly seen as yet another source of whistleblowing (e.g., Dyck et al., 2008; 2010). However, I argue and show that the media can also be a relevant factor in forming WBI. The media can be interpreted as conveying social norms to employees through their reporting behavior. If employees notice that the media single out fraud and corruption as harmful, this directly and positively influences their WBI. By framing behaviors as misconduct (Greve et al., 2010), the media can stimulate employees to report observed fraud cases within their firms.

How the media report on certain behaviors is also a relevant source when employees form their attitudes on behaviors they encounter at work, as they inform people about social norms. If the media regularly or strongly criticize fraud and corruption, such practices are more likely to be evaluated negatively by employees and thus more likely to be reported. This observed mediation effect extends prior whistleblowing studies that looked at attitudes and whistleblowing (e.g., Brown et al., 2016; Park & Blenkinsopp, 2009) regarding how these attitudes are formed in the first place.

While research has acknowledged the relevance of ethical co-worker behavior in forming WBI (e.g., Mayer et al., 2013), other research highlights the detrimental effects of unethical co-worker behavior, such as the spread of fraud in organizations (Davis & Pesch, 2013; Free & Murphy, 2015), especially when such practices become institutionalized (Gabbioneta et al., 2013). While my findings corroborate that unethical co-worker behaviors influence both attitudes and WBI, I extend this perspective by showing a way out of the cycle of the bad apple that spoils the barrel. The media can make social norms salient through extensive and critical coverage of fraud and corruption. This activation can then reduce harmful workplace norms as they materialize in the form of co-worker behavior and retaliation, in line with norm activation theory. Especially in terms of retaliation, prior research has highlighted its pivotal role in forming WBI (Brown et al., 2016; Cassematis & Wortley, 2013; Kenny et al., 2019; Oelrich, 2019; Park et al., 2020). Yet, few studies report on means to combat these fears. If people notice media strongly criticizing fraud and corruption, these employees seem to be less influenced by retaliation fears.

This activation of norms through media reports can also be understood in terms of legitimacy: By making salient that the observed behavior is publicly perceived as illegitimate, whistleblowing becomes the legitimate alternative (Butler et al., 2020; Watts & Buckley, 2017) and adverse co-worker behavior and fears of retaliation become less influential. This is particularly relevant and insightful for industries prone to corruption or fraud along the supply chain. Norm activation can be a powerful means to combat misconduct despite prevalent harmful workplace norms.

Overall, I observe three main mechanisms through which social norms, in particular the media, can operate: (1) by directly influencing WBI, (2) indirectly by influencing attitudes of the observed behavior, framing it as misconduct, which in turn influences employees' WBI; (3) media as norm activator, making social norms salient, and thus reducing the effect of (adverse) descriptive norms in the workplace. From the employee perspective, these three main mechanisms can be understood as "I report if they report" – they all increase reporting intentions when employees observe more frequent and more critical reporting of fraud and corruption by the media.

However, there are some limitations with this research. First, data are based on survey responses, where common method and social desirability biases cannot be ruled out. However, they have been carefully addressed through the research design and assurance of anonymity. This approach also only allows for correlation analyses and no causation statements. Although the advantage of such a field survey is that actual employees respond to questions regarding their real work situations and thus ensures stronger external validity, future experimental analyses could enhance the internal validity of these findings. Second, there may be a gap between the activation of norms and WBI and actual whistleblowing behavior. However, Oelrich (2021) showed that intentions and actual behaviors in whistleblowing contexts differ in effect magnitude and not influential factors per se. Third, I treated "the media" as a single variable, where respondents' perceptions were elicited in a broader and abstract sense. While this open perception approach has the advantage that respondents could report on their overall perception, I have no way of knowing if specific sources mattered more than others. For example, Neu et al. (2019) use Twitter as a media source, whereas Clemente and Gabbioneta (2017) use local and national newspaper sources. Future research could more closely look at whether these sources differ in their depiction of fraud, whistleblowing, and their influence.

In this paper, I looked at the important direct and indirect role of media in the context of fraud and corruption, arguing that critical media coverage in terms of frequent and strong criticisms of this behavior can increase their WBI. However, broader accounting and fraud literature research has criticized the media for their selective and biased coverage of organizational or white-collar crime (Levi, 2006; Miller, 2006). Stolowy et al. (2014) highlight how the media were complicit in framing Bernard Madoff, responsible for one of the largest investment frauds in the United States, as trustworthy. Others have cautioned that specific stakeholders may actively influence media reports (Forgues & May, 2018; Laguecir & Leca, 2019; Wieser et al., 2019). Future research could help to systematically understand how, when, and why media do (not) report on fraud, corruption, and whistleblowing.

I focused not only on the important role of social norms and media as one important social control agent to convey these norms but also on the interaction with other levels of analysis. While prior studies argued that whistleblowing research should move on from individual and situational aspects (Culiberg & Mihelič, 2017), I would argue that future research should not only concentrate on the mechanisms behind external factors and social norm influences but on the complex interactions of these several levels of analysis. One possibility for future studies could be to look at the boundary conditions of when media can override descriptive norms within the workplace. For example, when employees are strongly committed to the company, making social norms salient may be challenging. Watts and Buckley (2017) developed a complex multi-level model of whistleblowing with several testable propositions that could form the basis of further analyses. This paper can be understood as giving initial evidence that such interactions can be combined and studied in meaningful ways.

NOTES

1. I use whistleblowing according to Near and Miceli's definition (1985, p. 4): "the disclosure by organization members (former or current) of illegal, immoral or illegitimate practices under the control of their employers, to persons or organizations that may be able to effect action."

2. Retaliation is not thought to influence attitudes because it stands next to attitudes as a form of perceived behavioral control, according to Ajzen (1991; see also Chwolka & Oelrich, 2020; Park et al., 2008; Park & Blenkinsopp, 2009 for similar depictions in the context of whistleblowing, specifically).

3. https://www.transparency.org/en/cpi/2020/index/

4. The other respondents were asked about their actual experiences and is a different design compared to intention questions (scale vs dichotomous questionnaire). On the complexity, see, for example, Oelrich (2021), who compares these two approaches, designs, and variables using the same extended data set as is used here.

5. For example, differences in the legal system could directly or indirectly affect media coverage or fear of retaliation. However, in all three countries in our survey, no comprehensive legal protection for whistleblowers was in place by the time the survey was conducted; see, for example, Oelrich (2019) for Germany and Russia and Oelrich and Erlebach (2021) for China.

6. In untabulated control regressions, I corroborate the robustness of my moderation-mediation models using SPSS and PROCESS macro to model the same regressions with moderations. They yield similar results for all variables and the moderation effects and are thus not further discussed.

ACKNOWLEDGMENTS

I would like to thank Claudia Gabbioneta (issue editor), Nicole Siebold, Henry Walde, as well as an anonymous reviewer for very helpful and constructive comments on earlier versions of this manuscript. I would also like to thank Kai-D. Bussmann for allowing me to use this dataset freely and to have been part of this research project.

Data Availability

Data are available from the author upon request.

REFERENCES

ACFE. (2020). Association of Certified Fraud Examiners. *Report to the Nations 2020*.

Ajzen, I. (1991). The theory of planned behavior. *Organizational Behavior and Human Decision Processes*, *50*(2), 179–211. https://doi.org/10.1016/0749-5978(91)90020-T

Bian, Y., & Zhang, L. (2014). Corporate social capital in Chinese Guanxi Culture. *Research in the Sociology of Organizations*, *40*, 421–443. https://doi.org/10.1108/S0733-558X(2014)0000040021

Bicchieri, C. (2005). *The grammar of society: The nature and dynamics of social norms*. Cambridge University Press. https://doi.org/10.1017/CBO9780511616037

Brown, J., Hays, J., & Stuebs, M. (2016). Modeling accountant whistleblowing intentions: Applying the theory of planned behavior and the fraud triangle. *Accounting and the Public Interest*, *16*(1), 28–56. https://doi.org/10.2308/apin-51675

Bushnell, A. (2020). Reframing the whistleblower in research: Truth-tellers as whistleblowers in changing cultural contexts. *Sociology Compass*, *14*(8), 1–13. https://doi.org/10.1111/soc4.12816

Bussmann, K.-D., Oelrich, S., Schroth, A., & Selzer, N. (2021). *The impact of corporate culture and CMS. A cross-cultural analysis on internal and external preventive effects on corruption*. Springer. https://doi.org/10.1007/978-3-030-72151-0

Butler, J., Serra, D., & Spagnolo, G. (2020). Motivating whistleblowers. *Management Science*, *66*(2), 605–621. https://doi.org/10.1287/mnsc.2018.3240

Call, A., Martin, G., Sharp, N., & Wilde, J. (2018). Whistleblowers and outcomes of financial misrepresentation enforcement actions. *Journal of Accounting Research*, *66*(1), 123–171. https://doi.org/10.1111/1475-679X.12177

Callahan, E., & Dworkin, T. (1994). Who blows the whistle to the media and why: Organizational characteristics of media whistleblowers. *American Business Law Journal*, *151*, 153–158.

Carroll, C., & McCombs, M. (2003). Agenda-setting effects of business news on the public's images and opinions about major corporations. *Corporate Reputation Review*, *6*(1), 36–46. https://doi.org/10.1057/palgrave.crr.1540188

Cassematis, P., & Wortley, R. (2013). Prediction of whistleblowing or non-reporting observation: The role of personal and situational factors. *Journal of Business Ethics*, *117*(3), 615–634. https://doi.org/10.1007/s10551-012-1548-3

Chwolka, A., & Oelrich, S. (2020). Whistleblowing as a means for the prevention and detection of fraud in Germany – Amidst heroes and informers. *Betriebswirtschaftliche Forschung und Praxis (BFuP)*, *72*(4), 445–471.

Clemente, M., & Gabbioneta, C. (2017). How does the media frame corporate scandals? The case of German Newspapers and the Volkswagen Diesel Scandal. *Journal of Management Inquiry*, *26*(3), 287–302. https://doi.org/10.1177/1056492616689304

Courtois, C., & Gendron, Y. (2017). The "Normalization" of Deviance: A case study on the process underlying the adoption of deviant behavior. *AUDITING: A Journal of Practice & Theory*, *36*(3), 15–43. https://doi.org/10.2308/ajpt-51665

Culiberg, B., & Mihelič, K. (2017). The evolution of whistleblowing studies: A critical review and research agenda. *Journal of Business Ethics*, *146*(4), 787–803. https://doi.org/10.1007/s10551-016-3237-0

Dannals, J., Reit, E., & Miller, D. (2020). From whom do we learn group norms? Low-ranking group members are perceived as the best sources. *Organizational Behavior and Human Decision Processes*, *161*, 213–227. https://doi.org/10.1016/j.obhdo.2020.08.002

Daudigeos, T., Roulet, T., & Valiorgue, B. (2020). How scandals act as catalysts of fringe stakeholders' contentious actions against multinational corporations. *Business & Society*, *59*(3), 387–418. https://doi.org/10.1177/0007650318756982

Davis, J., & Pesch, H. (2013). Fraud dynamics and controls in organizations. *Accounting, Organizations and Society*, *38*(6–7), 469–483. https://doi.org/10.1016/j.aos.2012.07.005

Dong, W., Han, H., Ke, Y., & Chan, K. (2018). Social trust and corporate misconduct: Evidence from China. *Journal of Business Ethics, 151*(2), 539–562. https://doi.org/10.1007/s10551-016-3234-3

Dyck, A., Morse, A., & Zingales, L. (2010). Who blows the whistle on corporate fraud? *The Journal of Finance, 65*(6), 2213–2253. https://doi.org/10.1111/j.1540-6261-2010.01614.x

Dyck, A., Volchkova, N., & Zingales, L. (2008). The corporate governance role of the media: Evidence from Russia. *The Journal of Finance, 63*(3), 1093–1135. https://doi.org/10.1111/j.1514-6261.2008.01353.x

Forgues, B., & May, T. (2018). Message in a bottle: Multiple modes and multiple media in market identity claims. *Research in the Sociology of Organizations, 54*(B), 179–202. https://doi.org/10.1108/S0733-558X2017000054B006

Free, C., & Murphy, P. (2015). The ties that bind: The decision to co-offend in fraud. *Contemporary Accounting Research, 32*(1), 18–54. https://doi.org/10.1111/1911-3846.12063

Gabbioneta, C., Greenwood, R., Mazzola, P., & Minoja, M. (2013). The influence of the institutional context on corporate illegality. *Accounting, Organizations and Society, 38*(6–7), 484–504. https://doi.org/10.1016/j.aos.2012.09.002

Gamson, W., & Modigliani, A. (1989). Media discourse and public opinion on nuclear power: A constructionist approach. *American Journal of Sociology, 95*(1), 1–37.

Greve, H., Palmer, D., & Pozner, J.-E. (2010). Organizations gone wild: The causes, processes, and consequences of organizational misconduct. *The Academy of Management Annals, 4*(1), 53–107. https://doi.org/10.5465/196521003654186

Hair, J., Hult, G., Ringle, C., & Sarstedt, M. (2017). *A primer on partial least squares structural equation modeling (PLS-SEM)* (2nd ed.). Sage Publications.

Hair, J., Sarstedt, M., Ringle, C., & Gudergan, S. (2018). *Advanced issues in partial least squares structural equation modeling.* Sage Publications.

Kenny, K., Fotaki, M., & Scriver, S. (2019). Mental health as a weapon: Whistleblower retaliation and normative violence. *Journal of Business Ethics, 160*(3), 801–815. https://doi.org/10.1007/s10551-018-3868-4

Kepplinger, H., Geiss, S., & Siebert, S. (2012). Framing scandals: Cognitive and emotional media effects. *Journal of Communication, 62*(4), 659–681. https://doi.org/10.1111/j.1460-2466.2012.01653.x

Kish-Gephart, J., Harrison, D., & Treviño, L. (2010). Bad apples, bad cases, and bad barrels: Meta-analytic evidence about sources of unethical decisions at work. *Journal of Applied Psychology, 95*(1), 1–31. https://doi.org/10.1037/a0017103

Laguecir, A., & Leca, B. (2019). Strategies of visibility in contemporary surveillance settings: Insights from misconduct concealment in financial markets. *Critical Perspectives on Accounting, 62,* 39–58. https://doi.org/10.1016/j.cpa.2018.10.002

Levi, M. (2006). The media construction of financial white-collar crimes. *British Journal of Criminology, 46*(6), 1037–1057. https://doi.org/10.1093/bjc/azl079

Mayer, D., Nurmohamed, S., Treviño, L., Shapiro, D., & Schminke, M. (2013). Encouraging employees to report unethical conduct internally: It takes a village. *Organizational Behavior and Human Decision Processes, 121*(1), 89–103. https://doi.org/10.1016/j.obhdp.2013.01.002

McCombs, M., & Shaw, D. (1972). The agenda-setting function of mass media. *The Public Opinion Quarterly, 36*(2), 176–187. https://doi.org/10.1086/267990

Miller, G. (2006). The press as a watchdog for accounting fraud. *Journal of Accounting Research, 44*(5), 1001–1033. https://doi.org/10.1111/j.1475-679X.2006.00224.x

Near, J., & Miceli, M. (1985). Organizational dissidence: The case of whistle-blowing. *Journal of Business Ethics, 4*(1), 1–16. https://doi.org/10.1007/BF00382668

Neu, D., Saxton, G., Rahaman, A., & Everett, J. (2019). Twitter and social accountability: Reactions to the Panama Papers. *Critical Perspectives on Accounting, 61,* 38–53. https://doi.org/10.1016/j.cpa.2019.04.003

Nicholls, A., Fairs, L., Toner, J., Jones, L., Mantis, C., Barkoukis, V., Perry, J. L., Micle, A. V., Theodorou, N. C., Shakhverdieva, S., Stoicescu, M., Vesic, M. V., Dikic, N., Andjelkovic, M., Grimau, E. G., Amigo, J. A., & Schomöller, A. (2021). Snitches get stitches and end up in ditches: A systematic review of the factors associated with whistleblowing intentions. *Frontiers in Psychology, 12,* 1–20. https://doi.org/10.3389/fpsyg.2021.631538.

Oelrich, S. (2019). Making regulation fit by taking irrationality into account: The case of the whistle-blower. *Business Research*, *12*(1), 175–207. https://doi.org/10.1007/s40685-019-0094-6

Oelrich, S. (2021). Intention without action? Differences between whistleblowing intention and behavior on corruption and fraud. *Business Ethics, the Environment & Responsibility*, *30*(3), 447–463. https://doi.org/10.1111/beer.12337

Oelrich, S., & Erlebach, K. (2021). Taking it outside: A study of legal contexts and external whistleblowing in China and India. *Asian Journal of Business Ethics*, *10*(1), 129–151. https://doi.org/10.1007/s13520-021-00125-y

Park, H., Bjørkelo, B., & Blenkinsopp, J. (2020). External whistleblowers' experiences of workplace bullying by superiors and colleagues. *Journal of Business Ethics*, *161*(3), 591–601. https://doi.org/10.1007/s10551-018-3936-9

Park, H., & Blenkinsopp, J. (2009). Whistleblowing as planned behavior – A Survey of South Korean Police Officers. *Journal of Business Ethics*, *85*(4), 545–556. https://doi.org/10.1007/s10551-008-9788-y

Park, H., Blenkinsopp, J., Oktem, M., & Omurgonulsen, U. (2008). Cultural orientation and attitudes toward different forms of whistleblowing: A comparison of South Korea, Turkey, and the U.K. *Journal of Business Ethics*, *82*(4), 929–939. https://doi.org/10.1007/s10551-007-9603-1

Roulet, T. (2019). Sins for some, virtues for others: Media coverage of investment banks' misconduct and adherence to professional norms during the financial crisis. *Human Relations*, *72*(9), 1436–1463. https://doi.org/10.1177/0018726718799404

Semetko, H., & Valkenburg, P. (2000). Framing European politics: A content analysis of press and television news. *Journal of Communication*, *50*(2), 93–109. https://doi.org/10.1111/j.1460-2466-2000.tb02843.x

Stolowy, H., Gendron, Y., Moll, J., & Paugam, L. (2019). Building legitimacy of whistleblowers: A multi-case discourse analysis. *Contemporary Accounting Research*, *36*(1), 7–49. https://doi.org/10.1111/1911-3846.12453

Stolowy, H., Messner, M., Jeanjean, T., & Baker, R. (2014). The construction of a trustworthy investment opportunity: Insights from the Madoff fraud. *Contemporary Accounting Research*, *31*(2), 354–397. https://doi.org/10.1111/1911-3846.12039

van Es, R., & Smit, G. (2003). Whistleblowing and media logic: A case study. *Business Ethics: A European Review*, *12*(2), 144–150. https://doi.org/10.1111/1467-8608.00314

Watts, L., & Buckley, M. (2017). A dual-processing model of moral whistleblowing in organizations. *Journal of Business Ethics*, *146*(3), 669–683. https://doi.org/10.1007/s10551-015-2913-9

Wieser, V., Hemetsberger, A., & Luedicke, M. (2019). Protest rhetoric's appeal: How brands as moral entrepreneurs recruit the media into moral struggles. *Research in the Sociology of Organizations*, *63*, 151–166. https://doi.org/10.1108/S0733-558X20190000063016

CHAPTER 6

NETWORKED WHISTLEBLOWING, COUNTER-HEGEMONY AND THE CHALLENGE TO SYSTEMIC CORRUPTION

Iain Munro and Kate Kenny

ABSTRACT

Whistleblowing plays a crucial role in revealing organizational misconduct and systemic corruption in industry and government. This paper investigates changing practices of whistleblower activism, with particular reference to the role of solidarity and the increased role of support networks. Many modern whistleblower disclosures have revealed gaping flaws in the system of global governance related to a range of important social and economic issues, such as tax evasion, global mass surveillance, the use of torture and illegal wars of aggression. All these forms of systemic corruption are reliant on the use of secrecy havens to conceal the abuse from public scrutiny and democratic oversight. Counter-hegemonic social movements that oppose forms of systemic corruption can find important allies in those whistleblowers, who leak vital information about misconduct and corruption to the public. In this paper, we argue that there is a clear relationship of mutual support between whistleblowing and activist social movements, both in the process of whistleblowing and in furthering the campaigns of the social movements themselves. We theorize this, unpacking the processes and dynamics underlying the relationship, and offering a framework for analysis. The paper concludes with a discussion of the

Organizational Wrongdoing as the "Foundational" Grand Challenge: Consequences and Impact
Research in the Sociology of Organizations, Volume 85, 121–140
Published under exclusive licence by Emerald Publishing Limited
ISSN: 0733-558X/doi:10.1108/S0733-558X20230000085007

changing role of whistleblower activism and support networks in undertaking social reform and counter-hegemonic practice.

Keywords: Activism; corruption; counter-hegemony; secrecy; social movements; whistleblowing

INTRODUCTION

Whistleblowing plays a crucial role in revealing organizational misconduct and systemic corruption in industry and government. The paper investigates changing practices of whistleblower activism, with particular reference to the increased use of networks to reveal organizational misconduct. Major problems that whistleblowers face in disclosing corruption include the fact that they can be ignored within their own organizations (Alford, 2001; Kenny, 2019), or, if heeded, can find themselves isolated and targeted by other organizations including industry professional bodies and the media. Retaliation occurs in approximately one in every five acts of speaking out about organizational wrongdoing, and can include punitive legal action, smear campaigns, and blacklisting, among other measures (Alford, 2001; Mistry & Gurman, 2020). Systemic corruption refers to deep-seated misconduct that goes to the heart of how an organization, sector, or industry is structured, as opposed to wrongdoing that can be more easily eliminated – a single manager stealing, for example, or the knowing promotion of a single flawed product. Where systemic corruption is at stake, retaliation against whistleblowers is significantly harsher (Mesmer-Magnus & Viswesvaran, 2005).

Notable examples include Chelsea Manning's revelations of war crimes and human rights violations in Afghanistan and Iraq, where her approaches to the *New York Times* and the *Washington Post* were initially rebuffed, Paul Moore's attempts to raise concerns about mis-selling mortgages at HBOS prior to the financial meltdown of 2008, for which he was smeared and discredited in the business press and by a professional auditing body, and Rudolf Elmer's disclosures about tax evasion facilitated by the Swiss bank Julius Baer for which he was subject to similar treatment (Kenny & Bushnell, 2020; Maxwell, 2019). It is not only the organization that retaliates against the whistleblower, but a wider network of powerful interests can work to effectively exclude and silence her (Kenny, 2019; Munro, 2019; Stein, 2019).

Concern about the difficulties faced by whistleblowers has led to the rise of new whistleblower practices drawing on emergent technological innovations, as highlighted by cases such as the Panama Papers, Chelsea Manning's leaks of the Iraq War logs, and Edward Snowden's leaks related to the NSA's system of global mass surveillance, among others. We investigate these new whistleblowing practices not only as a matter of doing the right thing at the level of the individual speaking up, but also as a critical part of a counter-hegemonic struggle that is aimed at stopping immediate misconduct and wider systemic reforms. In so doing, we propose that current transformations in whistleblowing practices may be broadly understood as a form of counter-hegemonic practice that encompasses the formation of alliances with wider activist movements that can also help protect those who speak, ensure their message is heard and bring greater public pressure on the need for urgent reform.

This paper is structured by first explaining whistleblower activism in terms of alliance formation, solidarity tactics and civil disobedience, and then turning to an analysis of how whistleblower activism has helped address systemic corruption in two domains of practice – the global finance industry and anti-war activism. The analysis reveals similarities between critical problems faced by whistleblower activists in both of these domains of activism – particularly related to the formation of alliances and the limits of engendering reforms. We theorize these alliances and their capacity, developing a framework to inform future analysis. Highlighting major transformations in the role of whistleblower support networks, the paper concludes with a discussion of the changing role of whistleblower activism in undertaking social reform and counter-hegemonic practice.

WHISTLEBLOWING ACTIVISM: ALLIANCE FORMATION AND SOLIDARITY TACTICS

Alliance formation can help to mitigate the effects of retaliation against whistleblowers, but it has been identified as one of the most difficult aspects of the process of speaking out. Devine and Maassarani (2011, p. 47) discuss the importance of what they term "solidarity tactics" in the process of whistleblowing. Tactics can include soliciting the support of friends, family, sympathetic journalists, unions, politicians, whistleblower support groups, alternative avenues for safe disclosure like WikiLeaks, and social movement organizations such Amnesty International or the Tax Justice Network (Munro, 2017).

When the British diplomat Craig Murray blew the whistle on the UK's complicity in torture in Uzbekistan during the so-called "war on terror," he was subject to a smear campaign by the UK government, ostracism by his colleagues in the Foreign and Commonwealth Office, and other forms of retaliation (Murray, 2006). Murray described how the alliances he fostered as part of his campaign to raise concerns about the UK's complicity in torture were crucial for his emotional wellbeing during an extremely stressful time, for ensuring that his message was heard, and for protecting his livelihood. He explains the significance of these sources of support in the following way,

> Three things had kept me in my job [as a British diplomat] – the powerful media reaction in the UK in my favour, the extremely strong reaction of the British business community in Tashkent, and the support of the embassy staff. Of these the media reaction was, by far and away, the most important. (Murray, 2006, p. 321)

Describing the escalation of a "war on leakers," Gardner (2016) notes that other whistleblowers can become powerful allies and spokespersons for those who later follow in their footsteps. Veteran whistleblower, Daniel Ellsberg, is among the most outspoken supporters of recent disclosers. He has campaigned on behalf of Chelsea Manning, Edward Snowden and others who have raised concerns about government corruption. Ellsberg went about building and institutionalizing support networks for whistleblowers including ExposeFacts, which offered a secure dropbox to protect the anonymity of whistleblowers, and the Freedom of the Press Foundation, "with the stated goal of encouraging more whistleblowers" (Gardner, 2016, p. 168). Many whistleblower support networks have emerged. These groups aim to advise and support would-be disclosers. They include the Government Accountability Project (GAP) in the U.S., and, in the UK: the Courage Foundation, Protect and Compassion in Care. Devine and Maassarani (2011) have identified a range of groups that offer support to whistleblowers including the Electronic Frontier Foundation, the American Civil Liberties Union, and the Whistleblower-Netzwerk.e.V. Some of these organizations are run by former whistleblowers and volunteers, such as Compassion in Care, while others have greater involvement with professional advisers including human rights and employment lawyers (e.g., GAP) and journalists (e.g., WikiLeaks, the Intercept). Since its founding in 1978 GAP has advised over 8,000 whistleblowers. GAP plays a critical role in supporting whistleblower activism; the network offers guidance in alliance-building comprising legal advice and representation, political expertise to help mobilize local support for whistleblowers and their disclosures, and media advice (Hertsgaard, 2016). Tom Devine, a leading member of GAP, explains how these different forms of support are essential to engender "public solidarity that effectively turns information into power" (Devine quoted in Hertsgaard, 2016, p. 65). New media networks have also evolved with the aim of fostering and supporting contacts with whistleblowers, most notably WikiLeaks founded by Julian Assange, and The Intercept, founded by Glen Greenwald.

In addition to individual organizations that offer different levels of professional, legal, media and emotional support to whistleblowers, whistleblowers can also find support in broader social movements whose goals are furthered by their public interest disclosures (Bushnell, 2020). Existing research on the relationship between whistleblowing and activist campaigning is scant, but empirical studies have indicated that whistleblower disclosures can be a vital resource for the work of activists. The Julius Baer whistleblower, Rudolf Elmer worked with WikiLeaks and the Tax Justice Network to draw public attention to widespread tax evasion (Kenny & Bushnell, 2020). Whistleblower disclosures around the time of the 2008 financial crisis were critical to social movement campaigns calling for radical reform of the financial services system including Occupy Wall St (Kenny, 2019). Harvey Weinstein's sexual harassment whistleblowers added to the momentum that precipitated the #MeToo protest movement (Bushnell, 2020). Other compelling examples of whistleblowers who turned to activism are Daniel Ellsberg's engagement with the anti-Vietnam war movement when he spoke out about the Pentagon Papers and Katharine Gun's involvement in the anti-war movement after she blew the whistle on GCHQ and the NSA's attempts to manipulate the United Nations vote in favor of the Iraq War.

The relationship between activists and whistleblowers is not always straightforward. For example, UK whistleblower Katharine Gun highlighted the fact that although whistleblowers such as herself may get drawn into activism, this requires a distinctive set of skills that they had not previously had occasion to develop. In this regard, Gun explains that,

> What has to be understood is that most whistleblowers are not natural activists – this one certainly wasn't. We usually work in anonymous jobs, far from the spotlight. We are not campaigners or journalists or wannabe celebrities craving a platform. Our conscience tells us we must reveal what we know. We do that, we blow the whistle, and overnight the whole media circus descends on us. You just don't know what to do... that's why we stick together. (Gun, in Mitchell and Mitchell, p. 171)

Given the relatively weak legal protections offered to whistleblowers, social movements can become very important for whistleblowing because, as noted by Devine and Maassarani (2011, p. 69), "solidarity from a coalition whose combined membership numbers in the tens of millions can be more valuable than conventional legal rights." Thus it is clear that while whistleblowers can support activists' work, activists working in social movements can, in turn, offer help and support to whistleblowers. Here again, however, in-depth research and analysis is limited.

Whistleblowing has often been investigated in terms of the courage and action of the individual whistleblower (Contu, 2014; Weiskopf & Willmott, 2013, see Kenny, 2019 for a discussion), while the importance of those who support their actions has been a relatively neglected area of academic inquiry. Some research has framed whistleblowing in terms of civil disobedience (Pozen, 2020; Scheuerman, 2015), but even these studies tend to focus on the individual behavior of the whistleblower rather than its collective aspects. In the following section, we will thus explore the role of whistleblowing activism as a form of civil disobedience with a particular focus on its collective praxis.

WHISTLEBLOWER ALLIANCES: ACTIVISM AND CIVIL DISOBEDIENCE

Several whistleblowers have positioned their reasons for blowing the whistle not simply as a matter of public interest but more broadly in the tradition of social protest and civil disobedience. Civil disobedience entails an active but non-violent protest and the refusal to obey laws which are considered to be morally wrong. Daniel Ellsberg for example cites the ideas of non-violent protest and the civil disobedience of Gandhi, Rosa Parks and Martin Luther King as being influential in his decision to blow the whistle on the US government's wars in Cambodia and Vietnam. Discussing Thoreau's original conception of the term, Ellsberg (2002, p. 263) argues for the necessity of "something beyond verbal dissent and protest: the withdrawal of cooperation, militant disobedience by a *civilian*, akin to that of a 'soldier... who refuses to serve in an unjust war.'" The practice of civil disobedience is a counter-hegemonic practice which presents a principled challenge to the prevailing status quo and the laws that prop it up. Tom Devine of GAP has described Snowden's actions as a form of "civil disobedience whistleblowing" which he contrasts with strictly lawful whistleblowing.[1] Devine explains that, "in the national security arena, civil disobedience whistleblowing is what works" (Quoted in Herstgaard, 2016, p. 46). This is due to the fact that in many countries, including the United States, there is no public interest defense enshrined in law for national security whistleblowers – the legal process aims to determine whether or not illicit disclosure of classified information took place, and punish this act, regardless of the public interest served.

Snowden (2019, p. 239) defines his own act of whistleblowing in purely reformist terms. He asserts that his motivation lies in the defence of the US Constitution and he explicitly rejects alternative framings of his disclosure as "a radical act of dissent or resistance." He also emphasizes the importance of alliance-building as a necessary part of whistleblowing. Specifically, he describes how: "Cooperating with some type of media organization would defend me against the worse accusations of rogue activity, and correct for whatever biases I had…" (Snowden, 2019, p. 243). Snowden discusses his initial consideration of the WikiLeaks platform due to its evident concern for the protection of previous whistleblowers, such as Chelsea Manning, but notes he was not comfortable with its limited approach to redaction, opting instead to contact Ewan MacAskill and Glen Greenwald on the grounds that these journalists had already been targeted by the national security state and were thus likely to be independent from it. Snowden highlights the vital role of support that was provided to him in the early days of his disclosures when he was hiding from the US authorities in Hong Kong. During this time, he had very few supporters and was particularly vulnerable to capture and arrest. Chief among his allies were his lawyers Robert Tibbo and Jonathan Mann and the refugees who helped him to evade capture. Snowden (2019, p. 296) explains that,

> The solidarity they showed me was not political. It was human, and I shall be forever in their debt. They didn't care who I was or what dangers they might face by helping me, only that there was a person in need… they shared everything they had with me, and they shared it unstintingly, refusing my offers to reimburse them for the cost of taking me in… they protected me.

Mr Tibbo has since secured the political asylum of all but one of these refugees in Canada. He continues to represent the "Snowden refugees" and has expressed concern that his clients as asylum seekers have been subject to increased persecution by the Hong Kong and US governments due to their helping Mr Snowden.

The nature of alliances and the needs of the whistleblower may change considerably during the process of whistleblowing and after, but what does not change is the absolutely crucial role that solidarity tactics and the support of others plays in the process. These points notwithstanding, the cases of Snowden and Ellsberg are by no means typical. Civil disobedience whistleblowing involves actions that violate the law and sometimes national security laws, which can lead to accusations of treason which may deter potential allies. In this respect retaliating organizations often draw on common stereotypes to discredit whistleblowers and the importance of their disclosures. On the other hand, civil disobedience whistleblowing can open up the range of potential allies with existing social movements such as the anti-war movement, human rights campaigners and privacy activists.

Not all whistleblowers are civil disobedience whistleblowers, nor engage in counter-hegemonic activism. Some may focus on relatively modest revelations related to isolated incidents of wrongdoing. However, the cases discussed in this paper are clearly engaged with more systemic forms of misconduct and corruption related to mass surveillance, tax evasion and war crimes, where their revelations have clear significance for social movements working toward large-scale social change. We now turn to a more detailed investigation of two kinds of whistle-blower activism: attempts to reform of the finance industry and anti-war activism, in order to better map out the collective aspects of whistleblowing as an activist and counter-hegemonic practice.

FINANCIAL WHISTLEBLOWING AND THE REFORM OF FINANCIAL SECRECY HAVENS

Our knowledge of systematic corruption in the global financial system has been transformed in recent years by revelations from whistleblowers and whistleblower journalists (Kenny, 2019; Obermayer & Obermaier, 2016). These include revela-tions concerning misconduct by individual financial institutions such as HSBC, HBOS, Deutsche Bank, and UBS, among many others, and evidence of systemic corruption at work within the global banking system as a whole as evidenced in the Panama Papers and the Paradise Papers. Gabbioneta et al. (2019, p. 1) have observed that the Panama Papers, "reveal the shocking scale of this profes-sionally orchestrated tax avoidance, with around 214,000 companies and 14,000 individuals named…" The Panama Papers were leaked to German investigative journalist Bastian Obermayer by an anonymous whistleblower in 2015. These leaks revealed a system of tax havens supporting practices of tax evasion and money laundering by

> dozens of heads of state and dictators; stories explaining how billions are earned from arms, drug and blood-diamond trafficking and other illegal business, and bring home to readers the scale of tax evasion by the wealthy and the super-rich of this world. (Obermayer & Obermaier, 2016, p. 9)

The journalists who received the leaks explained that,

> the secret offshore industry – centred in tax havens like the British Virgin Islands – was not, as previously had been thought, a minor part of our economic system. Rather it *was* the system … The rich, it turned out, had exited from the messy business of tax long ago. (Harding in Obermayer & Obermaier, 2016, p. vii)

The leaks originated from the computer files of a Panamanian law firm called Mossack Fonseca, revealing not only the existence of widespread tax evasion by a wealthy global elite, but a network of law firms and banks that facilitated corrup-tion across the globe – "More than 500 banks world-wide have used the services of Mossfon [Mossack Fonseca]" (Obermayer & Obermaier, 2016, p. 244).

Whistleblower revelations of tax evasion had occurred previously, for example in the run-up to the global financial crisis, including Rudolf Elmer's disclosures about Julius Baer bank's facilitation of such practices (Kenny, 2019). However, the significance of the Panama Papers goes far beyond a concern for tax evasion and the identification of "bad apples" who believe that they are above the law, it also revealed the systemic corruption of a network of legal and banking professionals throughout the global financial system. The journalists who worked on these leaks explained that,

> In our globalised world it seems that there is hardly a single law that cannot be circumvented or have its impact lessened with the help of a few [offshore] shell companies. (Obermayer & Obermaier, 2016, p. 302)

They highlight how the system of corruption that is facilitated by the network of offshore tax havens played a crucial role in the lead up to 2008 global financial crisis, and as such tax havens are not only responsible for the reduction of funds available for public spending by governments, but have played a key role in the destablization of the global financial system as a whole. These leaks reveal more than the greed of certain powerful individuals (Vladimir Putin and David Cameron's family are identified as persistent tax evaders in the Papers); they illustrate deeper and fundamental problems with both the legal and financial professions and the governance of the global financial system.[2]

Professional firms have set up financial "secrecy havens" in order to provide services to wealthy clients which evade financial governance mechanisms and adequate democratic oversight (Assange, 2011). Secrecy havens are often a central feature of corrupt systems, which require the creation of spaces used by powerful elites to avoid appropriate governance and democratic oversight (Assange, 2011; Munro, 2016). In addition to the offshore tax havens described here, such spaces can be created by military and national security organizations, with examples including Guantanamo Bay and CIA black sites that have sought to conceal evidence of gross human rights abuses (Assange, 2011). One tactic by which the dominant hegemony maintains its power is through secrecy (Dean, 2006), and in this respect whistleblowers can play a vital role in revealing the secrecy havens of the powerful (Assange, 2011; Munro, 2016).

One important theme that runs throughout Obermayer and Obermaier's account of the Panama Papers is the crucial role that whistleblowers and whistleblower journalists play in exposing systemic corruption. New journalistic practices have evolved for dealing with the scope and scale of recent leaks. These have enabled a huge quantity of information to be made available in recent leaks such as the US Diplomatic cables, Snowden Files, the HSBC Files, and Luxleaks. The Panama Papers involved nearly 260 gigabytes of data. The two journalists who originally received the leaks quickly contacted a much larger network of journalists to help them – the International Consortium of Investigative Journalists. This network also created a searchable database and employed state-of-the-art software in developing search protocols to help navigate the database. In the closing pages of their book, Obermayer and Obermaier explicitly situate this new form of whistleblower journalism, inspired by previous projects including those of WikiLeaks and Edward Snowden's leaks, as part of a revolutionary movement –

> we live in a time of inexpensive, limitless data storage and fast Internet connections that transcend national boundaries. It doesn't take much to connect the dots: from start to finish, inception to global media distribution, the next revolution will be digitized. Or perhaps it has already begun. (Obermayer & Obermaier, 2016, p. 344)

These transformations in whistleblower support can be seen as new forms of networked counter-hegemonic practice directed against financial centers of power. One of the most important points about the impact of such leaks, therefore, is their role as part of a wider movement in the evolution of new whistleblowing and journalistic practices, and what might be understood as forms of counter-hegemonic practice (de Lagasnarie, 2016; Kenny & Bushnell, 2020; Munro, 2017). These recent leaks should be understood not only as revelations of isolated incidents of misconduct but as part of the evolution of the "networked fourth estate" (Benkler, 2011) and a digitized revolution which is playing a key role in the development of future reforms and changing practices of counter-hegemonic activism.

Social movements incorporating organizations such as Tax Justice Network for example continue to work with whistleblower revelations, including those of Rudolf Elmer, in order to "join the dots" and showcase the wider systemic failures that enable the disclosed wrongdoing to continue. Thus while alliance formation and solidarity tactics are a crucial aspect of effective whistleblowing – because they both protect whistleblowers and ensure their information reaches the public, we can see also that alliance formation and solidarity tactics are a crucial aspect of counter-hegemonic struggles (Carroll & Ratner, 2010). These points notwithstanding, it is important not to overstate the impact of new practices of disclosure. Obermayer and Obermaier (2016, p. 338) express skepticism concerning the ultimate impact of these leaks, specifically whether they can precipitate fundamental systemic change – "But real change? Genuine progress in the battle against the shady world of offshore business? Not really." At the same time, the new technologies, practices and alliances that they precipitate help both democratic reform and counter-hegemonic struggle.

WHISTLEBLOWING ACTIVISM AND THE ANTI-WAR MOVEMENT

Probably the most influential whistleblower who became an anti-war activist is the Pentagon Papers whistleblower, Daniel Ellsberg. Ellsberg, a former US marine, was working as a senior analyst for the government when he became aware of an apparatus of secrecy surrounding the US involvement in Vietnam. He was increasingly concerned about the stream of lies being told to the US public by its political representatives. Ellsberg leaked a secret RAND review of the US conduct of the Vietnam War in 1971 (Ellsberg, 2002). It became headline news in the *New York Times* and *Washington Post*, and helped to turn the US media narrative against the war, which had previously been strongly supportive of it. Ellsberg underwent a radical transformation becoming a whistleblower and a prominent spokesperson for the anti-war movement. His own account of whistleblowing explains the importance of meeting with and engaging in conversations with anti-war activists in his decision to blow the whistle. He recounts his first such meeting at a conference at Princeton in 1968 when he was still working as an analyst for the RAND Corporation. The activists were speaking out against US involvement in Vietnam and its conduct of the war. Ellsberg (2002, pp. 209–210) explains,

> the first activists I had ever met [were] from the anti-nuclear movement of the fifties and the civil-rights and antiwar movements of the sixties…. Their lives and mine were parallel in some respects, intersecting in others, both in ironic ways… Now we were all against the Vietnam war. … they were sympathetic to a variety of revolutionary causes. My own interest in the conference stemmed from my past and current work on averting or defeating Communist-led revolutions. I was there in effect as a professional counterrevolutionary [working for the Rand Corporation on counterinsurgency.]

In his memoir, *Secrets*, Ellsberg describes a turning point in his thoughts about the war, and his decision to blow the whistle, at a talk with an anti-war activist [Janaki] who introduced him to the idea of non-violent resistance and the work of Ghandi and Martin Luther King. Ellsberg's first direct action was shortly after a conversation with draft resister, Bob Eaton, who was going to prison as a conscientious objector. Ellsberg handed out leaflets against the war with a group of anti-war protestors in Philadelphia, "I was, it seems, in the process of shedding that skin on that morning. Before I had grown a new one. I felt naked – and raw" (Ellsberg, 2002, p. 268). He explains how participating in direct action with anti-war activists was an important inspiration for his decision to become a whistleblower,

> Something very important had happened to me. I felt liberated. I doubt if I could have explained that at the time. But by now I have seen this exhilaration often enough in others, in particular people who have just gone through their first action of civil disobedience, whether or not they have been taken to jail. The simple vigil, my first public action, had freed me from a nearly universal fear whose inhibiting force, I think is very widely underestimated. I had become free of the fear of appearing absurd, of looking foolish, for stepping out of line… By stepping into that particular vigil, in solidarity with Bob Eaton and in company with others whose views I shared and whose lives and commitment I respected, I had stepped across another line and invisible one of the kind that recruiters mark out on the floor of an induction centre. I had joined a movement. (Ellsberg, 2002, pp. 269–230)

The context in which Ellsberg made his decision was a vital aspect of how he reached his decision to go to the press and blow the whistle, particularly the wider culture of anti-war protest with which he began to engage.

In contrast to previous studies that tend to focus on the virtues of the individual in the decision to blow the whistle (e.g., Contu, 2014; Weiskopf & Willmott, 2013), Ellsberg's own account highlights desires for group solidarity, becoming part of a movement, the sharing of doubts and ideas with others, and the crucial role of engaging in direct action. These led to Ellsberg's increasing engagement with anti-war activism and taking the first steps to leak the Pentagon Papers to the press. Anti-war activists also played an important role in supporting Ellsberg after he had blown the whistle, helping him to evade capture by the FBI and campaigning for him during his trial. He writes, "I was far from alone when it came to crucial help from friends, family, and antiwar resisters" (Ellsberg, 2002, p. 407). So while Ellsberg had little or no support from his former friends in RAND, he gradually gathered the support of his family, journalists at prominent national newspapers, lawyers as well as the anti-war movement which proved to be a huge source of moral support.

Ellsberg's account of whistleblowing suggests that there is a clear relationship of mutual support between whistleblowing and activist social movements, both in the process of whistleblowing and in furthering the campaigns of the social movement itself. Varon (2020) has observed how in the 1960s and 1970s, national security whistleblowers benefited from a growing culture of direct action, particularly related to the anti-war movement and campus-based activism. He explains that,

> The CIA whistleblowers first emerged in a robust climate of protest, rife with truth-to-power politics and exemplary self-sacrificing resistance. Their message further blossomed in the shifting sands of dissent. (Varon, 2020, p. 164)

Varon observes, that since 9/11, intelligence whistleblowers like John Kiriakou, Jospeh Hickman, Lawrence Wilkerson, and Morris Davis have provided detailed knowledge on topics such as the US torture programme at Guantanamo Bay and the War on Terror. He explains that, "Their voices have been valuable in public activism that – if never on a par with Vietnam War-era protests – has arguably helped constrain the 'War on Terror'" (Varon, 2020, p. 174). Mistry (2020) has highlighted the appearance of a number of national security whistleblowers who followed in Daniel Ellsberg's footsteps, leaving roles in intelligence organizations and government and becoming anti-war activists. Mistry (2020, p. 135) characterizes this as "anti-imperial whistleblowing," which, he observes, "was part of a broader cultural shift that marked increased skepticism toward government, tangibly revealing the gap between words and actions of successive US administrations on foreign policy." These observations reinforce both the crucial role of national security whistleblowers in supporting anti-war activism and exposing war crimes and systemic corruption in the government, as well as highlighting the role of social activist movements in supporting whistleblowers and how their disclosures are received.

Another prominent whistleblower who became an anti-war activist in the process of revealing of human rights abuses and war crimes is Chelsea Manning. Troubled by what she was witnessing as an intelligence analyst for the US Army in Iraq, in 2010 Manning released a trove of classified files to the whistleblowing network WikiLeaks about the conduct of the wars in Afghanistan and Iraq which contained information related to the killing of civilians, the use of torture, and the increased use of drone strikes against a civilian population, among other things. Manning's actions were aimed at dismantling the secrecy structures hiding these crimes from the public. One of the most infamous leaks concerned the release of the "Collateral Murder" video which shows the actions of an Apache helicopter gunship killing 12 civilians including two Reuters reporters as well as injuring others including children. Manning became an outspoken critic of the war in Iraq, and was subsequently sentenced to 35 years in a maximum-security prison. She received support from numerous whistleblower organizations including WikiLeaks, the Courage Foundation and the ACLU, as well as from other whistleblowers like Daniel Ellsberg and John Kiriakou.

Manning's release of this information had a catalyzing effect within the anti-war community, particularly in prompting former soldiers to speak out about their concerns over the misconduct of the war. After seeing the video "Collateral

Murder" on a news channel, Ethan McCord spoke out about scenes he had personally witnessed as a soldier dealing with the aftermath, the cries of the injured children and smell of burning bodies –

> I had to clean the blood of the children off my uniform … and I started piecing it together and just started realising that it was the Apache that did that….Things from that day changed for me. (McCord, 2010)

McCord contacted other soldiers from his unit who were troubled by what they had witnessed in the war. Many veterans have since become vocal critics of the war,

> From our own experiences, and the experiences of other veterans we have talked to, we know that the acts depicted in this video are everyday occurrences of this war: this is the nature of how U.S.-led wars are carried out in this region. (McCord & Steiber, 2010)

After serving 7 years, Chelsea Manning's sentence was commuted by President Barack Obama and she was released from prison. She has since become a committed anti-war and transgender rights campaigner. Manning has received support and awards from numerous activist and human rights organizations including the Whistleblowerpreis (2011), The Global Exchange People's Choice Award (2012), The US Peace Prize, US Peace Memorial Foundation (2013), the Sean McBride Peace Prize, International Peace Bureau (2013), the Sam Adams Award for Integrity (2014), the EFF Pioneer Award for whistleblowing (2017). In January 2020, she was nominated for the Nobel Peace Prize alongside Edward Snowden and Julian Assange, "in honour of their unparalleled contributions to the pursuit of peace, and their immense personal sacrifices to promote peace for all" (Dağdelen et al, 2020).

Maxwell (2019) has placed Manning's act of whistleblowing in the context of a long history of anti-war and peace activism, particularly associated with the feminist movement. She characterizes Manning's whistleblowing as an "insurgent truth" which challenges not only the war in Iraq but the broader hegemonic structures of modern society –

> […] outsider truth-tellers suggest that our dominant system of representing the truth is shaped by a broader security regime (e.g. modern capitalism and militarism, violence in the name of "security," digital technology, patriarchy). (Maxwell, 2019, p. 16)

THEORIZING WHISTLEBLOWING ACTIVISM AND COUNTER-HEGEMONY

This paper has developed the concept of whistleblower activism which highlights the role of whistleblowing as a collective practice, and focuses on the crucial importance of solidarity tactics and the formation of broader alliances with social movements in the process of whistleblowing. In what follows we theorize the key components of the ways in which whistleblowers and social movements can engage in counter-hegemonic practices to shed light on systemic corruption. This framework is depicted in Table 1, and its categories are explained as follows:

Secrecy Havens as a Focus of Disclosure: Many modern whistleblower leaks have revealed systemic corruption and gaping flaws in the system of global governance related to a range of important social and economic issues, such as tax evasion, global mass surveillance, the use of torture and illegal wars of aggression. All these forms of systemic corruption are reliant on the use of "secrecy havens" to conceal the abuse from public scrutiny and democratic oversight. This paper shows how whistleblowers can shed light on the increasingly intricate ways in which information is hidden in secrecy havens, in the national security contexts and in offshore tax havens discussed here but also as shown in Table 1, extending to many other contexts. In this respect, an emerging characteristic of modern whistleblowing practice has been the increased use of technology to enhance whistleblower protections as well as the quantity of information leaked, and support for its analysis and global distribution. Journalists who have worked on whistleblower leaks have expressed pessimism concerning the extent of change that can be achieved through whistleblower activism and leaking in the short term, however we have shown that in the longer term activism contributes to profound social transformations regarding whistleblower protections, pioneering new forms of journalism and fostering new alliances with counter-hegemonic social movements.

Social Movements: Current transformations in whistleblowing practices include a growth in alliance formation with wider activist movements and the transformation of whistleblower journalism to protect those who speak up and ensure a global dissemination of their message, as evidenced in the work of the International Consortium of Investigative Journalists and the WikiLeaks network. The mutual support between whistleblowers and activists can be seen from the close relationship that certain whistleblowers have developed with NGOs and social movement organizations. Whistleblowers such as Daniel Ellsberg, Katharine Gun, Chelsea Manning and others have all received open support from a range of human rights, civil liberties and anti-war NGOs including Amnesty International, the American Civil Liberties Union, the Chaos Computer Club, Liberty, Freedom of the Press Foundation, the Electronic Frontier Foundation, and the Stop the War Coalition, among others. The whistleblower supports the movement by providing their unique insider information concerning corruption and misconduct of the organizations they had previously worked for and as high-profile campaigners for the social movements they engage with - e.g. anti-war (Ellsberg, Gun, Manning), privacy (Fellwock, Binney, Drake, Snowden), and financial reform (Elmer). In turn important NGOs can provide support for whistleblowers offering them platforms at which to speak and campaigning on their behalf. As well as furthering their mutual goals in revealing systemic corruption and campaigning for reform, these alliances are also an important source of moral and emotional support for whistleblowers.

Counter-Hegemonic Practices: We can understand these transformations as incorporating counter-hegemonic practice and alliance building. Recent whistleblowing practices are not limited to concerns with "doing the right thing" in

Table 1. Counter-Hegemonic Whistleblowing Practices and Alliances.

Secrecy Havens Revealed	Prominent Exemplars	Hegemonic Practice Revealed by Disclosure	Allied Social Movements	Whistleblower Support Networks
US government and the RAND Corporation's cover-up of activities in Vietnam	Daniel Ellsberg	Disclosure of the Pentagon Papers shed new light on the history of US imperialism and deception in Vietnam, Laos, Cambodia	Anti-War movement	Anti-War activists, Journalists, Family
Torture networks operated by UK allies	Craig Murray	Disclosure revealed UK and US intelligence agencies' complicity in widespread torture	Anti-war and human rights movements	British business community in Tashkent, Journalists, Interpersonal support from staff at British embassy
The NSA and GCHQ	Katharine Gun	Disclosure highlighted illegal NSA surveillance of United Nations delegates	Anti-War movement	Journalists, Anti-War activists, UK politicians, Human rights NGOs, Family
US Army intelligence	Chelsea Manning	Disclosure revealed war crimes in Iraq and Afghanistan	Anti-War movement	Other whistleblowers, (Ellsberg, Kiriakou) Wikileaks, Courage Foundation Human rights NGOs
NSA and allied intelligence agencies	Edward Snowden	Disclosures of system of Global Mass Surveillance	Privacy activism	Journalists, Lawyers, Freedom of the Press network, The "Snowden refugees," Other whistleblowers, Human grits NGOs, Civil rights groups, Family
An off-shore tax haven in the Cayman Islands and role of Swiss bank Julius Baer	Rudolf Elmer	Disclosure highlighted Swiss bank involvement in facilitating tax evasion for wealthy clients	Tax justice	Tax Justice Network, Journalists, (*Guardian* Newspaper), Human rights organization

Icelandic banking system	Leaked report of Kaupthing bank by WikiLeaks (via anonymous whistle blower)	Disclosure showed systemic financial misconduct and political corruption in Iceland	The "pots and pans" revolution Occupy	WikiLeaks
An off-shore tax haven in Panama	John Doe (anonymous whistleblower)	Disclosure of the global system of offshore tax evasion in the Panama Papers	Tax justice	Tax justice movement International Consortium of Investigative Journalists
System of tax havens supporting practices of tax evasion and money laundering	Anonymous whistleblower	Disclosure of the global system of offshore tax evasion in the Paradise Papers	Tax justice	Tax justice movement International Consortium of Investigative Journalists
Endemic Sexual harassment, sexual violence and discrimination	Ambra Battilana Gutierrez Zelda Perkins Multiple whistleblowers	Disclosures revealed systemic sexual harassment and gender-based discrimination	MeToo, women's rights movement	MeToo

specific settings, but are also related to counter-hegemonic struggles that are aimed not only at stopping individual misconduct but at wider systemic reforms. Some whistleblower activists may become prominent spokespersons and moral leaders of international movements, as the case in Daniel Ellsberg's anti-war activism and Edward Snowden's privacy activism. Whistleblowing activism can be understood as a form of moral leadership which transcends narrow corporate or even national obligations. In certain respects, one may draw fruitful comparison between whistleblower activists and the leaders of civil disobedience movements, and it is no coincidence that some whistleblowers have acknowledged a degree of inspiration from such leaders (Ellsberg, 2002). This point notwithstanding, the importance of "leader-less" movements in which whistleblowers can come together to voice concerns collectively and in some cases anonymously, cannot be overstated, not least given the dangers of reprisal against individuals who speak up.

One important development over recent years has been the increased use of technology and networks by journalists in the protection of whistleblower anonymity, the access and processing of data leaks, and their global dissemination. Counter-hegemonic social movements that oppose forms of systemic corruption can find important allies in those whistleblowers, who leak vital information about crimes to the public. Böhm et al. (2008, p. 13) have observed that, "Importantly, because of its contingency and unstable configuration, a hegemonic regime will always give rise to resistance and counter-hegemonic forces…" (see also Kenny & Bushnell, 2020). In the cases examined in this paper we can see this contingency at work in the way that former insiders become whistleblowers to reveal the systemic corruption, open up secrecy havens for scrutiny, and develop new alliances within civil society actors beyond their employing organization.

Support Networks: Whistleblowing support networks are important allies, and help to disseminate a whistleblower's message as well as providing moral and emotional support for their disclosures. The cases presented here have shown that support networks for whistleblowing are essential not only for the wellbeing and protection of the whistleblower, but also, as Tom Devine has observed, to turn information into power. These support networks can include informal networks of family, friends and volunteers as well as formal networks of professional lawyers and journalists. The crucial role that these support networks can play in the early days of whistleblowing has been a much-neglected area of study, as is the fact that individuals who provide such support may also find themselves the targets of retaliation.

Support networks have also played an important role in pioneering new forms of whistleblower protection, not only in campaigning for increased legal protections but also developing new technologies for protecting the anonymity of whistleblowers. The Panama Papers were made possible by an anonymous whistleblower who to our knowledge did not incur personal risk. In contrast Chelsea Manning intended for her disclosures to be made in an anonymous capacity via Wikileaks, but her identity was revealed by a hacker, Adrian Lamo, with whom she had shared her confidence. Her subsequent treatment exemplifies the danger of high-profile, individual whistleblowing. What is clear is that new technological practices have been pioneered by support networks that help increased protections for whistleblowers.

UNDERSTANDING THE CONTINGENCY OF CASES

In developing our framework, it is tempting to try to typologize the dynamics giving rise to such alliances and movements, into a neat set of categories describing exactly how this occurs. However, our research and practice informs us that the precise nature of the relationship between whistleblowing and social movements is highly contingent upon the individual circumstances of the whistleblower. For instance, Daniel Ellsberg's first engagement with anti-war activists happened when he was working for the RAND corporation on counter-insurgency; the alliance was a gradual process involving his changing views of the Vietnam war and his own role in the structures of power. In contrast, the Metoo social movement began with the actions of two women who blew the whistle on Harvey Weinstein and the culture of harassment in the film industry. This particular social movement, however, was preceded by a long history of feminist social movements from the Suffragettes to today's Women Against Rape. The Occupy Wall Street movement did not emerge directly from whistleblowing, although banking whistleblowers were a crucial source of information in revealing corruption within the banking industry during this period (Kenny, 2019), and the whistleblower journalist Julian Assange spoke at Occupy London to announce the determination of WikiLeaks to target corruption in this sector. In some instances, social movements have pre-existed the actions of individual whistleblowers – for example in the cases of Ellsberg, Gun, Manning, and Kiriakou, but in others the whistleblowers themselves were crucial in catalyzing the formation of social movements, such as the Metoo movement and the Occupy Wall Street movement. Each case must be examined in terms of its own specificity, while our framework provides a useful guide to the variety of networks of whistleblower support that have been developed across a range of individual cases as well as the variety of alliances that have been formed between particular whistleblowers and related social movements.

CONCLUDING REMARKS

Whistleblowers and their support networks play a vital role in revealing systemic corruption that is concealed by the secrecy havens of the powerful, and as activists in broader counter-hegemonic movements. Our paper is unique in detailing the relationship between whistleblowing and social movements in terms of explaining these novel alliances in terms of counter-hegemonic practice, answering calls to focus on this as-yet under-researched area. Practical implications are clear; the counter-hegemonic practices described include solidarity tactics and alliance-building to protect whistleblowers and turn information into power, the revelation of insurgent truths about secrecy havens that challenge the status quo, the increased use of technology by journalists for source protection, data analysis and dissemination, and the appeal to higher values which demand disobedience and direct action. Counter-hegemonic whistleblowing tends to be directed at concentrations of power, such as the in the financial industry, the military, political organizations and the media itself. Whistleblowing that challenges systemic corruption tends for that very reason to be seen as a greater threat to the status quo, even if the whistleblower themselves sees their demands in terms of basic democratic reform. In developing our analytic framing of the ways in which whistleblowers and social movements can engage in counter-hegemonic practices to shed light on the development of secrecy havens, we acknowledge some limitations. We focus on a subset of exemplary cases here, and whilst this is a limited sample it proves a groundwork for future studies to build on both in breadth of cases analyzed and in the depth of analysis of each component aspect of this framework. Future research is needed to provide in-depth analysis of the relationship between the circumstances of individual whistleblowers and the wider political dynamics which enable them to build broader counter-hegemonic alliances. What is the role of key supporting actors in building these alliances? Do different actors such as lawyers, journalists and activists play a more or less prominent role in different sectors? How do whistleblowers engage prominent spokespersons in the creation of alliances? What is the role of stigmatization and smear campaigns in the development or negation of alliances? Future research is also needed into new developments in networked whistleblowing and the different ways in which technological tactics can be combined with human factors in whistleblower support, which has been a prominent feature of recent cases of counter-hegemonic whistleblowing. Future research can also usefully extend the framework developed in this paper to include a wider range of whistleblowers and their alliances with social movements.

NOTES

1. Scheuerman (2015) also defends Mr Snowden's whistleblowing as a form of civil disobedience, where "his actions were required by constitutional and international law" (Scheuerman, 2015, p. 82). In contrast to this view, Pozen (2020) has argued that Snowden's approach to whistleblowing departs from civil disobedience because he did not accept a legal punishment for his breach of the law and because it was a relatively individualist rather than collective act.

2. New legislation has subsequently been passed in an effort to better regulate and prevent tax evasion in Ghana, the UK, the US and elsewhere. Examples include the US 2019 Corporate Transparency Act, which explicitly referred to the role of the Panama Papers in highlighting the urgent need for greater regulation (Fitzgibbon & Hudson, 2021). Within three years of these revelations, $1.2 billion dollars had been levied in fines as a result of prosecutions directly related to the Panama Papers investigations (Dalby, 2019).

REFERENCES

Alford, C. F. (2001). *Whistle-blowers: Broken lives and organizational power*. Cornell University Press.

Assange, J. (2011). *Julian Assange: The unauthorized autobiography*. Canongate Books Ltd.

Benkler, Y. (2011). A free irresponsible press: Wikileaks and the battle over the soul of the networked fourth estate. *Harvard Civil Rights-Civil Liberties Law Review, 46*, 311–397.

Böhm, S., Spicer, A., & Fleming, P. (2008). Infra-political dimensions of resistance to internationa-Scandinavian. *Journal of Management*, *24*(3), 169–182.

Bushnell, A. (2020). Reframing the whistleblower in research: Truth-tellers as whistleblowers in changing cultural contexts. *Sociology Compass*, e12816.

Carroll, W. K., & Ratner, R. S. (2010). Social movements and counter-hegemony: Lessons from the field. *New Proposals: Journal of Marxism and Interdisciplinary Inquiry*, *4*(1), 7–22.

Contu, A. (2014). Rationality and Relationality in the Process of Whistleblowing: Recasting Whis-tle-Blowing through Readings of Antigone. *Journal of Management Inquiry*, *23*(4), 393–406.

Dalby, D. (2019). Panama Papers helps recover more than $1.2 billion around the world, International Consortium of Investigative Journalists. https://www.icij.org/investigations/panama-papers/panama-papers-helps-recover-more-than-1-2-billion-around-the-world/

de Lagasnerie, G. (2016). *The art of revolt: Snowden, Assange, Manning*. Stanford University Press.

Dean, J. (2006). Secrecy since September 11. *Interventions*, *6*(3), 362–380.

Devine, T., & Maassarani, T. (2011). *The corporate whistleblowers' survival guide*. Berret-Koehler Publishers.

Ellsberg, D. (2002). *Secrets: A memoir of Vietnam and the pentagon papers*. London: Penguin.

Fitzgibbon, W., & Hudson, M. (2021). Five years later, Panama Papers still having a big impact. International Consortium of Investigative Journalists. https://www.icij.org/investigations/panama-papers/five-years-later-panama-papers-still-having-a-big-impact/

Gabbioneta, C., Faulconbridge, J. Currie, G., Dinovitzer, R., & Muzio, D. (2019). Critical Article: Inserting professionals and professional organizations in studies of wrongdoing: The nature, antecedents, and consequences of professional misconduct. *Human Relations*, *72*(11), 1707–1725.

Gardner, L. (2016). *War on leakers: National Security and American Democracy from Eugene V. Debs to Edward Snowden*. The New Press.

Hertsgaard, M. (2016). *Bravehearts: Whistle blowing in the age of Snowden*. Hot Books: New York.

Kenny, K. (2019). *Whistleblowing: Towards a new theory*. Harvard University Press.

Kenny, K., & Bushnell, A. (2020). How to whistle-blow: Dissensus and demand. *Journal of Business Ethics*, *164*, 643–656.

Maxwell, L. (2019). *Insurgent truth: Chelsea Manning and the politics of outsider truth-telling*. Oxford University Press.

McCord, E. (2010). US Solider on the aftermath of WikiLeaks Apache attack, BBC. http://news.bbc.co.uk/1/hi/programmes/newsnight/9136984.stm

McCord, E., & Steiber, J. (2010). Open letter of reconciliation and responsibility. https://www.common-dreams.org/views/2010/04/16/open-letter-reconciliation-and-responsibility-iraqi-people

Mesmer-Magnus, J. R., & Viswesvaran, C. (2005). Whistleblowing in organizations: An examination of correlates of whistleblowing intentions, actions, and retaliation. *Journal of Business Ethics*, *62*, 277–297.

Mistry, K. (2020). The rise of fall of Anti-Imperial Whistleblowing in the Long 1970s. In K. Mistry & H. Gurman (Eds.), *Whistleblowing nation: The history of national security disclosures and the cult of state secrecy* (pp. 123–152). Columbia University Press.

Mistry, K., & Gurman, H. (2020). *Whistleblowing nation: The history of national security disclosures and the cult of state secrecy*. Columbia University Press.

Mitchell, M., & Mitchell, T. (2008). *The spy who tried to stop a war: Katharine Gun and the Secret Plot to Sanction the Iraq Invasion*. Polipoint Press.

Munro, I. (2016). Organizational resistance as a vector of deterritorialization: The case of WikiLeaks and secrecy havens. *Organization*, *23*(4), 567–587.

Munro, I. (2017). Whistleblowing and the politics of truth: Mobilizing 'truth games' in the WikiLeaks case. *Human Relations*, *70*(5), 519–543.

Munro, I. (2019). An interview with Chelsea Manning's Lawyer: Nancy Hollander on human rights and the protection of whistleblowers. *Organization*, *26*(2), 276–290.

Murray, C. (2006). *Murder in Samarkand*. Mainstream Publishing Press.

Obermayer, B., & Obermaier, F. (2016). *The Panama papers: Breaking the story of how the rich and powerful hide their money*. Oneworld Publications.

Pozen, D. (2020). CODA: Edward Snowden, National security whistleblowing, and civil disobedience. In K. Mistry & H. Gurman (Eds.), *Whistleblowing nation: The history of national security dis-closures and the cult of state secrecy* (pp. 327–338). Columbia University Press.

Scheuerman, W. (2015). Taking Snowden seriously: Civil disobedience for an age of total surveillance. In D. Fidler (Ed.), *The Snowden reader* (pp. 70–90). Indiana University Press.

Snowden, E. (2019). *Permanent record*. Macmillan.

Stein, M. (2019). The Lost Good Self: Why the whistleblower is hated and stigmatized. *Organization Studies*. Online first.

Varon, J. (2020). Winter soldiers of the dark side: CIA whistleblowers and national security dissent. In K. Mistry & H. Gurman (Eds.), *Whistleblowing nation: The history of national security disclosures and the cult of state secrecy* (pp. 153–186). Columbia University Press.

Weiskopf, R., & Willmott, H. (2013). Ethics as Critical Practice: The "Pentagon Papers", deciding responsibly, truth-telling, and the unsettling of organizational morality. *Organization Studies*, *34*(4), 469–493.

CHAPTER 7

HISTORICAL APPROACHES TO RESEARCHING ORGANIZATIONAL WRONGDOING

Adam Nix and Stephanie Decker

ABSTRACT

Organizational wrongdoing researchers often look to past cases to empirically develop and support theoretical understanding. Their research is therefore conducted at a temporal distance to focal events and frequently relies on retrospective accounts and surviving documentary evidence. These methodological circumstances define historical research practice, and we demonstrate in this paper the valuable insights that historical approaches can provide organizational wrongdoing research. Specifically, we draw on a range of practices from history and the social sciences to introduce four historically informed approaches: narrative history, analytically structured history, historical process study, short-term process study. We differentiate these based on their particular affordances and treatment of two key methodological considerations: historical evidence and temporality. We demonstrate the specific value these approaches represent to organizational wrongdoing research with several exemplars showing how they have been used in related fields of research.

Keywords: Organizational history; qualitative research methods; secondary data; corruption; organizational misconduct; fraud

Organizational Wrongdoing as the "Foundational" Grand Challenge: Consequences and Impact
Research in the Sociology of Organizations, Volume 85, 141–158
Copyright © 2023 by Adam Nix and Stephanie Decker
Published under exclusive licence by Emerald Publishing Limited
ISSN: 0733-558X/doi:10.1108/S0733-558X20230000085008

1. INTRODUCTION

Acts of misconduct, corruption, and other forms of unethical organizational behavior are invariably studied after the fact, once the essential details are in the public domain. In part, this is a conceptual necessity, as the wrongful status of an event is largely seen as dependent on an appreciation of context and some level of social construction, which establishes whether the line separating right from wrong has been crossed (Andersson, 2017; Clemente & Gabbioneta, 2017; Greve et al., 2010; Palmer, 2012). While such judgments can sometimes be made during a prolonged occurrence of wrongdoing, they are more typically retrospective in nature, with interpretations solidified over time by legal process and the uncovering of empirical detail. Indeed, while scandals of Enron-like proportions are rare, the judgments of courts, regulators and the media are generally what link contextually specific actions and events to abstract conceptualizations of wrongdoing (Greve et al., 2010). There are also obvious practical challenges to observing wrongdoing as it occurs within an organizational context, with issues around pre-selecting and accessing relevant research sites, the impact of an observer's presence on behavior, and the potential risks to researcher safety (Castro et al., 2020; Cornelissen et al., 2014; Cowton, 1998).

It is perhaps for these reasons that contextually situated research into organizational wrongdoing so often makes use of historical case studies. For instance, Palmer (2012) effectively draws on both the recent and distant past, going back as far as 1919 to show how misconduct can represent a mindless extension of normal organizational behavior. Indeed, while his approach did not "resemble the rigorous case analyses found in most scholarly [management and organization] journals," his tracing of conceptual themes over time and space shares many similarities with historical research (Palmer, 2012, p. 39). There are also many examples of in-depth, single-case research on past incidents of wrongdoing (Baker & Faulkner, 1993; Black et al., 1995; Gambetta, 1993; Salter, 2008; Sims & Brinkmann, 2003; Vaughan, 1996), some of which are counted amongst the most influential of our field. Like historical research, these studies often leverage documentary evidence, which can be substantial in cases that generate significant judicial, political, and public interest. Despite these important parallels, however, historical case usage within organizational wrongdoing is seldom discussed, and work drawing explicitly on historical approaches is rarer still.

Our aim within this paper is to make clearer and more robust the bridge between organizational wrongdoing research and historical research practice. This contributes methodically to qualitative, contextually embedded research into organizational wrongdoing, by providing useful alternatives to traditional case study analysis (Eisenhardt & Graebner, 2007; Gioia et al., 2013; Yin, 2013). Historical approaches are naturally conducive to researching past events, building on well-established methodical precedents that account for both the challenges and affordances this presents. While there has been considerable progress in encouraging historically reflexive research within management and organization research, these considerations and practices remain unfamiliar to many (Barros et al., 2019; Decker et al., 2021; Stutz & Sachs, 2018). As such, we provide specific guidance for scholars who wish to use historical cases of wrongdoing in a manner attentive to the methodological particularities of researching the past. This provides a basis for getting the most out of historical cases of wrongdoing, and for reflecting on the extent to which using the past confers potential methodical issues.

The chapter starts with an overview of the relationship between history and theoretically oriented research into organizations. From here, two key methodological considerations are introduced: the use of historical sources to study cases of wrongdoing and the role that temporality plays in interpreting historical events. We then provide four approaches that show how organizational wrongdoing in the past can be studied in a historically informed way before closing with a discussion of the potential these approaches have for generating novel and alternative theoretical interpretations.

2. HISTORY AND THEORY IN MANAGEMENT AND ORGANIZATION STUDIES

While historians have traditionally been associated with contributions of an empirical nature, management and organization studies has been a catalyst for more theoretically oriented historical research. In particular, a community of scholars have argued for a "historical turn" (Clark & Rowlinson, 2004), combining more explicitly reflexive historical approaches (Decker et al., 2021) with a greater engagement in theory development (Maclean et al., 2016). Nevertheless, historical research methods remain unfamiliar to many, due to the absence of methodological discussion (Decker, 2013; van Lent & Durepos, 2019). On the surface, some features look similar to those seen in qualitative research, for instance, a shared preference for discrete empirical settings and a predominance of textual evidence (Yates, 2014). Moreover, an interpretation of past events is a common basis for interpretive insight and inductive theory building, often through an appreciation of participants' "lived experiences" (Silverman, 2013). Building on these synergies, there have been various attempts to integrate historical principles within social scientific approaches (Burgelman, 2011; Langley, 1999; Pettigrew, 1995; Skocpol, 1984; Welch, 2000; Welch et al., 2011).

Despite their similarities, however, there are important differences in the philosophical and methodological characteristics of social scientific and historical research. Particularly, this is seen in the differing assumptions around whether (1) findings are explained narratively or analytically, (2) evidence comes from found sources or created data, and (3) whether time should be treated as elastic periods or a constant chronology (Rowlinson et al., 2014). For those seeking to conduct research that is both historically situated and theoretically focused (Maclean et al., 2016; Vaara & Lamberg, 2016), managing these dualisms is vital. Ongoing elaboration of historical approaches in management and organizational research means the innovative potential of such approaches is now recognized (Bansal et al., 2018; Lê & Schmid, 2020). However, they require researchers to demonstrate "dual integrity" by balancing empirical veracity and theoretical fluency (Maclean et al., 2016).

Not only can history provide an empirical evidence base, but it can also represent a causal factor within theoretical interpretations (Kipping & Üsdiken, 2014). Clemente et al. (2016) use a historical approach to propose a recursive model of institutional change. Here, not only is the influence that different levels of history have on organizational phenomena accounted for, but also the fact that, in turn, critical events shape history. Such factors are clearly relevant to organizational wrongdoing, particularly when we consider the wider economic and social impact of scandals like Enron's bankruptcy (Benke, 2018). Andersson (2017) also demonstrates how theories of wrongdoing can be historically situated, showing how corruption is socially constructed over time. However, while incorporating history into theory (van Lent & Durepos, 2019 call "history as theory"), provides many opportunities, it is necessary to distinguish this from history as a methodological issue. As such, we limit our scope to "history as method" or rather, the integration of "historical data collection and analysis into empirical strategies for performing theoretically motivated studies" (van Lent & Durepos, 2019, p. 340).

Without explicit methodological consideration, scholars risk treating the past as merely a convenient source of case study material (Decker et al., 2021). This is especially relevant for empirical research into past cases of wrongdoing, where the prevalence of retrospective case studies makes historical approaches a practical and robust methodological choice. Unlike the social sciences, history has a long tradition of historical reflexivity (Barros et al., 2019; Stutz & Sachs, 2018), routinely considering issues of temporality, hindsight and contradictory or incomplete evidence (Kipping & Üsdiken, 2014; Lipartito, 2014; Wadhwani & Decker, 2017). These are considerations that any substantive retrospective cases will encounter, but which are generally absent from mainstream qualitative approaches (Schaefer & Alvesson, 2020). For research on organizational wrongdoing, we highlight two aspects that are particularly relevant: evidence and temporality.

2.1. Interpretation of Historical Sources

The empirical evidence used in qualitative social sciences and history share many similarities: they are often text-based, they are contextually rich, and they are generally interpreted through the subjective and value-based perspectives of both focal actors and researchers (Schaefer & Alvesson, 2020; Scott, 1990; Tight, 2019). Despite this, they are subject to quite different treatment, something seen in the conceptual distinction between "data" and "sources." Historians generally prefer to find evidence (often in documents and letters), whereas qualitative researchers generally prefer to create new evidence (often via interviews or observation) specific to their research questions (Rowlinson et al., 2014). Even when historians raise historical data in the form of oral history interviews, the resulting transcripts are archived alongside documentary evidence to be accessible to others in the future (Ritchie, 2014). The term "source" implies an epistemic attitude not normally employed for data: one of critical and skeptical evaluation (Schaefer & Alvesson, 2020) and a degree of interpretive distance (Mees-Buss et al., 2020). Thus, the veracity of historical analysis is predicated on the accuracy of sources (verifiability) and their validity and credibility as supporting evidence (Lipartito, 2014). Where non-historians undertake substantive empirical analysis on historical cases of wrongdoing, such scrutiny of found empirical evidence is similarly important.

The distinction between sources and data also has the potential to raise researchers' awareness of the fact that not all secondary data is created equal. When engaging in critical appreciation and interpretation, it is helpful to differentiate between "social documents" and "narrative sources." The former are sources close in time and display little concern with how their author(s) would be viewed by future readers, including most types of internal business correspondence. The latter are more distant in time and concerned with managing reputation, for example, corporate histories, speeches, annual reports and accounts, and communication to shareholders and stakeholders (Decker et al., 2021). Whilst most cases of wrongdoing become widely known through secondary accounts (the equivalent of narrative sources), it is in fact the availability of social documents that offer the greatest potential for analytical insight. Such social documents are not created with the intention of providing knowledge of the past to future observers (Megill, 2007), and due to their proximity to corrupt or wrongful activities, they provide a rich view into past events that is unattainable from retrospective interpretations (Alvesson & Sköldberg, 2009; Jordanova, 2006). Not unlike detective work, historians value these "traces of the past" because they can unearth new or previously missed information, which in turn change how we interpret past events (Ginzburg, 1989; Silverman, 1989).

The relevance of historical source interpretation has been remarked upon for qualitative analysis of interview data (Schaefer & Alvesson, 2020) and interpretive research more broadly. Silverman (1989), for example, suggested that researchers need to expand their analytical gaze by actively questioning how, why, and where data were produced – key questions that underpin much of historical source interpretation (Howell & Prevenier, 2001; Kipping et al., 2014). Sources are triangulated with other sources in the same or other archives, and with other historical accounts to ensure the reliability of the evidence and its analysis (Kipping et al., 2014). Moreover, relevant historical collections are already available, but remain underutilized, even in relation to well-known scandals. Such social documents are often available and rendered less problematic because narrative sources already provide insight into past organizational wrongdoing, often via books about notorious scandals, such as Enron (McLean & Elkind, 2013), ADM (Eichenwald, 2000), and MCI (Pavlo & Weinberg, 2007).

Once basic culpability has been established, available social documents rarely change these broader accounts or unveil further incriminating evidence, but they can still be used to advance empirical and theoretical understanding. For instance, Vaughan's historical ethnography of the Challenger launch disaster combines internal documents with oral and written retrospective accounts to show how actions and events that were externally viewed as rule violations by regulators, were actually negotiated and constructed over time as being in line with procedure (Vaughan, 1996). In terms of theoretical significance, this revelation challenged her own preconceptions about the case – from that of misconduct to mistake – and materially altered her theoretical interpretation (Vaughan, 2004). Thus, a critical evaluation of found sources is an important defence against the risks of uncritically following one's own initial interpretation of the available evidence as well as the conclusions reached by others.

2.2. Dealing with Temporality and Hindsight

In order to understand organizational wrongdoing and related scandals, it is important to comprehend such phenomena within their historical context (Andersson, 2017; Clemente et al., 2016). However, this is rarely developed as a methodological issue, with retrospective cases often naturalized as similar to contemporary equivalents, observed in the here and now, rather than after the fact. This is problematic given, unlike contemporary cases, the results are already known (Wolfram Cox & Hassard, 2007). Nevertheless, interest is rarely extended to temporality as a methodological issue, despite the acknowledged value of past cases as an alternative to traditional approaches, where it can be difficult or dangerous to get research access (Castro et al., 2020).

Such historical approaches are of relevance to studying hidden activities (Scott, 2015), or events only fully comprehensible in hindsight, due to their complex and interconnected nature. Grey (2014, p. 107), in his study of the culture of organizational secrecy at Bletchley Park, highlights the severe methodological problems in researching phenomena that are purposefully obscured, because "that which is secret is inaccessible to researchers." This makes historical research "virtually the only way of studying" some clandestine, secret, or illegal activities. Similarly, organizational wrongdoing is difficult to predict a priori or observe contemporaneously (Ashforth et al., 2008; Castro et al., 2020), meaning some temporal distance from the occurrence of such events is generally necessary. Moreover, being socially constructed, wrongfulness is hard to ascertain without the retrospective judgments of social agents like the courts or the press (Clemente & Gabbioneta, 2017; Greve et al., 2010; van Driel, 2019). Thus, if many occurrences of organizational wrongdoing are practically inaccessible in the present, it may be necessary to engage with historical methods to analyze the past more rigorously.

Unlike historians, it is normal for social scientists to collect primary data in the "present," meaning researchers and participants have no knowledge of the future (Rowlinson et al., 2014). In organizational research, such knowledge of the future represents "hindsight bias" and is often viewed as problematic for validity (Wolfram Cox & Hassard, 2007). In contrast, historical researchers need to position themselves against the temporal dimension (Wadhwani & Bucheli, 2014), because historical temporality is based on the assumption that past and present are distinct, and separated by temporal distance (Decker et al., 2021; Wadhwani & Decker, 2017). Temporal distance also implies that the past is not just distinct, but also different from the present (Gadamer, 2013), requiring an appreciation of unfamiliar settings and social dynamics not unlike ethnographic practices of portraying one culture in terms of another (Ginzburg, 2012; Van Maanen, 2011). This also provides an appreciation of the significance of events in hindsight, thus facilitating an interpretation of past events over time. Accordingly, temporal

distance implies that the retrospective appreciation of past events and their historiographical significance changes in response to concerns in the present.

Such an understanding of time differs from the standard chronological
assumption in organization studies that research designs are characterized as
either cross-sectional or longitudinal (Langley & Tsoukas, 2011; Mohr, 1982).
While historical research is sometimes described as longitudinal (da Silva Lopes
et al., 2019; Perchard & MacKenzie, 2020), in that it focuses on events over time
(Yates, 2014), in our view this is an oversimplification of the very different assumptions made in relation to time. For historians, time ontologically separates them
from the events they are interested in (Gaddis, 2002; Mills et al., 2014; Munslow,
2010). In contrast, social scientists can study events as they happen, with longitudinal collection of data over several separate points in time (e.g., 10 years, as in
Vaccaro and Palazzo (2015) study on organized crime) allowing an observation
of phenomena at various temporal positions (Langley, 2009; Pettigrew, 2012).

3. HISTORICALLY INFORMED APPROACHES TO ORGANIZATIONAL WRONGDOING

As a societal problem studied by many different fields, examples of research relevant to organizational wrongdoing are diverse in intended contribution and
approach. While this plurality offers a good deal of flexibility, it also complicates
the methodological landscape for those seeking established methods that help
them get the most out of historical case studies. Within this section, we focus on
four different approaches to researching organizational wrongdoing in a historically informed way (see Table 1). By this, we mean that they are explicit about
their focus on the past as an empirical context, and the use of data originating in
the past as a means of access. They achieve this in different ways and represent a
range of approaches to develop distinctive contributions based on historical cases
of wrongdoing. To help illustrate these approaches, we present them alongside
exemplars of research that use each of these approaches to contribute to organizational wrongdoing and related themes.

Our specific selection of approaches was guided by two main considerations.
First, they allow us to show how different ways of using history facilitate particular types of knowledge, which suit different audiences and research aims. Thus,
some of our approaches are more social scientific in their mode of inquiry, retaining a heavily analytical and conceptually oriented focus, despite their historical
dimension (Maclean et al., 2016). Others more closely resemble conventional histories, focusing on thick empirical elaboration, a subtler relationship to theory,
and a more narrative form of explanation (Rowlinson et al., 2014). Our second
reason for choosing these approaches is that they demonstrate the particular
affordances that history provides to researchers of organizational wrongdoing.
Specifically, they show the significant amount of rich historical evidence that is
accessible for studying wrongdoing, and how temporal distance adds to analysis,
rather than undermining validity. Thus, our below elaboration explains the value

Table 1. Historically Informed Approaches to Researching Organizational Wrongdoing.

Approach	Evidence	Temporality	Application	Exemplars
Narrative history	Critical use of social documents and narrative sources that originate from, or refer to, historical events. Analytical processes are rarely explicit	Historical and temporally distant. Often covers a long time period, following certain themes or actors through multiple historically relevant contexts	The development of new historical knowledge that contributes to an understanding of the past, with theory a means of making sense of empirical detail	Balleisen (2018) Shows the evolution of business fraud throughout US history, showing the link between openness to economic innovation and the periodic prevalence of fraud
Analytically structured history	Evidence based on historical norms and procedures, though source selection is guided by an interest in theoretical conceptualization rather than historical events	Historical and temporally distant. Focuses on events within a clearly specified period that is dictated by theoretical relevance	Offers a primarily theoretical contribution but retains an interest in historical significance. Draws on an analysis of historical events to inform the development of an emerging concept	Nix et al. (2021) Develops the concept of network-enabled corruption based on Enron's role in the California Energy Crisis
Historical process study	Uses historical sources as data but places this material in its historical context. Follows explicit qualitative analytical norms and procedures	Historical and temporally distant. Guided by an interest in long-term processes (several years or decades), often involving multiple stakeholders	The development of new theoretical interpretations, drawing explicitly on historical evidence and a contextual appreciation of events over time	Cappellaro et al. (2021) Provides a framework for better understanding strategic ambiguity by analyzing the Italian mafia's attempt to hide and obfuscate its activities
Short-term process study	Uses contemporary secondary data (documents, audio, video) from an event to reconstruct specific events. Follows explicit qualitative data analysis procedures	Focus on shorter time periods and more likely to deal with the recent past. Employs temporal distance to understand complex and fast-moving dynamics within specific event(s) and processes	The development of theoretical insight about micro-processes based on a reconstruction and interpretation of past events	Cornelissen et al. (2014) Employs documents released by the Stockwell Inquest to theorize how organizations come to false conclusions and commit to flawed interpretations

of each approach and how choices around evidence and temporality are reflected in their style of output and theoretical contribution.

3.1. Narrative history

Historical research typically takes a narrative form, often appearing as long-form monographs rather than articles. Such "narrative histories" provide detailed descriptions of historical actors and events and often cover these over long periods of time and multiple contexts. They are focused primarily on historical knowledge contributions; seeking a better understanding of events in the past through a (re)interpretation of historical sources. Nonetheless, some narrative histories do add significantly to our theoretical understanding of wrongdoing, even if it is not in a manner accustomed to social scientists (Berghoff & Spiekermann, 2018; van Driel, 2019). A relevant example of this is Balleisen's (2018) *Fraud*, which tracks deceptive practices through US history showing how periods of openness to innovation and entrepreneurship have consistently driven bouts of systemic fraud.

Narrative histories are generally built on extensive source usage, drawing on numerous archives and many thousands of documents. *Fraud* follows this norm, building on multiple collections, including those of the New York Stock Exchange and the National Archives (US), as well as various press and legal repositories. This is representative of established historical source analysis, whereby a variety of both narrative and social document sources are triangulated to form an empirical evidence base (Kipping et al., 2014; Lipartito, 2014). However, the specific analytical procedures used to critique, select, and ultimately rely upon particular materials are largely tacit (Rowlinson et al., 2014). Thus, Balleisen does not use evidence as "data" in the social scientific sense, by analyzing it through discrete and transparent procedures.

Narrative histories often encompass a significant period of time, in this case starting in the 1810s and ending in the 2010s with the fallout from the global financial crisis. A historical treatment of time is readily apparent in the management of such scope, with the narration stretched or contracted to highlight patterns and historically embed key events. The ability to track fraudulent behavior over extended periods of time is crucial here, as well as the distance offered by his position in the present. These provide a view of commonalities in causation over time, and with this, illuminate patterns of similar action occurring within different contexts. The result is an analysis that provides a view of how similar certain phenomena are over time, as well as the effects that markedly different contextual factors have on their prevalence and evolution.

3.2. Analytically Structured History

By contrast, some histories are principally motivated by theory, often taking an "analytically structured" approach that uses historical events to inform the development of emerging concepts (Rowlinson et al., 2014). While an understanding of the past remains critical, decisions about which actors or events to focus upon are driven by conceptual interests rather than new historical knowledge (e.g., Hamann & Bertels, 2018; Popielarz, 2016; Thompson, 2017). This shifts the primary contribution toward conceptualization – while at the same time retaining historical veracity and narrative quality – and such approaches have proven highly effective in explaining how complex socio-economic phenomena occur over time (Maclean et al., 2016). In this manner, Nix et al. (2021) used this approach to research Enron's history, elaborating a particular form of "network-enabled" corruption in relation to its role in California's turn-of-the-millennium energy crisis.

Because conceptual elaboration guilds the period(s) under analysis, they need not necessarily cover events of general historical importance. For instance, Nix et al.'s historical account of Enron does not deal significantly with its wider history but instead centers around a relatively short (crisis) period and a single energy trading division. Nonetheless, temporal distance afforded a stable and historically embedded "long view" of corruption (Ashforth et al., 2008), which was vital for interpreting the case and developing conceptual findings (Nix et al., 2021). In particular, their "networked-enabled" view of corruption was strongly influenced by the firm's development of industry "partnerships" in the years before the crisis as well as its wider influence on deregulation and finalization. In this way, a temporally distanced appreciation of broader events over time facilitated an understanding of specific organizational phenomena as outcomes of broader historical factors.

As with narrative histories, sources are often accessed from archival collections and subject to assessments of historical veracity. For instance, Nix et al. (2021) make use of the Federal Energy Regulatory Commission's e-library, which has preserved extensive social documents from legal cases dealing with Enron's role in the energy crisis. These included telephone transcripts from Enron's trading floor, which offered a detailed and reliable view of how relevant historical events occurred. These were supported by company documents, email correspondence, and witness testimonies, which helped validate their interpretation of the highly technical trading telephone dialogue. In this manner, an analytically structured approach provided a means of analyzing the highly intimate view into wrongdoing that these surviving documents provided, while also pursuing a substantively theoretical contribution.

3.3. Historical Process Study

Historical evidence can be used in the same way as social scientific data to better understand long-run processes. Such historical process studies employ explicit procedures to analyze qualitative historical data and provide some information on the historical context. The presentation is less narrative than that of analytically structured histories above, and more explicitly focused on the theorization of the data. In an in-depth historical process study of the Sicilian Mafia from the 1960s to 2018, Cappellaro et al. (2021) highlight how criminal organizations maintain ambiguity in their engagement with external audiences. They highlight three distinct strategies of maintaining opacity, fostering equivocality, and seeking to disrupt public opinion through absurd and illogical statements.

Historical process studies rely on temporal distance in their elaboration of distinct periods, which are in part defined by key events relevant to the organization.

Often such studies rely on documentary evidence that is in the public domain (Ansari et al., 2013). This is certainly true for our exemplar, which relied on reports and documents about the Mafia by the police, judiciary, and media. These were extensive, due to the high-profile nature of the Sicilian Mafia, and provided an excellent window into what is otherwise an archetypally "hidden organization" (Scott, 2013). As is normal with social scientific studies, the sources used are explicitly specified and summarized as a component of the methods section (Cappellaro et al., 2021).

Cappellaro et al. (2021) also make explicit their analytical procedure, starting with a historical reconstruction of key events and actions. Next, they identify organizational strategies. Compared to analytically structured histories, historical process studies combine historical and organizational techniques in their analysis. However, they present their results as a theoretically-driven analysis that largely dispenses with a narrative retelling of the twists and turns of Mafia history during this time period. The strategies that Cappellaro et al. (2021) observe span decades in their development and execution, and can only be considered in their entirety from a temporal distance. Their historical analysis allows them to understand long-term strategic shifts involving multiple stakeholders. From the vantage point of the present, they consider the dialogical interaction between the development of obfuscation strategies and stakeholder responses, as the Italian state seeks to effectively frame and prosecute the Mafia families for their actions, whilst the "*Mafiosi*" seek to obfuscate their activities and their intentions.

3.4. Short-Term Process Study

In contrast to a historical process study, short-term process studies do not cover long time periods, and instead investigate short episodes in minute detail. This approach is particularly suitable to unpack occasions of crisis and disaster, where every minute or possibly every second counts (Weick, 1993). This approach also focuses on replicable and explicitly described data analysis methods, but pays less attention to historical context, as short-term process studies either deal with more recent events or are more concerned with the generalizability of specific patterns of behavior or decision-making. Here, we use a case of organizational mistakes: Cornelissen et al.'s (2014) analysis of the so-called Stockwell shooting, in which an innocent member of the public, Jean-Charles de Menezes, was wrongly identified as a terrorist and suicide bomber and shot by a police officer.

As this case was subject to a public inquest, it is well documented and used as an example of an extreme situation in which sensemaking practices, such as commitment to specific frames of meaning, led to a collective decision with disastrous consequences. The study uses data collected for the inquest, similar to Nix et al. (2021), Cappellaro et al. (2021), and others (Brown, 2004, 2005; Gephart, 1993). Due to the nature of the inquest at which testimony and evidence were presented, this data included retrospective sensemaking accounts, but Cornelissen et al. (2014, p. 705) "focus primarily on recorded real-time instances of sensemaking on the day of the shooting." Such evidence also conforms to historical practice, which prefers social documents over narrative sources, precisely because the latter demonstrate retrospective sensemaking to a greater degree. The use of inquiry documents, recordings and testimony allow the reconstruction of complex and fast-moving situations as if dissected under a microscope.

Despite the relative recency of such cases, temporal distance remains important as it allows multiple sources of information, from a range of perspectives. As in the case discussed by Cornelissen et al. (2014), no single individual at the time had all the information, not even the senior officer, Cressida Dick. Such a historical "bird's eye view" presents the information from multiple perspectives, and across the whole time period, thus revealing patterns not accessible to individual participants. Short-term process studies develop explicitly theoretical contributions by drawing on and reinterpreting documentary (or audiovisual) evidence, with a methodological approach that is closely aligned to historical practice.

4. DISCUSSION

We have argued that research into organizational wrongdoing would benefit from history as an alternative empirical strategy to qualitative and contextually embedded case research. In doing so, the four approaches we describe provide researchers of organizational wrongdoing with a spectrum of methodological options, ranging from those familiar to historians (narrative and analytically structured histories) to those heavily informed by social scientific norms (historical and short-term process studies). Despite their different modes of inquiry, these approaches all provide solutions to the particular methodological implications of historical evidence and temporal distance, while also making the most of the unique viewpoint they provide. Together, they represent a methodological toolkit from which researchers might engage in historically informed research into organizational wrongdoing.

Whilst narrative history may not appear immediately relevant to researchers of organizational misconduct, many theoretically important long-form analyses closely align with a narrative approach (e.g., Gambetta, 1993; Salter, 2008; Vaughan, 1996). Additionally, understanding the conventions of narrative histories as one empirical approach can help researchers to draw on such detailed investigations, which often also contain highly relevant theoretical implications and empirical detail. In this way, Balleisen's (2018) interest in fraud as a historical phenomenon, provides insights into how socio-political efforts to facilitate something broadly seen as positive (innovation), had the side effect of encouraging something accepted as negative (fraud). As is taken for granted among historians, narrative histories, therefore, offer both a basis for conducting empirical research into the past and a source of empirical value in and of themselves.

While narrative histories do not generally seek theoretical contributions, analytically structured histories pursue theorization without dispensing with the historical context. Such contextual information is important for interpretation, which offers novel insights grounded in empirical accounts. In this way, Nix et al. (2021)

illustrates that, by returning to even the most infamous and well-documented cases with a historical toolkit, organizational wrongdoing scholars can develop new conceptual interpretations that are contextually detailed and historically situated. By drawing on a "fly-on-the-wall" view of historical events, they explain how Enron used the uncertainty around deregulation to establish an inter-organizational network of energy market clients. By ceding market information and resource control to Enron, these relationships enabled its energy traders to effectively invent and implement a playbook (and there was a literal book) of how to exploit California through loopholes within its new energy markets. Given the highly technical nature of these practices and the wholesale energy industry, interpreting the significance of individual events would have been very difficult without an appreciation of their wider historical context. This is also true for readers, and presenting conceptual conclusions narratively means they can be accompanied by an empirical elaboration of historical events as they become relevant to the emerging conceptualization.

Historical process studies and short-term process studies provide solutions to issues of scale. Organizational wrongdoing and the strategies associated with it may play out over the very long term, even decades as in the case of Cappellaro et al. (2021) study of the Sicilian mafia. Here, the historical approach allows them to establish the dialogic interaction between the changing perception of the mafia by the authorities and civil society over time, and the obfuscation strategies employed by *mafiosi*. On the other end of the spectrum lies the short-term process study, which can be likened to a microscope in its focus on the minutiae of a case and the sequence of events. Cornelissen et al. (2014) use this kind of detailed empirical analysis to draw out the breakdown of meaning and the asymmetries in knowledge in a tense and fast-moving police operation. Such an approach enables researchers to better appreciate factors that are difficult to perceive, and which may not have been consciously noted by participants as drivers of organizational wrongdoing.

Thus, while the first two approaches differ in terms of their balance between historical narrative and theoretically-focused analysis, the last two offer templates for investigating organizational misconduct at very different time scales. What they have in common is that they all draw on the kind of historical evidence that might be otherwise overlooked or subordinated in the social sciences. Documents, legal and media reporting, and recordings provide a rich evidence base for empirical analysis, even when the key "facts" of the case are already known. For example, the real-time insights on officers' sensemaking that Cornelissen et al. (2014) rely upon would be hard to replicate, even where interview access was possible, which is why the authors preferred social documents over witnesses' narrative accounts. Our article makes the case for organizational wrongdoing researchers to consistently consider this kind of evidence in their research and the four approaches outlined above provide a basis for doing so in a historically informed way.

While we have described discrete approaches to conducting historically informed research, there is scope for combination, particularly in long-form narrative analyses. This is particularly noticeable in *The Challenger Launch Decision,* which draws on elements from several of these approaches (Vaughan, 1996). In many respects, this analysis aligns with the historical process approach, in that it uses historical sources as data for a historically-informed and theoretically-driven investigation of organizational decision-making processes. However, there are also micro-processual elements, particularly in how she reconstructs the two alternative versions of the teleconference calls between engineers on the eve of the fateful launch. This allows the reconstruction of sensemaking processes at the level of the decision, which are then integrated into an explanation of more long-term, higher-level organizational processes. Finally, there is a clear historical significance to the study's findings, which revise historically accepted interpretations of the tragedy.

Reconstructing events and sensemaking after the fact is a fundamental methodological component of historical approaches. Given that potential acts of organizational wrongdoing are defined as such *after* they occur, it should be an essential part of the methodological toolkit of wrongdoing researchers. This is because a level of temporal distance is inherent in the social construction of transgressive behavior, which is retrospectively reported on and judged as details of the case become known (Andersson, 2017; Clemente & Gabbioneta, 2017; Greve et al., 2010). This temporal distance also means that researchers draw on different types of empirical material, which are found rather than created, and as evidence, requires critical interpretation (Schaefer & Alvesson, 2020). However, these sources (especially those close in time to historical events) not only enable a robust reconstruction but also open a window into the sensemaking and rationalizing by actors involved in wrongdoing. In this way, the affordances offered by historical approaches can significantly contribute to our empirical and theoretical understanding of organizational wrongdoing, offering new conceptual ideas and even challenging the way we think about theoretically important events.

5. CONCLUSION

Researching organizational wrongdoing via historical cases provides a valuable – and often necessary – pathway to empirical insight. However, analyzing events located in the past creates particular methodological implications that are often left unaddressed. This chapter elaborates on the methodological relevance of history to organizational wrongdoing research and, in doing so, provides alternatives to traditional case study analyses into organizational wrongdoing. Historically informed approaches are naturally conducive to researching past events, as they are grounded in well-established methodical precedents that account for both the challenges and affordances of researching the past. In particular, we argue that a researcher's temporal distance to the past and engagement with historical sources are material to how they reconstruct and interpret historical events. The four approaches we present manage these considerations in different ways, providing a range of options suited to diverse contributions and modes of inquiry. Together they offer a methodological toolkit for those wishing to use past cases of organizational wrongdoing in a more historically informed way.

REFERENCES

Alvesson, M., & Sköldberg, K. (2009). *Reflexive methodology: New vistas for qualitative research* (2nd ed.). SAGE.

Andersson, L. (2017). Of great vampire squids and jamming blood funnels: A socially constructed and historically situated perspective on organizational corruption. *Journal of Management Inquiry, 26*(4), 406–417.

Ansari, S. S., Wijen, F., & Gray, B. (2013). Constructing a climate change logic: An institutional perspective on the "tragedy of the commons." *Organization Science, 24*(4), 1014–1040.

Ashforth, B., Gioia, D., Robinson, S., & Trevino, L. (2008). Re-viewing organizational corruption. *Academy of Management Review, 33*(3), 670–684.

Baker, W., & Faulkner, R. (1993). The social organization of conspiracy: Illegal networks in the heavy electrical equipment industry. *American Sociological Review, 58*(6), 837–860.

Balleisen, E. (2018). *Fraud: An American History from Barnum to Madoff*. Princeton.

Bansal, P., Smith, W., & Vaara, E. (2018). From the editors: New ways of seeing through qualitative research. *Academy of Management Journal, 61*(4), 1–7.

Barros, A., de Toledo Carneiro, A., & Wanderley, S. (2019). Organizational archives and historical narratives: Practicing reflexivity in (re)constructing the past from memories and silences. *Qualitative Research in Organizations and Management: An International Journal, 14*(3), 280–294.

Benke, G. (2018). *Risk and Ruin: Enron and the culture of American Capitalism*. University of Pennsylvania Press.

Berghoff, H., & Spiekermann, U. (2018). Shady business: On the history of white-collar crime. *Business History, 60*(3), 289–304.

Black, W., Calavita, K., & Pontell, H. (1995). The Savings and Loan Debacle of the 1980s: White-Collar Crime or risky business? *Law & Policy, 17*(1), 23–55.

Brown, A. (2004). Authoritative sensemaking in a public inquiry report. *Organization Studies, 25*(1), 95–112.

Brown, A. (2005). Making sense of the collapse of Barings Bank. *Human Relations, 58*(12), 1579–1604.

Burgelman, R. (2011). Bridging history and reductionism: A key role for longitudinal qualitative research. *Journal of International Business Studies, 42*(5), 591–601.

Cappellaro, G., Compagni, A., & Vaara, E. (2021). Maintaining strategic ambiguity for protection: Struggles over opacity, equivocality, and absurdity around the Sicilian mafia. *Academy of Management Journal, 64*(1), 1–37.

Castro, A., Phillips, N., & Ansari, S. (2020). Corporate corruption: A review and an agenda for future research. *Academy of Management Annals, 14*(2), 935–968.

Clark, P., & Rowlinson, M. (2004). The treatment of history in organisation studies: Towards an "Historic turn"? *Business History, 46*(3), 331–352.

Clemente, M., Durand, R., & Roulet, T. (2016). The recursive nature of institutional change: An annales school perspective. *Journal of Management Inquiry, 26*(1), 17–31.

Clemente, M., & Gabbioneta, C. (2017). How does the media frame corporate scandals? The case of German Newspapers and the Volkswagen Diesel Scandal. *Journal of Management Inquiry, 26*(3), 287–302.

Cornelissen, J. P., Mantere, S., & Vaara, E. (2014). The contraction of meaning: The combined effect of communication, emotions, and materiality on sensemaking in the stockwell shooting. *Journal of Management Studies, 51*(5), 699–736.

Cowton, C. (1998). The use of secondary data in business ethics research. *Journal of Business Ethics, 17*(4), 423–434.

da Silva Lopes, T., Casson, M., & Jones, G. (2019). Organizational innovation in the multinational enterprise: Internalization theory and business history. *Journal of International Business Studies, 50*(8), 1338–1358.

Decker, S. (2013). The silence of the archives: Business history, post-colonialism and archival ethnography. *Management & Organizational History, 8*(2), 155–173.

Decker, S., Rowlinson, M., & Hassard, J. (2021). Rethinking history and memory in organization studies: The case for historiographical reflexivity. *Human Relations, 74*(8), 1123–1155.

Eichenwald, K. (2000). *The informant: A true story*. Broadway.

Eisenhardt, K. E. M., & Graebner, M. E. (2007). Theory building from cases: Opportunities and challenges. *Academy of Management Journal, 50*(1), 25–32.

Gadamer, H. (2013). *Truth and method*. Bloomsbury.

Gaddis, J. L. (2002). *The landscape of history: How historians map the past*. Oxford University Press.

Gambetta, D. (1993). *The Scicilian Mafia: The business of private protection*. Harvard University Press.

Gephart, R. (1993). The textual approach: Risk and blame in disaster sensemaking. *The Academy of Management Journal, 36*(6), 1465–1514.

Ginzburg, C. (1989). Clues: Roots of an evidential paradigm. In *Clues, myths, and the historical method* (pp. 96–214). Johns Hopkins University Press.

Ginzburg, C. (2012). Our words, and theirs: A reflection on the historian's craft, today. In S. Fellman & M. Rahikainen (Eds.), *Historical knowledge: In quest of theory, method and evidence* (pp. 97–120). Cambridge Scholars Publishing.

Gioia, D., Corley, K., & Hamilton, A. (2013). Seeking qualitative rigor in inductive research notes on the Gioia methodology. *Organizational Research Methods, 16*(1), 15–31.

Greve, H., Palmer, D., & Pozner, J. (2010). Organizations gone wild: The causes, processes, and consequences of organizational misconduct. *The Academy of Management Annals, 4*(1), 53–107.

Grey, C. (2014). An organizational culture of secrecy: The case of Bletchley Park. *Management and Organizational History, 9*(1), 107–122.

Hamann, R., & Bertels, S. (2018). The institutional work of exploitation: Employers' work to create and perpetuate inequality. *Journal of Management Studies, 55*, 394–423.

Howell, M., & Prevenier, W. (2001). *From reliable sources: An introduction to historical methods*. Cornell University Press.

Jordanova, L. (2006). *History in practice* (2nd ed.). Bloomsbury.

Kipping, M., & Üsdiken, B. (2014). History in organization and management theory: More than meets the eye. *The Academy of Management Annals, 8*(1), 535–588.

Kipping, M., Wadhwani, D., & Bucheli, M. (2014). Analyzing and interpreting historical sources: A basic methodology. In M. Bucheli & R. Wadhwani (Eds.), *Organizations in time: History, theory, methods* (pp. 305–330). Oxford University Press.

Langley, A. (1999). Strategies for theorizing from process data. *Academy of Management Review, 24*(4), 691–710.

Langley, A. (2009). Studying processes in and around organizations. In D. Buchanan & A. Bryman (Eds.), *The Sage handbook of organizational research methods* (pp. 409–429). Sage.

Langley, A., & Tsoukas, H. (2011). Introducing "Perspectives on Process Organization Studies." In *Process, sensemaking, and organizing*. Oxford University Press.

Lê, J., & Schmid, T. (2020). The practice of innovating research methods. *Organizational Research Methods*, 1–29.

Lipartito, K. (2014). Historical sources and data. In M. Bucheli & R. Wadhwani (Eds.), *Organizations in time: History, theory, methods* (pp. 284–304). Oxford University Press.

Maclean, M., Harvey, C., & Clegg, S. (2016). Conceptualizing historical organization studies. *Academy of Management Review, 41*(4), 609–632.

McLean, B., & Elkind, P. (2013). *The smartest guys in the room: The amazing rise and scandalous fall of Enron*. Penguin.

Mees-Buss, J., Welch, C., & Piekkari, R. (2020). From templates to heuristics: How and why to move beyond the Gioia Methodology. *Organizational Research Methods, 25*(2), 405–429.

Megill, A. (2007). *Historical knowledge, historical error: A contemporary guide to practice*. University of Chicago Press.

Mills, A., Weatherbee, T., & Durepos, G. (2014). Reassembling Weber to reveal the-past-as-history in management and organization studies. *Organization, 21*(2), 225–243.

Mohr, L. (1982). *Explaining organizational behaviour*. Jossey-Bass.

Munslow, A. (2010). *The future of history*. Palgrave Macmillan.

Nix, A., Decker, S., & Wolf, C. (2021). Enron and the California Energy Crisis: The role of networks in enabling organizational corruption. *Business History Review, 95*(4), 1–39.

Palmer, D. (2012). *Normal organizational wrongdoing: A critical analysis of theories of misconduct in and by organizations*. Oxford University Press.

Pavlo, W., & Weinberg, N. (2007). *Stolen without a gun: Confessions from inside history's biggest accounting fraud – The Collapse of MCI WorldCom*. Etika.

Perchard, A., & MacKenzie, N. (2020). Aligning to disadvantage: How corporate political activity and strategic homophily create path dependence in the firm. *Human Relations*, 1–39.

Pettigrew, A. (1995). Longitudinal field research on change: Theory and practice. *Longitudinal Field Research Methods. Studying Processes of Organizational Change*, *1*(3), 91–125.

Pettigrew, A. (2012). Context and action in the transformation of the firm: A reprise. *Journal of Management Studies*, *49*(7), 1304–1328.

Popielarz, P. A. (2016). Moral dividends: Freemasonry and finance capitalism in early-nineteenth-century America. *Business History*, *5*, 655–676.

Ritchie, D. A. (2014). *Doing oral history*. Oxford University Press.

Rowlinson, M., Hassard, J., & Decker, S. (2014). Research strategies for organizational history: A dialogue between historical theory and organization theory. *Academy of Management Review*, *39*(3), 250–274.

Salter, M. (2008). *Innovation corrupted: The origins and legacy of Enron's collapse*. Harvard University Press.

Schaefer, S., & Alvesson, M. (2020). Epistemic attitudes and source critique in qualitative research. *Journal of Management Inquiry*, *29*(1), 33–45.

Scott, J. (1990). *A matter of record: Documentary sources in social research*. Polity Press.

Scott, C. (2013). Hidden organizations and reputation. In Craig E. Carroll (Ed.), *The handbook of communication and corporate reputation* (pp. 545–557). Wiley. https://onlinelibrary.wiley.com/doi/book/10.1002/9781118335529

Scott, C. (2015). Bringing hidden organizations out of the shadows: Introduction to the special issue. *Management Communication Quarterly*, *29*(4), 503–511.

Silverman, D. (1989). Six rules of qualitative research: A post-romantic argument. *Symbolic Interaction*, *12*(2), 215–230.

Silverman, D. (2013). *Doing qualitative research: A practical handbook*. Sage.

Sims, R., & Brinkmann, J. (2003). Enron ethics (or: culture matters more than codes). *Journal of Business Ethics*, *45*(3), 243–256.

Skocpol, T. (1984). *Vision and method in historical sociology*. Cambridge University Press.

Stutz, C., & Sachs, S. (2018). Facing the normative challenges: The potential of reflexive historical research. *Business & Society*, *57*(1), 98–130.

Thompson, N. A. (2017). Hey DJ, don't stop the music: Institutional work and record pooling practices in the United States' music industry. *Business History*, in press (April), 1–22.

Tight, M. (2019). *Documentary research in the social sciences*. Sage. https://uk.sagepub.com/en-gb/eur/documentary-research-in-the-social-sciences/book258398#contents.

Vaara, E., & Lamberg, J.-A. J. (2016). Taking historical embeddedness seriously: Three historical approaches to advance strategy process and practice research. *Academy of Management Review*, *41*(4), 633–657.

Vaccaro, A., & Palazzo, G. (2015). Values against violence: Institutional change in societies dominated by organized crime. *Academy of Management Journal*, *58*(4), 1075–1101.

van Driel, H. (2019). Financial fraud, scandals, and regulation: A conceptual framework and literature review. *Business History*, *8*(61), 1259–1299.

van Lent, W., & Durepos, G. (2019). Nurturing the historic turn: "History as theory" versus "history as method." *Journal of Management History*, *25*(4), 429–443.

Van Maanen, J. (2011). *Tales of the field: On writing ethnography*. University of Chicago Press.

Vaughan, D. (1996). *The Challenger launch decision: Risky technology, culture, and deviance at NASA*. University of Chicago Press.

Vaughan, D. (2004). Theorizing disaster: Analogy, historical ethnography, and the Challenger accident. *Ethnography*, *5*(3), 315–347.

Wadhwani, D., & Bucheli, M. (2014). The future of the past in management and organization studies. In M. Bucheli & D. Wadhwani (Eds.), *Organizations in time: History, theory, methods* (pp. 3–32). Oxford University Press.

Wadhwani, D., & Decker, S. (2017). Clio's Toolkit: Historical methods beyond theory building from cases. In R. Mir & S. Jain (Eds.), *Routledge companion to qualitative research in organization studies* (pp. 113–127). Routledge.

Weick, K. E. (1993). The collapse of sensemaking in organizations: The Mann Gulch Disaster. *Administrative Science Quarterly*, *38*(4), 628–652.

Welch, C. (2000). The archaeology of business networks: The use of archival records in case study research. *Journal of Strategic Marketing*, *8*(2), 197–208.

Welch, C., Piekkari, R., Plakoyiannaki, E., & Paavilainen-Mäntymäki, E. (2011). Theorising from case studies: Towards a pluralist future for international business research. *Journal of International Business Studies*, *42*(5), 740–762.

Wolfram Cox, J., & Hassard, J. (2007). Ties to the past in organization research: A comparative analysis of retrospective methods. *Organization*, *14*(4), 475–497.

Yates, J. (2014). Understanding historical methods in organization studies. In M. Bucheli & R. D. Wadhwani (Eds.), *Organizations in time: History, theory, methods* (p. 265). Oxford University Press.

Yin, R. (2013). *Case study research: Design and methods* (5th ed.). Sage.